Political Environmentalism

The Hoover Institution
gratefully acknowledges the generous support of

Martin and Illie Anderson

for substantially underwriting
this research project and publication.

Edited by Terry L. Anderson

Political Environmentalism

Going behind the Green Curtain

Hoover Institution Press Stanford University Stanford, California

The Hoover Institution on War, Revolution and Peace, founded at Stanford University in 1919 by Herbert Hoover, who went on to become the thirty-first president of the United States, is an interdisciplinary research center for advanced study on domestic and international affairs. The views expressed in its publications are entirely those of the authors and do not necessarily reflect the views of the staff, officers, or Board of Overseers of the Hoover Institution.

www-hoover.stanford.edu

Hoover Institution Press Publication No. 467

First printing, 2000

Manufactured in the United States of America

05 04 03 02 01 00 9 8 7 6 5 4 3 2 1

The paper used in this publication meets the minimum requirements of American National Standard for Information Sciences—Permanence of Paper for Printed Library Materials, ANSI Z39.48-1984. ∞

Library of Congress Cataloging-in-Publication Data

Political environmentalism : going behind the green curtain / edited by Terry L. Anderson.
p. cm.
Includes bibliographical references (p.) and index.
ISBN 0-8179-9752-0 (alk. paper)
1. Environmental policy—United States. I. Anderson, Terry Lee, 1946–
GE180.P65 2000
363.7—dc21 99-058944

Contents

Contributors

Jonathan H. Adler, Senior Director of Environmental Policy at the Competitive Enterprise Institute, Washington, D.C.

Terry L. Anderson, Senior Fellow at the Hoover Institution, Stanford University, and Executive Director of the Political Economy Research Center, Bozeman, Montana

Daniel K. Benjamin, Professor of Economics at Clemson University and Senior Associate with the Political Economy Research Center, Bozeman, Montana

Elizabeth Brubaker, Executive Director of Environment Probe, a division of Energy Probe Research Foundation, Toronto, Canada

David Gerard, Research Associate at the Political Economy Research Center, Bozeman, Montana

Dean Lueck, Associate Professor of Economics at Montana State University

Andrew P. Morriss, Professor of Law and Associate Professor of Economics, Case Western Reserve University

Thomas Stratmann, Associate Professor of Economics at Montana State University

Kurtis J. Swope, Department of Economics at Indiana University

Bruce Yandle, Professor of Economics at Clemson University and Senior Associate with the Political Economy Research Center, Bozeman, Montana

Terry L. Anderson

Introduction

Since the 1960s, the environmental movement has taken the moral high ground, calling for political action in the name of public interest. Environmental legislation, such as the Wilderness Act (1964), the Clean Air Act (1970), the Clean Water Act (1972), the Endangered Species Act (1973), and Superfund (1980), took aim at the failure of the market system to care for the environment and called on politicians in Washington to regulate actions in the private sector. The majority of the public accepts that these acts were motivated by environmental concerns and that they achieve their goals. In short, these acts are put on a public-interest pedestal above self-interest.

Such renditions of environmental legislation, however, fly in the face of the vast literature of public choice that says legislation is better understood in the context of special interest groups, which lobby for laws to benefit themselves regardless of the net effect on society. Certainly environmental groups constitute one of these special interest groups, but it is unlikely that their diffuse interest in environmental amenities is sufficient to drive legislation that costs the American economy billions of dollars per year.

Although an old legal adage admonishes that the weak-of-stomach should not watch the making of sausage or law, this book goes behind the green legal curtain to examine critically how politics and environmentalism mix to produce some strange bedfellows and some perverse results. This book addresses specific laws, asking whether they were motivated by environmental concerns, whether they achieve their goals, whether they are cost-effective, and whether they generate perverse results.

It is said that an economist is a scoundrel whose faulty vision sees things as they are, not as they ought to be, which is what the authors of the chapters of this book attempt to do with environmental policy. Viewing the plethora of federal environmental laws of the past three decades through two economic lenses provides a robust explanation of why they passed and how they work (or don't work, as the case may be). The first economic lens is rent-seeking, the process whereby individuals and groups invest in influencing politics to get wealth transferred to them or to prevent wealth from being transferred away. Lobbying and making campaign contributions are two of the more obvious examples of rent-seeking, but there are many others, including organizing interest groups, influencing public opinion, and conducting smear campaigns. The transfer of wealth from one group to another should be a zero-sum game, but resources expended in the process of affecting or preventing the transfer of wealth make rent-seeking negative sum. This is the theme of chapter 1, "Clean Politics, Dirty Profits," by Jonathan Adler.

The second lens is the bootleggers-and-Baptist theory, espoused by Bruce Yandle in chapter 2, "Public Choice and the Environment." Yandle bases his theory on the observation that laws in the southeastern United States banning the sale of liquor on Sundays get moral support from religious groups (he uses *Baptists* for the alliterative quality), while providing a direct benefit to bootleggers who profit from selling illicit booze. Bootleggers would have little chance of lobbying for these restrictions without Baptists providing the moral high ground for the laws. This theory explains why otherwise disparate interest groups coalesce to make rent-seeking more effective. Accordingly, environmental special interest groups provide the moral high ground for economic special interest groups that stand to gain from legislation that hampers competitors.

Perhaps the best-known example of the bootlegger-and-Baptist theory at work in the environmental policy arena is the passage of the Clean Air Act Amendments in 1977. These amendments require coal-fired electric-generating facilities to install expensive scrubbers on their smokestacks to remove particulate matter, especially sulfur dioxide (SO_2). Given the concerns at the time about the possibility of acid rain, this expensive technological fix had an environmental rationale despite the fact that SO_2 emissions could be reduced at a much lower cost if midwestern utilities simply switched to burning low-sulfur western coal (instead of high-sulfur eastern coal). Nonetheless, environmentalists, utility companies, and eastern coal miners supported the higher-cost, less-effective technology. The bootleggers in this case are the eastern high-sulfur coal mining interests, who did not want competition from western coal, and the existing utilities, who got themselves exempted from the new requirements while imposing significantly higher costs on new competitors. But such transparent self-interest motivation would probably not have carried the day without the moral justification, provided by the environmental Baptists, for regulating big utilities.

A similar story is told in chapter 3, "The Law and Politics of Federal Wildlife Preservation," by Dean Lueck. Timber companies with large private landholdings supported the endangered species listing of the spotted owl, because the listing reduced timber harvests on federal lands and raised timber prices. Environmentalists wanted the owl listed to control federal land use. Not surprisingly, large landowners even paid biologists to help environmentalists locate spotted owls on public lands so that those lands would be placed off-limits to logging. Through the bootleggers-and-Baptist lens, such behavior is seen to be perfectly rational.

Lueck argues that in the tradeoff between traditional land uses, such as agriculture, and endangered species habitat, we do not get more private land allocated to endangered species habitat. The Endangered Species Act (ESA) puts property rights up for grabs in the political arena where environmental groups and agencies attempt to use their political power to control these property rights and landowners fight to keep what they think is theirs. Similar rent-seeking occurs for control of public lands where environmentalists use the ESA to reduce traditional land uses such as logging and grazing. The result is a negative-sum game that does little to save species but consumes considerable resources in the process.

If the Endangered Species Act is an example of interest groups using the political process to get something for nothing, the Duck Stamp Act would first appear to be an example of a user group, duck hunters, taxing itself to get more duck habitat. Economists argue that user fees should lead to a more optimal allocation of resources. The fee demonstration program, implemented by Congress in 1996, offers an example of another law designed to force amenity users on federal lands to pay for their land uses. But how well do user fees work? In chapter 4, "Bucks for Ducks or Money for Nothin'?" Kurtis Swope, Daniel Benjamin, and Terry Anderson find that the early years of the Duck Stamp Program generated substantial revenues, but that those revenues did more to increase the bureaucracy than to enhance duck habitat. As the Duck Stamp Program matured, agricultural interest captured the habitat expenditures to purchase marginal agricultural lands as opposed to quality duck habitat. The duck stamp story suggests that even well-intended user fees can be captured in the political process, thus reducing their effectiveness.

From fowl to fish, from the United States to Canada, politics seems to get in the way of conservation goals. In chapter 5, "Unnatural Disaster," Elizabeth Brubaker examines Canadian fishery policy and shows that, despite obvious mechanisms for increasing fishery stocks, Atlantic fish populations continue to decline. As she puts it, because of politics "the wrong people have been making the wrong decisions for the wrong reasons." Politics has subsidized the expansion of fisheries around the world, and Canada's experience is no different. Despite ample evidence that the transfer of ownership and control to fishermen, fishing companies, and fishing communities can greatly improve stocks, yields, and profits, government management bureaucracies remain entrenched and fisheries continue to decline. Unfortunately, getting politics out of the way is not easy.

The Wilderness Act of 1964 would seem to be a classic case of environmentalists following the leadership of such legends as Aldo Leopold and John Muir, who pushed for the preservation of our natural heritage. However, David Gerard (chapter 6, "The Origins of the Federal Wilderness System") finds that even this icon of environmental policy has roots in politics. In the early 1900s, soon after Congress placed national forests in the hands of the Department of Agriculture and national parks in the hands of the Department of the Interior, the two agencies began to compete for control of more acres in the public domain. The National Park Service did this by pushing for more wilderness-type lands that would be off-limits to logging. To combat this expansion, the Forest Service, at its expense, had to sacrifice some of its logging opportunities to show that it, too, could preserve natural qualities. Not surprisingly, the Forest Service did not set aside its best timber lands, but it did establish a de facto wilderness system long before environmentalists were lobbying for legislation. In this case, it was rent-seeking competition between governmental agencies, rather than by environmental groups, that gave us the precursor to our modern wilderness system, which encompasses more than 100 million acres.

If natural resources, such as endangered species, ducks, fish, and wilderness areas, are more a function of politics than environmentalism, surely hazardous wastes and clean air are examples of well-intentioned, well-functioning environmental laws. Again, however, the myth is debunked. Thomas Stratmann, in chapter 7, "The

Politics of Superfund," considers the determinants of Superfund expenditures. With data on the environmental threat of each Superfund site, we might expect that more funds would be spent sooner on the more hazardous sites. But Stratmann hypothesizes that politics might have something to do with expenditures. To test his hypothesis, Stratmann correlates expenditures to clean up Superfund sites with measures of environmental hazards, political variables, and state income. On the wealth-enhancing side of the ledger, he finds that more funds are spent on the more hazardous sites and that expenditures are income-sensitive, suggesting that cleanup is a luxury good. On the rent-seeking side of the ledger, he finds that politics matters, with influential legislators delivering the bacon by getting more Superfund spending in their home states.

Finally, in chapter 8, "The Politics of the Clean Air Act," Andrew Morriss carefully details the history of clean air laws, showing how politics has manipulated the legislation for the benefit of special interest groups. Morriss argues that state implementation plans (SIPs) filling multiple file cabinets with detailed regulations are hardly necessary to establish air-quality standards. Rather, those filing cabinets are the way by which some firms win and others lose in the regulatory process. Because of politics, he concludes, we are paying a lot and getting little from the federal Clean Air Act.

The title of this book, *Political Environmentalism*, purposefully contrasts with another book, *Free Market Environmentalism*, written by Donald R. Leal and me in 1991. For the past thirty years, citizens have naively accepted political environmentalism as the main, if not the only, way of solving environmental problems. Laws and regulations were supposed to represent the public interest and counter the greed of the marketplace. The evidence in this volume, however, questions this naive assumption and provides added impetus for market approaches to environmental problems. As we enter a new century and face new environmental problems, we must do better than presume that public interest will dominate. Andrew Morriss ends the book calling for environmental regulations that are transparent, universal, and property-rights based. Transparency would require that regulations be "clear, available, and readily comparable across media, type of source, and regulatory authority." Universality would make regulations "generally applicable to new sources and to old . . . to avoid opportunities for rent-seeking." And finally, regulations based on property rights would allow "contractual means of reallocating burdens" to achieve efficiencies. In summary, because political environmentalism does not always work the way we wish it would, perhaps the time has come to give free market environmentalism a chance.

Jonathan H. Adler*

Clean Politics, Dirty Profits

Rent-Seeking behind the Green Curtain

On August 4, 1992, Vice Presidential candidate Al Gore appeared in Orange County, California, to attack the incumbent President's record on regulation. In a speech at an Evergreen Company used-oil treatment facility, Gore attacked President George Bush for making it "impossible [for] companies like this one to survive." Gore charged "a lot of jobs were lost" because of the Bush administration's inaction (Gore 1992).

Then-Senator Gore was not calling for "reinventing" regulation or reducing the paperwork burden. He attacked President Bush not for presiding over too much regulation, but rather too little. Gore complained that the Bush administration hurt companies that rely on federal regulations to turn a profit by failing to promulgate more regulatory standards.

In particular, Gore attacked the Bush administration's failure to regulate used motor oil as a hazardous waste under the Resource Conservation and Recovery Act (RCRA). Such regulation would have increased the cost of oil changes for consumers and discouraged the recovery and recycling of used oil. However, it would have guaranteed additional business for the Evergreen Company and for

*This chapter is adapted and expanded from an article that appeared in *Regulation,* Vol. 19, No. 4 (1996). Reprinted with permission.

members of the Hazardous Waste Treatment Council (HWTC). This policy proposal had as much to do with promoting narrow economic interests as with protecting environmental concerns.

Green Politics Is Still Politics

When most Americans think of special-interest policies, what comes to mind is usually farm subsidies, pork-barrel spending, tax loopholes, and the like. Although most Americans recognize that politics has a lot to do with the pursuit of power, privilege, and special interest—and examples abound (Barnes 1994; Moore 1994; How to Make Lots of Money 1995; Hosansky 1998)—there seems to be a general presumption that environmental politics are different. When it comes to the environment, many take it for granted that laws are what they seem, that the legislators who enact those laws and the bureaucrats who implement them are earnestly struggling to protect public interests, and that these laws and rules will be enforced in a fair and sensible manner. Far more often than is commonly realized, the purpose and effect of environmental regulation is to serve narrow political and economic interests, not environmental objectives (Greve and Smith 1992).

The details of environmental policy have major economic consequences. America spends well over 2 percent of the Gross Domestic Product on pollution control, and the figure is rising (EPA 1990). By the year 2000, environmental regulations are expected to cost over $200 billion per year, over 25 percent of the total federal regulatory burden (SBA 1995, 28; Crews 1999, 5). As the costs of environmental regulations increase, so does the value of potential comparative advantages that environmental regulations can create. Seeking regulatory policies that will carve out niche markets or inhibit competitors becomes an increasingly profitable investment of time, money, and other resources. One should expect economic interests to lobby, litigate, and make alliances with "public interest" organizations to ensure favorable treatment for their own industries or companies and to utilize environmental regulations to transfer wealth.

Thus, attempts "to gain a competitive advantage through manipulation of the regulatory process" are "occurring with increasing frequency," according to former Environmental Protection Agency (EPA) Deputy Administrator A. James Barnes (1994). Examples are everywhere:

- The Business Council for a Sustainable Energy Future, a coalition of gas, wind, solar, and geothermal power producers and related firms, is lobbying for deep cuts in greenhouse gas emissions (How to Make Lots of Money 1995).
- The Environmental Technology Council, a successor organization to HWTC, is seeking to ensure that various wastes, such as fluorescent bulbs, are covered by hazardous waste regulations (Adler 1996).
- The Alliance for Responsible Thermal Treatment (ARTT), an HWTC spin-off of incinerator operators, wishes to prevent the burning of hazardous waste in cement kilns and thereby eliminate its members' toughest competition (Moore 1994; Bennett 1995).
- Major utilities joined with environmental groups to support mandating the sale of electric vehicles in the northeastern United States and have sought policies that would subsidize the purchase of electric cars at ratepayers' expense (Moore 1994).
- Ethanol producers wish to ensure that their product is guaranteed a portion of the lucrative oxygenate market for federally mandated reformulated gasoline (Adler 1992).
- The Conservation Reserve Program, heralded by leaders in both parties as a commonsense environmental program, has as a primary purpose to increase farm commodity prices by

taking acreage out of production and does little to control agricultural runoff (Tolman 1995).

The list can go on and on, for painting special interest policies green makes them easier to enact, irrespective of whether they further environmental protection. In this sense, the politics of the environment are no different than for any other issue.

Desperately Seeking Rent-Seekers

For years, academics have suggested that many regulatory policies are more the result of interest-group pleading and manipulation than a dispassionate consideration of the public interest. Many firms find it easier to lobby for wealth transfers than to create wealth in an open marketplace—a practice commonly referred to as rent-seeking. The rents that they seek are economic returns in excess of that which a competitive marketplace would allow. As defined by economist Robert Tollison (1982) in his survey of the subject, "Rent-seeking is the expenditure of scarce resources to capture an artificially created transfer" (578).

Rent-seeking occurs, in part, because firms have the ability to receive concentrated benefits through government action, the costs of which are dispersed throughout the whole of society. For example, in the case of sugar subsidies, the benefits accrue directly to U.S. sugar producers, while the costs, estimated at $1.4 billion per year, are spread across all consumers of sugar in the form of higher sugar prices (GAO 1993, 4). When such policies are enacted, a narrow interest arguably wins, while everyone else loses.

In the regulatory context, rent-seeking typically consists of pursuing those government interventions that will provide comparative advantage to a particular industry or subsector. By restricting entry or reducing output, regulations can serve to reduce competition and cartelize an industry and potentially increase returns. Tariffs and licensing restrictions are rather common regulatory measures sought by rent-seekers. Other, less overt, measures can heighten preexisting comparative advantages or manufacture a comparative advantage out of an incidental difference in firms or industrial sectors.

While often disparaged, rent-seeking can be viewed as the natural outgrowth of firms seeking their self-interest in a regulatory environment. If regulations are here to stay, the reasoning may go, a firm might as well make the best of the situation. In fact, given the courts' current interpretation of antitrust laws, one could consider rent-seeking as the only legal form of predation. Whether defensible or not, rent-seeking has become rather pervasive in regulatory programs. As economist Robert McCormick (1989) notes, "There is abundant evidence in the economic literature that when the flag of public interest is raised to support regulation, there is always a private interest lurking in the background" (27–28).

There is no reason to expect environmental regulation to be immune from the economic pressures that create rent-seeking in other contexts. In fact, by its very nature, environmental regulation may be more prone to rent-seeking, for in the environmental context, both regulated firms and public interest representatives stand to gain from reductions in output or the creation of barriers to entry. Such measures can produce cartel-like gains for the regulated firms while having the ostensible environmental benefit of reducing output and/or the use of natural resources (Maloney and McCormick 1982). There may not be agreement on the nature and design of a specific regulatory program, but there is a common interest nonetheless.

One definite effect of environmental regulation, indeed of most regulation, is to privilege older and larger facilities. Many environmental regulations impose stricter requirements on newer facilities than on older ones, thus protecting established facilities from new competition (Bartel and Thomas 1987). Regulatory burdens can also weed out smaller or less efficient competitors. "Compliance with environmental laws has not only reduced the number of plants in the affected industries but has placed a greater burden on small than on large plants," concluded B. Peter Pashigian in a 1984 study. "Small plants have found it more difficult to compete and survive with larger plants under environmental regulation" (23).

This effect should be expected. Small firms, by their very nature of being small, are particularly vulnerable to regulatory costs. With few employees to spare, reporting and other paperwork requirements that appear insignificant when drafted become significant drains on labor power once they are implemented. As the EPA concluded, small firms "do not have legal and engineering staffs to assist them, nor do they have the financial resources available to larger firms. Often their costs per unit of production to comply with environmental regulations are much larger than those of their large competitors" (EPA 1988, 1-1). Thus, larger companies may view regulatory hurdles as nuisances that can be absorbed by lowering profit margins or delaying capital investments, but for small businesses, regulation can threaten a firm's existence. It should be no surprise that larger firms sometimes seek to take advantage of this disparity in pursuit of comparative advantage.

Warring Coal-itions

The paradigmatic example of environmental policy by and for special interests is the mandatory imposition of scrubbers on coal-fired power plants under the Clean Air Act Amendments of 1977. Bruce Ackerman and William Hassler's (1981) thorough history of this development, *Clean Coal, Dirty Air,* bears the subtitle "How the Clean Air Act Became a Multibillion-Dollar Bail-Out for High Sulfur Coal Producers and What Should Be Done about It."

Under the 1970 Clean Air Act, the EPA had established a policy whereby all coal plants were required to meet a set emission standard for sulfur dioxide. The original standard of 1.2 pounds of sulfur dioxide (SO_2) per million British thermal units (BTUs) of coal could be met in a variety of ways.

Despite its apparent flexibility, this regulation had disparate regional effects. Most of the coal in the eastern United States is relatively "dirty" due to its high sulfur content. Western coal, on the other hand, is far cleaner. Using western coal enabled utilities and other coal-burning facilities to meet the federal standard without installing costly scrubbers to reduce the sulfur content of their emissions. At the time, scrubbers were so expensive that many midwestern firms found it less expensive to haul tons of low-sulfur coal from the West than to utilize closer, dirtier deposits.

When the Clean Air Act was revised in 1977, it was time for the eastern coal producers to get even. As Ackerman and Hassler (1981) noted, eastern producers of high-sulfur coal elected "to abandon their campaign to weaken pollution standards and take up the cudgels for the costliest possible clean air solution—universal scrubbing" (31). The result was a "bizarre coalition of environmentalists and dirty coal producers" that successfully advanced a new set of environmental standards that probably did more harm than good in much of the country (Ackerman and Hassler 1981, 27).

Under the 1977 law, coal plants had to meet both an emission standard and a technology standard. In particular, the law contained new-source-performance standards (NSPS) that forced facilities to attain a "percentage reduction in emissions." In other words, no matter how clean coal was, a new facility would still be required to install scrubbers. This law destroyed low-sulfur coal's comparative advantage, particularly in the Midwest and the East. If all new facilities had scrubbers, then there was no need to transport low-sulfur coal across the country. Less expensive, high-sulfur coal from the East would work just as well, even if it produced substantially greater emissions.

Unsatisfied with this measure alone, eastern coal producers and the eastern-based United Mine Workers, with the support of the Sierra Club and the National Clean Air Coalition, successfully pushed for additional provisions to encourage the use of "local" coal in the eastern United States (Ackerman and Hassler 1981, 46). In particular, Congress adopted Section 125, "Measures to Prevent Economic Disruption or Unemployment." This provision enabled state and federal officials to order power plants to use regionally available coal, if the use of coal from elsewhere in the United States might put local mine workers out of work.

This amendment was naked regional protectionism, pure and simple. "The dominant thrust of this amendment is not its relationship to clean air, but its relationship to the economics of the areas it is designed to protect," complained Senator Edmund Muskie (D-ME) on the floor of the Senate (quoted in Ackerman and Hassler 1981, 46). No matter; the amendment was adopted on an unrecorded vote in the House and squeaked to a 45–44 victory in the Senate, with most Senators voting along regional lines.

Ironically, one effect of the 1977 amendments was to extend the life of older, otherwise obsolete, coal-fired plants. By imposing scrubber requirements on all new coal plants, Congress made older plants more cost-effective by comparison, delaying the environmental gains that would be achieved by a switch to more modern, less polluting facilities. As a result, some regions of the country actually saw an increase in sulfur dioxide emissions as a result of the new law, and the amount of scrubber sludge requiring disposal increased substantially.

More Regional Rent-Seeking

Another element of the 1977 Clean Air Act Amendments clearly affected by special interest considerations was the prevention of significant deterioration (PSD) policy, which was designed to ensure that those areas already attaining federal clean air standards would continue to do so. As refined in the 1977 amendments, "clean" areas were classified according to their prescribed level of growth.

Each classification imposed limits on the rate at which new industrial facilities could emit into the regional air shed. Moreover, new facilities in clean areas became subject to new-source-review reporting requirements, and new facilities of sufficient size were required to adopt emission-control technologies, such as scrubbers.

All of this meant that the PSD policy imposed disproportionate costs on those parts of the country that had less air pollution. Thus, the policy benefited northern urban areas vis-à-vis rural areas, particularly in the West and South. In one sense, the PSD policy lessened the North's comparative disadvantages brought about by the first round of environmental regulation. As Pashigian concluded in a 1985 analysis, "PSD policy raised the cost factor of mobility and thereby allowed northern locations with lower air quality to improve local air quality without as large a loss of factors to areas with superior air quality" (553).

If this theory is correct, one would expect to find a regional disparity in support for the PSD policy. When Pashigian analyzed five congressional votes on the PSD policy in 1976 and 1977, that disparity is exactly what he found. There was a greater regional difference in support for PSD policy than for other air pollution control policies considered at the same time, and it could not be explained by ideological or party differences. The most likely cause of the pattern of support and opposition to PSD policy was regional self-interest.

Green Pork in the Corn Barrel

It is difficult to discuss rent-seeking without a mention of the ethanol lobby, in particular the agricultural powerhouse Archer Daniels Midland (ADM). As has been well documented on numerous occasions (e.g., Bovard 1995), ADM has perfected the art of rent-seeking as well as, if not better than, any other company in America. The agricultural conglomerate has benefited from a range of subsidies, agricultural and otherwise. ADM is "totally immersed in these government programs," according to CEO Dwayne Andreas (quoted in Grain King's Business Is Daily Grind 1990, 11). It has also been the beneficiary of environmental policy.

A key component of the 1990 Clean Air Act Amendments was a set of provisions governing the content of automotive fuels. The amendments mandated that in cities with high carbon monoxide (CO) levels, oxygenates be added to gasoline during the winter, and in cities with high ground-level ozone ("smog") levels, reformulated gasoline be used. Both of these provisions created opportunities for the use of ethanol, a corn-based alcohol fuel. Ethanol is an oxygenate that can be added to gasoline to reduce CO emissions and is a potential fuel additive for reformulated gasoline as well.

The ethanol lobby, supported by midwestern agricultural interests, swung into action. The lobby sought to ensure that both provisions required the maximum amount of oxygenates possible, so as to provide the greatest boost to ethanol markets. In particular, ethanol interests sought to require a minimum oxygen content that could not be met by other oxygenates (Adler 1992). Reducing air pollution quickly became a secondary concern. As one Senate committee report noted, "In the absence of other avenues through which to encourage domestically produced ethanol to enter the fuel stream, this [requirement] is necessary."[1]

Regrettably, the solicitation of the ethanol lobby did not end there. Desperate to attract votes from agricultural interests during the 1992 presidential campaign, George Bush proposed relaxing clean air standards to encourage the use of ethanol, a corn-based fuel. At the time, the Clinton campaign blasted the move as a cynical attempt "to buy the votes of the corn growers."[2]

1. *Clean Air Act Amendments of 1989*, Report of the Committee on Environment and Public Works, Senate Report No. 101-228, p. 449 (minority views of Senator Steve Symms).

2. Statement of Bill Burton, Clinton-Gore campaign chief energy policy director, quoted in Peckham (1992).

Fifteen months later, it was the Clinton administration's turn to rewrite environmental regulations, guaranteeing ethanol a 30 percent share of the oxygenate market for reformulated gasoline mandated in the nine smoggiest cities under the 1990 Clean Air Act. In 1993, the Clinton administration finalized a new rule outlining the program and defining what constitutes a suitably reformulated fuel. At the time, the ethanol lobby expressed concerns that the definition of reformulated gasoline would make it difficult for ethanol to compete. Ethanol can be added to gasoline to reduce certain emissions, but it is more expensive than some of its competitors and, under certain conditions, can actually increase automotive emissions. Ethanol producers were afraid that petroleum companies would be able to use other fuel additives, such as MTBE, to meet the regulatory guidelines at a lower cost.

Thus, the guaranteed 30 percent share was proposed, in EPA Administrator Carol Browner's words, to "create additional markets for ethanol and ETBE [an ethanol derivative]." According to Browner, the "EPA's proposal would help farmers by boosting the demand for ethanol and ETBE while protecting the environment" (quoted in EPA 1993). At the time, the EPA estimated that the rule "could increase the production and use of ethanol by as much as 60 percent over current levels." Agriculture Secretary Mike Espy crowed that "One of my top priorities is improving farm income, and this initiative will do just that" (quoted in EPA 1993).

Guaranteeing ethanol's market share would come at a significant price. The EPA estimated a direct cost to consumers of $48 million per year.[3] Other analyses put the annual price tag at $350 million (Hahn 1994). Because ethanol is exempt from most fuel taxes at both the state and federal level (another rent-seeking story in itself), the program would have hit government revenues as well. EPA analysts predicted that the Federal Highway Trust Fund, which

3. 58 *Federal Register* 68343, 68350 (December 27, 1993).

is used for highway maintenance and construction, would lose as much as $340 million per year in revenues from the federal gas tax.[4]

There are few things upon which the Sierra Club and the American Petroleum Institute agree, but they both argued that the EPA's proposal was bad for consumers, producers, and environmental protection. "This proposal is illegal, and it's bad policy," A. Blakeman Early of the Sierra Club told the *National Journal.* In Early's view, "It's not the role of the Clean Air Act to make mandatory markets for ethanol" (quoted in Kriz 1994, 898). Some of the law's authors clearly felt otherwise (Adler 1992).

Eager to paint the ethanol giveaway green, the EPA claimed that the proposal would reduce greenhouse gas emissions, energy demand, and the importation of foreign oil. A report published by Resources for the Future, however, cast serious doubts on the EPA's claims, concluding that there are "unsubsidized, lower-cost, domestically produced" oxygenates that can "produce environmental benefits indistinguishable from those" of ethanol (Stagliano 1994). A Department of Energy study went further, concluding that the proposal would increase energy use and greenhouse gas emissions (Southerland 1994). Despite these concerns, the EPA went ahead with the regulation.

Eventually, the federal judiciary intervened after the American Petroleum Institute filed suit. In April 1995, the District of Columbia Circuit Court of Appeals ruled that the Clinton administration never had the authority to propose the policy in the first place. The court held that "The sole purpose of the RFG [reformulated gasoline] program is to reduce air pollution, which it does through specific performance standards for reducing VOCs [voltaile organic compounds] and toxics emissions. EPA admits that the [ethanol rule] will not give additional emission reductions for VOCs or toxics . . . and has even conceded that the use of ethanol might possibly make

4. 58 *Federal Register* 68343, 68350 (December 27, 1993).

air quality worse."[5] No matter how important the ethanol lobby, the court declared, the Clinton administration did not have the statutory authority to subsidize it through environmental regulations. Such results are rare indeed.

Green Baptists and Brown Bootleggers

The prevalence of rent-seeking in environmental policy is due, in part, to the cover that protestations of environmental concern can provide for otherwise ill-fated policies. Paint a policy proposal green, and it will receive less scrutiny than in any other color. Moreover, the ability of economic interest groups to supplement their lobbying efforts with public interest allies from the environmentalist community greatly enhances their political clout.

Whereas ethanol producers rarely receive the support of environmental organizations, other interests have been more fortunate. The ability of economic interests to team up with moral or ideological forces makes them far more powerful in the policy debate. Clemson University professor and former Federal Trade Commission official Bruce Yandle called such efforts "bootlegger-and-Baptist" coalitions. "Both bootleggers and Baptists favor statutes that shut down liquor stores on Sunday," Yandle explains. "The Baptists because of their religious preferences. The bootleggers because it expands their market" (quoted in Brimelow and Spencer 1992).[6]

It is much the same in the environmental arena. Environmental activists may prefer a policy such as the tightening of hazardous waste regulations because of their "religious" preferences, while hazardous waste treatment firms see the same policy as an opportunity to expand

5. *American Petroleum Institute v. U.S. Environmental Protection Agency,* 52 F3d 1113, 1119 (D.C. Cir. 1995).

6. The "bootlegger-and-Baptist" phenomenon is discussed in greater detail by Yandle (1983; 1989). See also Yandle's chapter in this volume.

their market and stifle opposition. The HWTC, a trade association of companies that operate incinerators and other hazardous waste treatment facilities, often works in coalitions with environmental groups. In the late 1980s and early 1990s, the HWTC published reports and held numerous press conferences with major environmental groups, including the Natural Resources Defense Council, the Environmental Defense Fund, the Izaak Walton League, the National Audubon Society, and the Sierra Club, that criticized EPA enforcement of hazardous waste laws (Adler 1995, 73). The HWTC even allowed environmental group officials to testify on its behalf before Congress.

The HWTC's membership benefits from tighter enforcement as its members specialize in meeting stringent cleanup and treatment standards. Therefore, on a wide range of issues, from the burning of hazardous waste in cement kilns and Superfund cleanup standards to the recycling of fluorescent bulbs and the disposal of used motor oil, the HWTC and its successor organization, the Environmental Technology Council, have consistently sought to increase regulatory controls and require that more and more waste streams be classified as hazardous. The HWTC supports these controls because they create a greater market for the waste management services of its members.

This support has not always been to the benefit of the environment. "[T]he environmental movement and the waste treatment industry have tried to block efforts to promote the reduction of sources of hazardous waste generation," according to Marc K. Landy and Mary Hague (1992, 79) of Boston College. They note that the HWTC joined with environmental groups to oppose financing Superfund cleanups with a waste-end tax that would have provided industrial firms with an incentive to reduce the production of waste, thereby reducing the need to purchase the services of HWTC member companies.

HWTC and environmental groups have also teamed up to push for more stringent regulation of hazardous waste recycling, thus making such recycling more expensive and less competitive. From 1987 through 1994, the HWTC joined with the Natural Resources Defense Council, Izaak Walton League, and other environmentalist groups in a series of lawsuits seeking to force the EPA to impose more stringent regulations on the management of used motor oil. These regulations would require the treatment of used oil before disposal, thus providing HWTC members with increased business. As the District of Columbia Circuit Court of Appeals ruled in 1988, the HWTC's efforts were clearly aimed at "having government drive business its way."[7]

Ironically, the regulation of used motor oil as a hazardous waste has the potential to cause environmental harm. Several hundred million gallons of used motor oil is disposed of every year. While a substantial portion of it is reclaimed for reuse, recycling, or energy recovery, much of it is simply discarded into landfills or into sewers. Much of this used oil is generated by small service stations or individual car owners performing oil changes. If used oil were regulated as a hazardous waste, the costs of handling it would increase, as would insurance for potential environmental liability exposure. This, in turn, would increase the cost of an oil change and discourage voluntary collection programs, such as those run by many service stations at no charge to their customers. "The added costs expected as a result of listing used oil as a hazardous waste would only further decrease the attractiveness of handling these materials," testified one Energy Department official in 1992 (Schroeder 20). The primary effect would be to drive smaller firms out of the used oil collection business and reduce the overall percentage of oil collected

7. *Hazardous Waste Treatment Council v. U.S. Environmental Protection Agency*, 861 F2d 277, 285 (D.C. Cir. 1988).

for reuse, recycling, or energy recovery. It would, however, increase the amount of oil going to those firms that lobbied and litigated in support of such a rule.

When Bootleggers Fund Baptists

Those companies and associations that benefit from increased regulation have become quite aware of the benefits of "Baptists" to provide cover for their "bootlegging." This is one reason why some corporations are substantial funders of environmentalist causes (Adler 1995, 95–99). Although the National Wildlife Federation (NWF) supports zero discharge standards under the Clean Water Act and has endorsed phasing out the industrial use of chlorine, such corporate giants as Browning-Ferris, Dow Chemical, DuPont, 3M Company, Procter & Gamble, Shell Oil, and WMX Technologies paid a minimum of $10,000 each to be members of NWF's Corporate Conservation Council (Adler 1995, 98).

Obviously, some firms believe that supporting environmental causes is good public relations. Some executives openly acknowledge that supporting environmental lobbying groups advances policies that support their bottom line. For instance, according to William Y. Brown, director of environmental affairs for Waste Management (now WMX Technologies), the company's environmental grants "focus on policy issues that clearly are in the interest of the environment and that would advance our own business interests. . . . We're in a position to benefit from the same objectives that [environmental groups] are pursuing" (quoted in Gifford 1990). In particular, WMX Technologies benefits from the tightening of environmental regulations governing waste disposal because smaller firms have a more difficult time staying in compliance. It "helps our business," explains Brown (quoted in Gifford 1990). This certainly may explain why WMX has provided substantial funding to the National Audubon Society, the National Wildlife Federation, the Natural Resources Defense Council, the Wilderness Society, and the World Resources Institute. For several years, WMX Technologies donated more than $700,000 annually to environmental causes (EDRI 1995, 486). Among the projects that WMX funded are a National Audubon Society campaign to tighten the regulation of industrial wastes ($135,000) and efforts by the Center for Marine Conservation and the Sport Fishing Institute to ban ocean waste dumping ($75,000 and $32,500, respectively) (Gifford 1990). Waste not dumped in the sea is waste consumers may pay WMX to handle.

Another example of donations to environmental groups being used to support the bottom line involves the Surdna Foundation, founded by the Andrus family in 1917 (Surdna is Andrus spelled backward). In 1993, Surdna donated more than $5.2 million to environmental causes (EDRI 1995, 447). The Surdna Foundation also owns approximately 75,000 acres of timberland in northern California and earned $2.7 million in timber income in 1992–93. Surdna board member Frederick F. Moon III also served on the board of Andrus Timber Partners, which also has substantial timberland holdings in northern California (Arnold 1994, 24).

If timber harvesting on public lands is restricted in the Pacific Northwest, the value of timber on nearby private lands should increase due to the constriction of timber supplies. It is interesting to note that in 1989, the Surdna Foundation began to provide significant support to organizations seeking to limit timber harvesting on federal lands, including the Wilderness Society, the National Audubon Society, the Western Ancient Forests Campaign, the Oregon Natural Resources Council, and Americans for the Ancient Forest. Whether deliberate or not, Surdna's contributions to efforts aimed at stopping timber harvesting on government-owned lands have the potential to increase the value of private timber, thus benefiting Surdna and the Andrus's timber holdings. Surdna is not alone. In the early 1990s, timber giant Weyerhauser funded biological surveys on federal lands in the hopes of finding endangered species that would trigger logging restrictions, thereby increasing profits on sales from Weyerhauser's own lands (Yandle 1997, 74).[8]

The purpose of Surdna's grants to environmentalist causes may be conjectural, but there is no question why ARTT and its member companies have supported environmentalist groups. ARTT, which represents hazardous waste incinerators, was explicitly created to protect its members against competition from cement kilns (Bennett 1995, 1). In the early 1990s, the volume of hazardous waste sent to commercial incinerators began to decline, and cement kilns began burning waste as fuel at less than one-half the cost charged by commercial incinerators. Upon its founding, ARTT announced that it would oppose the "dismantling" of federal hazardous waste regulations that allowed the burning of regulated waste in cement kilns, which are less expensive to operate.[9] Cement kiln operators oppose ARTT's efforts and maintain that their facilities are cleaner and more tightly regulated than incinerators, albeit under different regulations.

In addition to lobbying Congress and the EPA to tighten federal hazardous waste regulation, ARTT also began funding environmental attacks on cement kilns. For instance, in 1994 and 1995 ARTT gave the American Lung Association (ALA) $260,000 to fund educational campaigns against cement kilns in several states (Kiln Group Asks IRS to Probe Lung Association 1995). In 1994, three ALA state affiliates, all of which received portions of the grant, began campaigns against the burning of waste in local cement kilns while remaining largely silent about emissions from hazardous waste incinerators (Bennett 1995, 3–4). "This is not to say we believe commercial hazardous waste incinerators are benign," an ALA

8. Yandle (1997) also notes that when the Clinton administration passed the 1993 Northwest Timber Plan, which substantially restricted harvesting in national forests, paper company stocks increased, indicating that some firms were likely to benefit from the resulting reductions in supply (1–2).

9. ARTT press release of December 3, 1993, quoted in Bennett (1995, 1–2).

spokesman told the *Hazardous Waste News.* In deciding to accept the grant, he explained, "we said, 'You have your interests, we have ours.' This was just a case of the two interests complementing each other" (quoted in Lung Association Head Rebuts Cement 1995).

ARTT's funding of ALA is not the only instance in which the incinerator industry has sought to use environmental organizations in its campaign against cement kilns. Incinerator companies have also funded citizen suits against cement kilns by local "grass-roots" groups. In November 1995, the newly formed Pennsylvania Environmental Enforcement Project (PEEP) filed suit against Keystone Cement Company, alleging that the burning of hazardous waste at Keystone's Bath, Pennsylvania, kiln posed an imminent threat to public health. Although PEEP was a small and purportedly grass-roots group, among its lawyers was former Representative James Florio, the chief lobbyist for ARTT (Rubenstein 1996).

Keystone's lawyers became suspicious and sought discovery of PEEP's funding sources and the scientific bases for its allegations. The suit was soon dismissed, but not before Keystone learned that PEEP had received $250,000 from the Environmental Responsibility Fund (ERF), which is controlled by a subsidiary of Rollins Environmental Services, a major incinerator operator (Rubenstein 1996). This information was kept confidential under court seal until Keystone sued to force public disclosure of Rollins's use of environmental groups to attack the competition. In lifting the protective order, the federal district court declared that "when a corporation attempts to use the litigation process to injure a competitor under the guise of a public interest lawsuit, this Court will remove the shield of confidentiality protecting that masquerade and allow the public to judge the merits of the dispute with full knowledge of the debate's participants."[10]

10. *Pennsylvania Environmental Enforcement Project v. Keystone Cement,* Civil Action No. 96-585 (D.C. Del. 1997), at 7.

In the Public Interest?

Perhaps it is the exceptional citizen suit that serves as a mask for corporate efforts to quash competition. But this does not mean that the typical environmental citizen suit promotes the public interest. The idea behind environmental citizen suit provisions is to empower local groups to ensure that federal regulations are enforced and that environmental problems are corrected. National environmental groups file a disproportionate share of environmental citizen suits, and most of these suits are filed against private industry—even when other entities are responsible for the lion's share of the pollution.

The citizen suit provisions of the Clean Water Act (CWA) have been among the most frequently used. A review of citizen suit activity under the CWA in the 1980s found that five national organizations—the Natural Resources Defense Council, the Sierra Club Legal Defense Fund, the Atlantic States Legal Foundation, the Public Interest Research Group, and the Friends of the Earth—were responsible for the majority of suits filed from May 1984 to September 1988 (Greve 1990, 353).

More interesting to note is that these groups filed most of their suits against private industry even though municipalities and agriculture were responsible for a greater share of water pollution. In the years between 1984 and 1988, there were more than six times as many CWA citizen suits against industrial facilities as there were against governmental entities. "This pronounced preference for proceeding against private industry cannot be explained by environmental considerations—municipal facilities cause far more water pollution than private industry and violate their [CWA] permits far more frequently" notes Greve (1990, 362).

Greve's research suggests that corporations are more inviting targets because environmental organizations stand to gain substantially from suing industry under federal environmental laws. "Substantial portions of [citizen suit] settlements constitute direct transfer payments to environmental groups," including above-cost attorney's fees and payments to third-party environmental groups to fund conservation efforts (Greve 1990, 356). The result can be settlements of several million dollars or more. When the Sierra Club Legal Defense Fund sued the oil company Unocal, the settlement totaled over $5 million, including approximately $2.5 million for the Trust for Public Land, another nonprofit environmental group (Greve 1990, 358). A 1987 Natural Resources Defense Council suit against Bethlehem Steel produced similar gains for environmental activist groups. In addition to more than $1 million in fines, Bethlehem was required to make substantial contributions to the Trust for Public Lands ($200,000), the National Fish and Wildlife Foundation ($100,000), and Save Our Streams ($50,000) (Adler 1995, 46).

For a Good Cause?

The fact that environmental policy measures are often influenced by special interest considerations does not mean that they are wholly ineffective at achieving environmental ends. More likely, policies influenced by the push and pull of warring interests span the spectrum from those, like the ethanol giveaway, that are bare wealth transfers benefiting from the apparent association with environmental goals to measures that are arguably sensible responses to valid environmental concerns.

A possible example of the latter can be found in the history of the chlorofluorocarbon (CFC) phaseout. CFCs, once the most widely used class of refrigerants, are less expensive and less dangerous than practical alternatives. As a result, CFCs were found in virtually every refrigerator, car air conditioner, and commercial chiller in the United States and much of the world. For a time, CFCs were also used for aerosol can propellants, cleaning agents, and foam-blowing agents.

In the 1970s scientists found evidence, later confirmed, suggesting that CFCs were contributing to a thinning of Earth's stratospheric ozone layer, which deflects substantial amounts of ultraviolet solar radiation. Some feared that this thinning could pose a significant ecological threat, if not to people, then to other animal and plant life. To this day, uncertainties remain about the extent of the risk posed by thinning (Lieberman 1994a). In response to this concern, Congress banned the use of CFCs in aerosol cans in 1978, and the United Nations sponsored negotiations with the purpose of drafting a treaty to protect the ozone layer.

Although the initial response of the CFC industry was resistance, this posture did not last long. In 1986, the industry suddenly signaled that it would support global limits on the use of CFCs and related compounds, while simultaneously claiming there was no solid evidence of a real environmental threat. In 1988, DuPont, the world's largest CFC producer, called for a complete global phaseout. The company appears to have been motivated less by concern for the global environment than for the opportunity to increase profits. In fact, at the same time it called for CFC controls, the industry's primary association maintained that evidence linking CFCs to tangible environmental harms remained speculative (McInnis 1992).

During the early 1980s, as concern about CFCs increased, DuPont stepped up research into possible substitutes. Everything DuPont's researchers came up with was substantially more expensive or impractical (McInnis 1992, 147). At the same time, foreign CFC producers were beginning to erode DuPont's market share. Yet under a global phaseout, consumers would have no alternative to replacing CFCs and CFC-reliant equipment with substitutes designed and patented by DuPont and other American producers. Thus, the American CFC industry morphed from a staunch opponent of CFC regulations to a prime backer of international limits. The end result will cost American consumers as much as $100 billion over the course of the decade-long phaseout (Lieberman 1994b).

Others got into the act as well, boosting the phaseout's overall cost. The Mobile Air Conditioning Society, a trade association representing those who repair automotive air conditioners, successfully pushed to accelerate the restrictions on smaller cans of CFC-12, such as those used by car owners to recharge car air conditioners. Under the phaseout, the purchase of containers with less than twenty pounds of refrigerant was limited to EPA-certified technicians two years earlier than for larger purchases. This rule effectively forced people who would recharge their own car air conditioners to take their vehicles to a service shop.

Green Rents Go Global

The history of the CFC phaseout points to the larger push toward environmental rent-seeking on a global scale. Natural gas and alternative energy companies see in the proposed United Nations global warming treaty the potential to cripple their primary competitors, petroleum and coal (How to Make Lots of Money 1995). Thus, Kenneth Lay, CEO of natural gas giant Enron Corporation, signed his name to op-eds in favor of a global warming treaty distributed by the National Environmental Trust, an environmental activist organization based in Washington, D.C. Similarly, advertisements by the American Gas Association, the natural gas industry's primary trade group, tout natural gas as "the cleanest fossil fuel available" because it produces substantially fewer greenhouse gas emissions than does oil or coal.[11]

Industries that have traditionally sought protection from global competition through tariffs and other trade barriers see a new opportunity in the push for increased international environmental

11. For example, the American Gas Association sponsored an ad in the *National Journal* (20 June 1998, 1416), headlined "A source of energy that reduces greenhouse gas emissions. And hours of congressional debate," that compared natural gas emissions with those from other fuel sources and that closed with the lines "Clean natural gas. Think what you'll save."

efforts. C. Ford Runge (1990) of the University of Minnesota notes, "Because environmental standards have a growing national constituency, they are especially attractive candidates for disguised protectionism" (47). Daniel Esty, who participated in the NAFTA negotiations on behalf of the Environmental Protection Agency, concurs, noting that "Environmental standards can be crafted chiefly to benefit domestic producers, not to protect the environment" (Esty 1994, 45).

A prime example of trade protectionism disguised as environmental protection is the European Community's (E.C.) 1989 ban on the importation of U.S. beef produced with bovine growth hormones. The E.C. defended the restriction as a health measure. Conversely, there was no credible scientific evidence linking hormones in U.S. beef to any health threat. Growth hormones occur naturally in beef. Most observers see this action as an attempt to exclude U.S. producers from the lucrative European beef and offal markets (Esty 1994, 103).

The United States has also used environmental measures to restrict foreign imports. When Corporate Average Fuel Economy (CAFE) standards for automobiles were first enacted in the 1970s, Congress explicitly rejected alternative means of reducing automobile fuel consumption that might encourage foreign imports. The 1975 House report on the legislation explained that Congress "did not want the auto efficiency tax to provide a stimulus to increased imports of autos . . ." (cited in Esty 1994, 45). CAFE standards have had the deliberate effect of discriminating against high-end foreign manufacturers such as Mercedes-Benz, BMW, and Volvo. Because these manufacturers do not make many smaller cars with high fuel economy ratings, they are penalized in a way that America's "Big Three" automakers, with their complete automobile lines, are not.

In theory, Article XX of the General Agreement on Tariffs and Trade (GATT) has always allowed for exceptions to general free-trade principles for measures "relating to the conservation of exhaustible natural resources." It has also been designed to protect public health. Cases in which GATT panels upheld trade-restrictive environmental measures, however, are few and far between. The use of environmental measures as trade barriers may get a boost from the World Trade Organization Committee on Trade and Environment, which is considering proposals that give companies greater discretion in enacting environmental regulations that have discriminatory effects. These proposals could potentially open the door to nontariff trade barriers enacted under environmental pretenses. "If anything, the temptation to use environmental and health standards to deny access to home markets is stronger now than in the 1980s," notes Runge (1990, 51).

Gray Hats

There is no doubt that many environmental statutes and regulations have been enacted for reasons other than the private gains of interested firms, but the fact that environmental causes have also become public interest shields for private gain cannot be ignored. It is difficult to argue that environmental policy is relatively immune to special interest pressures. Due to the tremendous cost and complexity of environmental rules, the environmental policy arena presents an extremely attractive target for those who wish to seek rents in Washington, D.C. If there is one consistent interest, it is that of the inside-the-beltway consultants, lobbyists, and litigators who benefit from the continuation of a Byzantine regulatory structure, the intimate knowledge of which is valuable and rare.

Rent-seeking in environmental policy is not new, and it is not likely to go away. As long as environmental decisions made in Washington have the potential to reallocate billions of dollars from one set of interests to another, those interests will be sure that they have their say. Lifting the green curtain and exposing the rent-seeking that lies behind it to the light of day is a useful educational exercise that can demystify the public interest aura attached to any policy labeled "pro-environment."

The foregoing suggests that the traditional framing of the environmental debate is a false one. There is no corporate monolith that opposes regulation across the board, and one can never assume that support for more regulations comes primarily from those who have the public's well-being at heart. Environmental policy conflicts are not epic struggles between white-hat public interest crusaders and greedy black-hat corporate interests. Indeed, in the environmental arena, as in most policy debates, there are few black hats and white hats—most are shades of gray.

REFERENCES

Ackerman, Bruce, and William T. Hassler. 1981. *Clean Coal, Dirty Air: How the Clean Air Act Became a Multibillion-Dollar Bail-Out for High Sulfur Coal Producers and What Should Be Done About It.* New Haven: Yale University Press.

Adler, Jonathan H. 1992. Clean Fuels, Dirty Air. In *Environmental Politics: Public Costs, Private Rewards,* edited by Michael S. Greve and Fred L. Smith, Jr. New York: Praeger.

Adler, Jonathan H. 1995. *Environmentalism at the Crossroads: Green Activism in America.* Washington, D.C.: Capital Research Center.

Adler, Jonathan H. 1996. Wasted Lights. *Regulation* 19, no. 2: 15–18.

Arnold, Ron. 1994. *Getting Rich: The Environmental Movement's Income, Salary, Contributor, and Investment Patterns.* Bellevue, WA: Center for the Defense of Free Enterprise.

Barnes, A. James. 1994. How to Milk EPA's Smog Rules for Fun and Profit. *Sacramento Bee,* 30 March, B7.

Bartel, Ann P., and Lacy Glenn Thomas. 1987. Predation through Regulation: The Wage and Profit Effects of the Occupational Safety and Health Administration and the Environmental Protection Agency. *Journal of Law and Economics* 30 (October): 239–264.

Bennett, James T. 1995. Selling Its Reputation: The American Lung Association. *Alternatives in Philanthropy* (January).

Bovard, James. 1995. *Archer Daniels Midland: A Case Study in Corporate Welfare.* Cato Policy Analysis No. 241 (September). Washington, D.C.: Cato Institute.

Brimelow, Peter, and Leslie Spencer. 1992. Should We Abolish the EPA? *Forbes,* 14 September, p. 42.

Crews, Clyde Wayne, Jr. 1999. *Ten Thousand Commandments: An Annual Policymaker's Snapshot of the Federal Regulatory State.* 1999 Edition. Washington, D.C.: Competitive Enterprise Institute.

Environmental Data Research Institute (EDRI). 1995. *Environmental Grantmaking Foundations: 1995 Directory.* Rochester: Environmental Data Research Institute.

Environmental Protection Agency (EPA), Office of Policy Planning and Evaluation. 1988. *The Small Business Sector Study: Impacts of Environmental Regulations on Small Business.* EPA 230-09/88-039. Washington, D.C.: Environmental Protection Agency.

Environmental Protection Agency (EPA), Office of Policy Planning and Evaluation. 1990. *Environmental Investments: The Cost of a Clean Environment.* EPA-230-12/90-084. Washington, D.C.: Environmental Protection Agency.

Environmental Protection Agency (EPA). 1993. EPA Finalizes Reformulated Gasoline Rule. *Environmental News.* EPA 93-R-298. Washington, D.C.: Environmental Protection Agency.

Esty, Daniel C. 1994. *Greening the GATT: Trade, Environment, and the Future.* Washington, D.C.: Institute for International Economics.

General Accounting Office (GAO). 1993. *Sugar Program: Changing Domestic and International Conditions Require Program Changes.* GAO/RCED-93-84. Washington, D.C.: General Accounting Office.

Gifford, William. 1990. Waste Management's Unlikely Allies. *Legal Times,* May, 1.

Gore, Al. 1992. Remarks of Senator Al Gore at Evergreen Co. in California. *U.S. Newswire,* 4 August.

Grain King's Business Is Daily Grind for Profit. 1990. *Insight,* 19 February, 11+.

Greve, Michael. 1990. The Private Enforcement of Environmental Law. *Tulane Law Review* 65: 339–394.

Greve, Michael S., and Fred L. Smith, Jr., eds. 1992. *Environmental Politics: Public Costs, Private Rewards.* New York: Praeger.

Hahn, Robert W. 1994. Testimony on the Renewable Oxygenate Requirement before the U.S. Environmental Protection Agency (January 14).

Hosansky, David. 1998. The Art of Business Lobbying: Finding Profit in Regulation. *Congressional Quarterly,* 18 April, 953, 966–972.

How to Make Lots of Money, and Save the Planet Too. 1995. *The Economist,* 3 June, 57.

Kiln Group Asks IRS to Probe Lung Association Tax-Exempt Status. 1995. *Environment Week* 8, no. 5.

Kriz, Margaret. 1994. Fight Over Clean Fuels Gets Dirty. *National Journal* 26, no. 16 (April 16): 898.

Landy, Marc K., and Mary Hague. 1992. The Coalition for Waste: Private Interests and Superfund. In *Environmental Politics: Public Costs, Private Rewards,* edited by Michael S. Greve and Fred L. Smith, Jr. New York: Praeger.

Lieberman, Ben. 1994a. Stratospheric Ozone Depletion and the Montreal Protocol: A Critical Analysis. *Buffalo Environmental Law Journal* 2 (Spring): 1–31.

Lieberman, Ben. 1994b. *The High Cost of Cool: The Economic Impact of the CFC Phaseout in the United States*. Washington, D.C.: Competitive Enterprise Institute.

Lung Association Head Rebuts Cement Kiln Industry Charges. 1995. *Hazardous Waste News* 1, no. 2.

Maloney, Michael T., and Robert E. McCormick. 1982. A Positive Theory of Environmental Quality Regulation. *Journal of Law and Economics* 25 (April): 99–123.

McCormick, Robert E. 1989. A Review of the Economics of Regulation: The Political Process. In *Regulation and the Reagan Era: Politics Bureaucracy and the Public Interest*, edited by Roger E. Meiners and Bruce Yandle. New York: Holmes & Meier.

McInnis, Daniel F. 1992. Ozone Layers and Oligopoly Profits. In *Environmental Politics: Public Costs, Private Rewards*, edited by Michael S. Greve and Fred L. Smith, Jr. New York: Praeger.

Moore, W. John. 1994. Golden Rules. *National Journal*, 14 May, 1124–1128.

Pashigian, B. Peter. 1984. The Effect of Environmental Regulation on Optimal Plant Size and Factor Shares. *Journal of Law and Economics* 27 (April): 1–28.

Pashigian, B. Peter. 1985. Environmental Regulation: Whose Self-Interests Are Being Protected? *Economic Inquiry* 23 (October): 551–584.

Peckham, Jack. 1992. Clinton Camp Attacks Bush Over Ethanol Waiver. *U.S. Oil Week* 29, no. 40.

Rubenstein, Bruce. 1996. Outraged Citizens or Public Relations Ploy? *Corporate Legal Times* (December), p. 1.

Runge, C. Ford. 1990. Trade Protectionism and Environmental Regulations: The New Nontariff Barriers. *Northwestern Journal of International Law & Business* 11: 47–61.

Schroeder, Marc C. 1992. Statement of Marc C. Schroeder, Deputy General Counsel, Department of Energy. In *Used Oil Energy Production*

Act: Hearing before the Committee on Energy and Natural Resources (May 20). Washington, D.C.: United States Senate.

Small Business Administration (SBA), Office of the Chief Counsel for Advocacy. 1995. *The Changing Burden of Regulation, Paperwork, and Tax Compliance on Small Business: A Report to Congress.* Washington, D.C.: Small Business Administration.

Southerland, Daniel. 1994. U.S. Study Questions Ethanol's Effect on Pollution. *Washington Post,* 13 May, p. F1.

Stagliano, Vito. 1994. *The Impact of a Proposed EPA Rule Mandating Renewable Oxygenates for Reformulated Gasoline: Questionable Energy Security, Environmental, and Economic Benefits.* Discussion Paper 94–17. Washington, D.C.: Resources for the Future.

Tollison, Robert D. 1982. Rent Seeking: A Survey. *Kyklos* 35: 575–602.

Tolman, Jonathan. 1995. Paying Farmers not to Farm. *CEI UpDate,* May, 3.

Yandle, Bruce. 1983. Bootleggers and Baptists—The Education of a Regulatory Economist. *Regulation,* May/June, 12–16.

Yandle, Bruce. 1989. *The Political Limits of Environmental Regulation: Tracking the Unicorn.* New York: Quorum Books.

Yandle, Bruce. 1997. *Common Sense and Common Law for the Environment.* Lanham, Md.: Rowman & Littlefield.

Bruce Yandle

Public Choice and the Environment

From the Frying Pan to the Fire

Introduction

Environmental problems can be placed into two categories: those that seem tough to understand and deal with and those that are apparently simple (Anderson and Leal 1991). Problems such as global warming, ozone depletion, and endocrine disrupters show up on the tough list. Although knowledgeable people can surely speculate about these problems and may be able to specify scientific relationships that identify potential harm from related pollution, policies that might address these problems remain unclear. By comparison, issues associated with the uncontrolled discharge of sewage into rivers, emission of suspended particulates to the air, discharge of noxious slurry from swine operations, and disposal of hazardous waste in landfills seem simple. Here, the cause-and-effect links are rather stark, and the potential policy solutions seem to be straightforward. Why not hold the polluter responsible for common law violation of adjoining environmental rights and either shut the polluter down or make the polluter pay damages?

But although one might think that fortifying institutions to cause forbearance in the discharge of conventional wastes is simple, that turns out not to be the case at all, especially when the logic of common law is replaced with the law of politics (Yandle 1997). Now, some twenty-five years after embarking on a major federal effort to clean the air, water, and soil, we are still hectored by news about uncontrolled discharge of sewage, hazardous waste sites waiting to be cleaned, and major cities that have not come to grips with clean air standards. Along with the hectoring comes a clear recognition of environmental gridlock (Anderson 1997). For a combination of complex reasons, progress seems to be at a standstill. Having abandoned earlier environmental protection afforded by common law, city and state regulations, and regional compacts in favor of more effective federal control, we sometimes seem to have jumped from the frying pan to the fire.

Why should something as simple as protecting rivers from the discharge of sewage, for example, be so difficult to achieve? What is complicated about cleaning up abandoned hazardous waste dumps? Why is so much attention focused on industrial emitters of toxic chemicals when they collectively account for a minor part of the toxic emission problem and when the chemical emissions themselves are not ranked for toxicity or potential damage? If we cannot resolve these simpler problems, how could we expect to deal with things as complex as the ozone layer? When all is said and done, collective decision making—politics—is the complicating factor, not environmental science or economics.

A dispassionate review of less-than-successful federal programs designed to protect the environment leads to the conclusion that what we got is what we wanted. After all, the outcomes observed reflect a series of choices, later learning, revisions, and continuation of programs that do not work very well. Consider a simple analogy. If after twenty-five years of difficulty with leaking pipes from a chemical plant, following a long series of repairs by the same contractor accompanied by an unstinting commitment of funds, the leaks continue, a dispassionate observer would have to conclude that the leaks are desired. Conscious decisions to stay with the same contractor, and perhaps the same repair technologies, suggest that pipe repair is motivated by something other than stopping leaks. A similar conclusion must be reached when we think about this nation's cleanup record.

Drawing on lessons from public choice, this chapter focuses on collective choice and environmental control. The chapter begins with a discussion of the simple analytics of pollution control and related policy prescriptions. Two possible paths for dealing with water and air pollution are described. Choosing one path or the other involves more or less government intervention. The operating and cost characteristics of the two approaches are assessed, with an emphasis on the economist's efficiency focus. With the simple analytics of the situation described, the next section explains what happens when politics enters the environmental protection decision, with descriptions of some research findings to help explain why environmental outcomes and economic efficiency are compromised. Research that relates to air pollution, hazardous waste, global warming, and the management of publicly owned timberlands comes into play. The last major section of the chapter reflects on the environmental challenge and on why it has been so difficult to meet. Lessons from the past are called on to provide a basis for recommending approaches that offer the promise of "stopping the leaks."

The Simple Analytics: Before Politics Enters

Two Approaches to the Problem

Economists searching for efficient solutions take two fundamentally different approaches when analyzing pollution (Yandle 1997). A first approach, historically related to the work of A. C. Pigou (1920), involves discussion of externalities. Stated in terms of an industrial firm, an operating plant produces a product demanded by a group of consumers. The firm involved sends bills for the product, which cover all the costs recorded in the course of operating a going concern. Consumers pay the bills. The firm has internalized production costs and, by their willingness to purchase the firm's product, consumers have indicated that the value of the product or service is at least equal to the cost of providing it. So far, so good. Now, introduce external costs.

If the producing firm discharges waste into the air, water, or soil, and if the waste imposes costs on people not recorded by the firm, then the firm produces an externality. All pollution is not an externality: only pollution that imposes an unwanted cost. Because the externality represents unwanted costs, the efficiency-seeking economist offers a solution. Let the government regulate the firm in one way or another. The related policy instruments include standards accompanied by specified technologies, standards without specified technologies or performance standards, and economic incentives such as taxes and emission fees. Of course, the three instruments can be bundled in different ways to yield an apparent solution to the externality problem. The only hurdle involves writing the desired statute that yields efficiency in the face of an externality. As we shall see, that hurdle challenges even Olympic-grade high jumpers.

The second analytical approach, which is associated with Nobel laureate Ronald H. Coase (1960), concentrates on marketable property rights and related legal rules. Focusing on the same industrial plant discussed in conjunction with externalities, evidence of pollution that imposes costs is evidence of a violated property right, if the right exists in the first place. The property rights economist calls for a different solution from that of the externality economist. Instead of calling for involvement by government in managing technologies, permits, and controls, this economist recommends institutional change. Define environmental rights or enforce those now in place. Then, with rights defined and protected, let the related parties deal with the problem. Dealing with the problem may involve bargaining between affected landowners, the use of environmental liability insurance, applying the common law of nuisance when property rights are invaded or damaged, the purchase of easements or the affected land by the polluter, or the writing of contracts between the polluters and receivers of pollution so that unwanted costs are eliminated.

The first approach calls on government to correct what is termed "market failure." The second calls for contract and property-rights enforcement and relies on market successes. The use of the body politic is expanded in the first and maintained or minimized in the second, but government has a role to play in both situations.

The Choice of Instruments

A choice to expand government's role requires a second choice: which instrument? performance standards? technology standards? market instruments? Each instrument generates its own incentives and administrative costs.

Performance standards set specific goals and penalties for not achieving those goals. Outcomes must be monitored and penalties applied. If leaks are to be corrected, someone must check to see. Performance standards induce a continuous process of discovery and implementation. Start-up costs are relatively low. Monitoring costs are relatively high, and outcomes must be identified and reported. Performance standards do not specify the means. The regulated units have profit-based incentives to discover the problem and to apply the least-cost means for achieving the specified goal. Competition-based incentives cause the regulated to search for and protect new cleanup assets. Patents and copyrights matter a great deal. Political influence also matters when the performance standard itself is selected.

As with performance standards, technology standards require setting a goal. Large amounts of information must be assembled at one time. This information must be studied to select technologies that work. The selected technologies must be used by all similar polluters. The technology approach uses a batch process that is information-intensive and time-sensitive; it induces momentary discoveries and then freezes the chosen technology. Start-up costs are high, but monitoring costs are low. Inputs, not outcomes, matter most. If leaky pipes are corrected, the correct technology must be discovered in a once-and-for-all process. Once identified, the technology is imposed. If installed and operated correctly, the leaks are assumed to be fixed. No one has to check to see. Because one technology will be selected for each similar polluter, competitive incentives cause the regulated to invest in efforts to influence the outcome. Political influence matters a lot; patents and copyrights matter less.

The use of economic instruments, such as emission taxes and fees, requires setting a standard, just as with performance and technology standards. Then, prices or taxes must be determined and applied to each polluter so that the polluter will adjust its discharge. Theoretically, every polluter would be charged a different price if the cost imposed by each polluter varied. Facing a price for environmental use causes the polluter to search for less environmentally intensive production techniques or for less damaging locations. Economic instruments require pollution activity to be monitored, bills to be sent and collected, and taxes or fees to be modified as conditions dictate. System start-up costs are relatively low; operating costs, relatively high.

Table 1 summarizes the relative costs of the three instruments that may be adopted by governments seeking to resolve perceived externality problems. If higher information and lobbying costs are viewed negatively, then technology standards are less attractive. If these factors are viewed positively, then technology standards take the day. As shown in the table, performance standards have two low-cost cells. The other two instruments have only one low-cost cell each.

TABLE 1 Relative Cost Analysis

	Information	*Monitoring/Administration*	*Lobbying*
Performance	Low	High	Low
Technology	High	Low	High
Economic	High	High	Low

Choosing Property Rights Enforcement

Relying on property rights and free market forces for managing environmental assets means another set of considerations falls into place. Existing court and arbitration systems that resolve disputes can provide the formal element of the system. This component of institutional costs is relatively low or at least no higher than the court costs associated with regulation and market intervention (Ceplo and Yandle 1997). Those who write environmental contracts or seek to bring private and public suits against polluters need information. To provide evidence of harm, they must provide hard, monitor-based data. But unlike the case with taxes and fees or performance standards, not every pollution source needs to be monitored continuously or randomly. Monitoring activities, perhaps privately provided, are matched to those situations that appear to be violating property rights. The incentives that come from predicting with some confidence that property rights will be protected cause cost-avoiding people to minimize the harm they impose on others.

Pollution liability insurance provides an example of how property rights enforcement might work. Firms seeking to minimize the risk of common law suits from environmental spills and accidents purchase liability insurance to cover future claims. Insurance companies typically require the insured to install and maintain state-of-the-art equipment and management systems that reduce environmental hazards. When claims are filed, the insurer requires information from the insured, and the insurer monitors performance.

Competition in the insurance market brings lower-cost environmental protection. Internal and external monitoring is delivered by market forces. Insurance premiums and unpaid claims cause potential polluters to avoid environmental harms.

There is yet another example. The demand for environmental quality may show itself in other ways when a property rights–based approach is taken to the pollution problem. If consumers value environmental information about products and services and also seek to purchase products that impose low environmental costs, the information market will deliver labels, advertisements, and specialized books and magazines providing this information. If firms are the lower-priced information provider, product labels and brands will provide environmental impact information. If consumers are the lower-cost providers, specialized books, magazines, and consumer groups will provide the information. In short, a mix of decentralized information will be provided.

It is not easy to compare the relative costs of these decentralized approaches with those associated with government intervention and centralized regulation. However, it is difficult to believe that information and monitoring costs would be any higher than for the market approach. It is easy to believe that market incentives and connection of benefits to costs would generate cost-beneficial improvements. However, it is impossible to believe that one would find uniform approaches being taken across a country as vast and varied as the United States. After all, the people worried most about leaks would be living with the result. Each case could be different, and some people would want tighter and more costly repairs than others would want. On a theoretical basis, the property rights approach generates variable outcomes across communities, states, and regions even though each community adopts a strict property rule for protecting environmental rights. This variety is due to different perceptions of risk and harm that combine with different environmental conditions and income levels.

Summary

Before politics enters the picture, two distinctly different approaches may be described for managing environmental use. Both are dedicated to the economist's efficiency standard. Both claim to seek outcomes that maximize net benefits and wealth. One approach calls for government intervention and control. The other calls for property rights definition and protection and relies more on market forces. Government intervention can be based on several control instruments, each of which has different cost characteristics while theoretically delivering the same outcome. The decentralized approach relies on property rights protection, market forces, and actions taken by individuals who seek to protect environmental assets. While the same property rule can apply across diverse groups and regions, environmental outcomes will vary, just as they do under the current centralized system. The choice—public law and regulation or private law and markets—depends largely on the extent to which efficiency-enhancing forces survive when steps are taken to move from the world of theory to the world of practice. That is, we have to consider what happens when public choices are made.

What Happens When Public Choices Are Made

The discussion of simple analytics focused almost exclusively on economic efficiency with occasional comments about the importance of political influence. To the extent that politics entered the mind of the reader, the imaginary politician was dedicated to finding lower-cost ways to "stop the leaks." To continue this line of logic, let the politician emerge in full form at the level of the national government. Suppose the politician is convinced that federal control must be exercised, that past actions taken at the individual, community, state, and regional levels will not adequately protect the environment. Federal programs must be built. Reaching this conclusion, the politician must decide on the instrument: command and control, performance standards, or economic incentives.

Based on the summary in table 1, the politician would favor performance standards, which provide fixed targets, are rich in incentives, and offer lower information-gathering costs over technology command-and-control or emission fees and taxes. Alternately, the politician might blend performance standards with permit trading. Lower cost outcomes—stopping the leaks—would take the day if efficiency were the motivating factor. But political decision making does not take place in a vacuum. Although efficiency may matter, other things must matter more. Otherwise, we would be hard-pressed to explain why politicians always seem to start with command and control.

What Public Choice Tells Us

In an early examination of the problem of instrument selection, Nobel laureate James M. Buchanan and his noted co-author Gordon Tullock (1975)—the two founders of the Public Choice School in economics—asked why command and control always seems to be favored over lower-cost, and generally more effective, methods of environmental protection. Their article has an insightful title: "Polluters' 'Profit' and Political Response." Arguing strictly in theoretical terms, and applying a heavy dose of politics, Buchanan and Tullock demonstrate that a competitive industry has something to gain from federally mandated command-and-control regulation that can never be obtained by any other legal means. The industry can be cartelized. How can this be?

Like most things, the point is rather simple once explained. Command-and-control regulation sets an output constraint, mandates methods and standards for individual plants to meet the constraint, and restricts expansions and entry. (This sounds just like an OPEC meeting.) Innovating firms have nothing to gain by discovering and applying technologies that allow output to be expanded.

New entrants that might bring lower-cost pollution control are ushered away from the industry door. No fees or taxes are placed on pollution. And to add icing to the cake, a point not mentioned by Buchanan and Tullock, older plants are generally treated better than newer ones.

In a growing economy, the constrained industry experiences increases in demand and higher profits. Meanwhile, environmental police stop all producers seeking to expand their output. (New-source-performance standards see to that.) Profitable stagnation follows. Command-and-control technology standards are best suited to accomplish this result, because performance standards and emission fees do not limit expansions and entry. But notice, the system is based on input specification; it does not require rigorous monitoring of pollution or air and water quality. In terms of the leaking pipe analogy, the command-and-control instrument may fail to patch the pipes.

The Buchanan-Tullock story introduces a key industry group, which logically supports a particular form of regulation at the national level. Industries with plants nationwide can cartelize, simplify the legal environment within which they operate, and obtain that much sought-after level playing field mentioned so often by industries. On this basis, national regulation is much preferred to community, state, and regional management of environmental quality. One suit that fits everybody seems better than struggling with fifty tailors for a different fit in each state.

Long before Buchanan and Tullock wrote about polluters' profit, Ralph Turvey (1963) explained what might happen when environmentalists seeking to reduce the cost imposed by unwanted pollution confront polluters. Turvey's theoretical story focused on emission fees imposed on polluters to reduce their discharge to an efficient level, which would be the point where the benefits to society of products and services that come with further discharge are just equal to the pollution cost imposed at that point. Turvey pointed out that fees or penalties imposed on polluters only address half the problem. If those who value environmental quality for its own sake pay nothing for additional units, they will lobby for even higher pollution taxes or stricter controls. Turvey's analysis identifies another key interest group—environmental organizations—that favor rules that impose costs on polluters but not on themselves. This theoretical story does not concern itself with a key element of environmentalism that tilts the instrument preference in the direction of command and control. As it turns out, the most dedicated environmentalists see pollution fees and taxes as a way for rich polluters to buy licenses to pollute, which in the extreme view is seen as the equivalent of selling permits to commit murder (Nelson 1993). Command and control takes the day again. Environmentalists join industrialists in seeking national regulations that dictate uniform control technologies. Again, the focus is on inputs, not on environmental quality outcomes.

In his work on environmental policy, Paul Downing (1984) adds another element of spice to the political soup that forms environmental policy—the bureaucracy. Downing explains how federal legislation provides what might be termed a national marketing opportunity for environmental organizations. From the standpoint of attracting new members and revenues, national programs, and the publicity that accompany them, are far better than state or regional debates about environmental rules. If a large bureaucracy is to be formed, opportunities surface for environmentalists to become entrenched in government. Those who favor command and control for other reasons become employed in designing and enforcing the rules.

With industry, environmental organizations, and the bureaucracy connected by command-and-control regulation, we now have the famous iron triangle of politics. But the iron triangle focuses on inputs, not outcomes. Somehow the purpose of environmental policy is almost forgotten. Little attention is focused on systematically monitoring and reporting environmental outcomes. Much effort is exerted on writing detailed rules, limiting entry, and identifying new margins for applying command-and-control regulation. Along these lines, it is interesting to note that even today, researchers face a severe challenge in obtaining a consistent set of time series data on air and water pollution and other measures of environmental quality. By comparison, it is easy to obtain data on rules, regulation, required technologies, and enforcement activities.

Lessons Learned about Political Favor Seeking

The preceding brief outline of key public choice insights, although overlooking a vast amount of significant related research, sets the stage for discussing some watershed thinking that crystalized the public choice problem encountered by efficiency-bound politicians. This crystallization came when James M. Buchanan, Robert D. Tollison, and Gordon Tullock (1980) published a collection of articles under the title *Toward a Theory of the Rent-Seeking Society*, a book that coincided with the release of a companion volume by Terry L. Anderson and P. J. Hill (1980), *The Birth of a Transfer Society*. The former volume focuses on public choice theory, the latter on history and institutions. Both tell similar stories. In a political system where votes determine outcomes, special interest groups have operational incentives to seek favors or rents in the resulting political economy. Political competition ensues, and efficiency loses out to restrictions that assist or protect successful special interest groups.

Sam Peltzman (1976) and Nobel laureate George J. Stigler (1971) explore the nature of competition in the political marketplace where regulations are being devised and implemented. Whereas Stigler describes the politician strictly as a broker auctioning off favors to the highest bidder and never seeking efficiency for its own sake, Peltzman visualizes a richer competition where interest groups matter a great deal, as do the mass of consumers and unorganized voters. These two stories combined tell us that tradeoffs will be made. After all, as Robert McCormick and Robert Tollison

(1981) explain, one group will bear the burden of benefits obtained by another and politicians bear the burden of pleasing both groups. Efficiency, on the one hand, is traded away partly for special interest benefits on the other hand. Neither group holds sway completely. In terms of leaking pipes, the politicians will contract for repairs that stop some of the leaks. But the contracts written will reflect special interest concerns that relate to other objectives.

Yet a third Nobel laureate in economics, Gary Becker (1983), adds another important component to the theory of regulation and public choice. Becker's theoretical story accepts existing constitutional constraints, voting rules, and congressional committee assignments, in addition to all the other political trappings, and argues the following line: If politicians could find a lower-cost, more effective approach to environmental or any other kind of regulation, wouldn't they do so? In these restricted terms, what politicians do is efficient. Responding systematically and balancing all meaningful pressures imposed on them, politicians design rules that, though compromising efficiency in some more narrow sense of the word, are indeed efficient when all political costs are considered. Becker's argument suggests that if we desire more effective pollution control, we might best seek solutions in other quarters. As Fred Smith, president of Competitive Enterprise Institute has put it on several informal occasions, "If we are seeking efficient outcomes from Congress, we are looking for love in all the wrong places."

Payoffs from Protection against Regulation

The focus on political decision making described thus far puts a bright light on the demand side of the political market. Interest groups that have something to gain, be they environmentalists, industrialists, or members of the bureaucracy, organize efforts to communicate and bid for legislation. The unorganized and rationally ignorant play a minor role in all this (Downs 1957). Consumers/taxpayers end up bearing a substantial part of the cost of restrictions delivered by politicians, but the costs are spread thinly over a thick set of people. Until and unless the collective burden becomes large and burdensome, the unorganized, by definition, have little incentive to make their voices heard.

But Fred S. McChesney (1991; 1997) describes another component to the regulation story and sheds a different light on interest group behavior. Politicians can orchestrate responses from groups that feel threatened by the prospects of regulation. Instead of simply announcing a write-up on proposed clean air legislation, for example, the politician can indicate that electric utilities are being targeted for dramatic decreases in sulfur dioxide emissions. Then, instead of the industry organizing to seek favors or rents derived from regulation, the industry organizes to deflect or soften the pending rules. McChesney describes the politician's strategy as "rent extraction," where the politician receives "money for nothing," which is the title of McChesney's 1997 book on the topic. In contrast, the Buchanan-Tullock, Stigler, Peltzman, and other stories relate to "rent-seeking behavior."

Efforts to defend against extractions of wealth can be as important as efforts to gain political favors outright. Consider the struggle over fuel economy standards, which were first justified as a means to reduce dependence on imported crude oil and to reduce harmful tailpipe emissions from automobiles (Crandall et al. 1986). In 1975, Congress announced a 1985 end point goal and instructed the U.S. Department of Transportation to define goals for corporate fleets for intervening years. From that point on, a struggle ensued with some firms seemingly using the regulation to advantage and others struggling to deflect it (Yandle 1980). As time passed and fuel prices rose and fell, auto producers took different positions. Some argued that they had followed the will of Congress and downsized their fleets. They were prepared to produce even more fuel-efficient vehicles. Others argued the reverse. Consumers wanted larger vehicles, which they were prepared to produce, and failing to do so would lead to large worker layoffs. The two competing parties engaged in lobbying activities as they sought to keep rules on the one hand and deflect them on the other.

The Kyoto Conference on global warming offers a pending episode worth watching. Representatives of the industrialized nations agreed to establish 1990 baseline carbon reductions by the year 2010 that translate into a 40 percent carbon and other greenhouse gas emissions below-trend reduction for the United States. If ratified by the U.S. Senate, which was doubtful at the time, the agreement would then be translated into regulations. There are differential effects to be considered: industries that will gain, industries that will lose, and some that will be severely regulated for the first time. Each organized interest group will spend resources to influence the politicians. Some will seek to deflect costs and prevent rent extraction. Others will seek to impose costs on others in hopes of gaining additional profits or rents. While all this happens, consumers and taxpayers could become better informed, and as they do, communicate their concerns, one way or the other, to the politicians.

Bootleggers and Baptists

The aforementioned theories of regulation and public choice tell us that addressing environmental or any other perceived social problem by political means is never simple. Indeed, it is clearly possible that after political repairs are completed, the repaired pipes may leak more than before, or they may be tighter but with reduced capacity. The theory also tells us that pipe repairs will have differential effects. The leaks will be strategically positioned, as will the repaired portion. It is indeed possible that we will jump from the frying pan to the fire.

But as logical and sound as these theories may be, the matter of how the political message is communicated needs to be addressed. How do messages get organized and transferred from special interests to politicians? How are the messages packaged? We know that packaging matters a great deal in the market for consumer goods.

How things are packaged may matter even more in political markets (Olasky 1987).

Almost systematically it seems, two interest groups emerge together, calling for the same outcome when environmental rules are being constructed. Notice the focus on the construction of the rules, not the urge to write rules in the first place. These two groups always include some economic interest groups—such as certain manufacturers, labor unions, or trade associations—and environmental organizations. One group takes a publicly perceived high road calling for a better life. The other takes the low, looking for improved profits and wealth. Years ago, in struggles over whether to allow the Sunday sale of alcoholic beverages in rural America, the local bootleggers saw opportunities to expand markets if legal outlets were shut tight (Yandle 1983). The bootleggers could count on the Baptists, who officially opposed the consumption of alcoholic beverages at any time, to raise their voices in opposition to Sunday sales. The bootleggers and Baptists worked the political aisles to gain passage of Sunday closing laws. It is worth noting that none of the alcohol strictures limited consumption of spirits on Sunday, just the legal sale of such. Limits on consumption would lose bootlegger support.

We find a similar blending of voices in the demand for environmental regulation (Greve and Smith 1992). As noted earlier, environmentalists oppose the use of emission fees and markets for allocating environmental use by polluters. They favor command and control. Industries seeking cartelization join the chorus. Environmentalists support eco-labels that provide detailed information of the environmental consequences of specified consumer goods. Domestic producers who can use the label requirements to exclude foreign goods support them as well. For example, organized labor in eastern coal fields, which provide high-sulfur coal, supported the requirement that all coal-fired electric utilities install and operate scrubbers to reduce sulfur oxides, whether the coal burned produced sulfur oxides or not. Environmentalists support scrubbers, too. Organized labor in U.S. manufacturing opposed the North American Free Trade Agreement for environmental reasons. Environmentalists welcomed the support.

We can see how the blending of disparate voices to form harmonious support of command-and-control regulation makes it easier for politicians to trade off efficiency for future political support. But what about rank-and-file voters? Will they catch on to all this and deny support to politicians who restrict output, raise costs, and actually limit environmental protection?

Recent work by Geoffrey Brennan and Loren Lomasky (1993) explains why voters in general stick with less-than-effective and inefficient environmental programs. Brennan and Lomasky's theory is based on the notion of expressive voting, the idea that voters with no financial interest in an outcome will choose to support what appear to be morally or socially important issues when they are uncertain about the facts involved. If, for example, voters are asked to indicate support for something with high-sounding titles, such as the Resource Conservation and Recovery Act or the Clean Air Act, they will more likely than not vote yes. Burrowing beneath the concept of rational ignorance and apathetic citizens, Brennan and Lomasky argue that technically uninformed citizens still have a logical basis for pulling the voting booth lever. Otherwise disinterested voters will more likely than not support properly packaged command-and-control regulation, never knowing about outcomes and never asking for a report card on past successes.

What Does the Evidence Tell Us?

A number of empirical studies have been done on environmental decision making using public choice logic. To support the public choice story, these studies must show evidence that environmental regulations provide identifiable benefits to special interest groups, which include industrial firms, environmentalists, and others who can appropriate gains from command-and-control regulation. A

1985 study by Peter Pashigian examined congressional voting patterns on the 1977 Clean Air Act Amendments that had to do with setting stricter standards for regions with cleaner air. The amendment examined was for prevention of significant deterioration (PSD). The amendment required expanding plants in PSD regions to meet newly specified stricter technology standards than similar plants in industrialized and dirtier regions had to meet.

We might expect a vote based on human health and public interest to favor stricter standards in dirty regions. This was not the case. After adjusting for a number of other variables such as income, population density, and manufacturing concentration, Pashigian found that representatives from the older industrialized regions systematically supported tighter standards in those regions that were beginning to attract new industrial plants. Owners of plants and unionized workers in older and dirtier regions were favored, as were other important interest groups in those regions. Michael T. Maloney and Robert E. McCormick (1982) examined portfolios of stocks of U.S. copper producers to see if those portfolios rose significantly at the precise time when the Environmental Protection Agency (EPA) announced its strict emission guidelines for copper smelters. As noted at the time of the EPA's announcement, the stricter standards would preclude the construction of additional U.S. capacity. The portfolios showed significant positive returns in association with the announcement.

Public choice analysis also suggests that a shift from state and local environmental control to federal control would bring different outcomes for identifiable interest groups. Robert Quinn and I (Quinn and Yandle 1986) examined regulatory expenditures on air pollution control across the fifty United States, both prior to and following the time of federal regulation of air pollution. We found a significant shift in the allocation of regulatory expenditures. In the pre-federal period, expenditures were higher in association with private investment in real property and human exposure to air pollution. In the post-federal period, expenditures were explained by the presence of federally owned land and other national landmarks. Private investment in residential property and human exposure did not seem to matter.

Richard Meyer and I (Meyer and Yandle 1987) examined House and Senate votes on acid rain amendments to the Clean Air Act that ultimately required reductions in sulfur dioxide (SO_2) emissions. Our statistical models included variables that adjusted for population exposure to sulfur dioxide, tons of SO_2 emitted by electric utilities, the economic presence of other industries that might be adversely affected, and whether the politician represented states in the eastern acid rain control region. The results showed that senators were less likely to vote in favor of SO_2 emissions the greater the presence of forest products industries and federal lands. The more deteriorated a state's water quality, the more likely a senator would vote yes. Population exposure to SO_2 did not seem to matter, nor did the amount of SO_2 emitted from electric utilities. In other words, as Sam Peltzman's theory of regulation predicts, the senators provided some environmental benefits and some industry protection.

Although some empirical research provides evidence of special interest influence and bootleggers-and-Baptists coalition, only a few studies indicate that federal regulation may have actually harmed the environment. A study by Maloney and Brady (1988) falls into this latter category. Maloney and Brady examined capital turnover in electric utility generating capacity in conjunction with EPA regulations that set higher standards for new plants than for older ones. All else equal, economists predicted that plant operators would delay rebuilding or replacing generating capacity if the regulatory penalty was significant. Using vintage data on generators nationwide, Maloney and Brady determined a steady-state trend for replacement prior to the implementation of EPA new-source-performance standards for utilities. As theory predicts, Maloney and Brady found a significant slowdown in capital turnover. Going further, the two researchers estimated the amount of emissions that would come from older technologies versus newer ones. They found that stricter new source standards increased the level of air pollution from the industry.

The Maloney-Brady study is the empirical counterpart of a highly documented historical story told by Bruce A. Ackerman and William T. Hassler (1981) about the struggle over mandating scrubbers for newly constructed coal-fired electric utilities, a stricture required by the 1977 Clean Air Act. Ackerman and Hassler provide inside-EPA documentation of exchanges of information between White House and EPA officials who favored another regulatory instrument and Senator Robert Byrd, the senior senator from West Virginia who, by coincidence, chaired EPA's budget committee. The scrubber requirement emerged as a way to protect the interests of unionized coal workers and owners of eastern coal mines against the competition that was emerging from nonunionized producers of clean coal in the western states. Apparently the significant cost of scrubbers was enough to encourage electric utility operators to postpone replacement of older vintage and dirtier capital. This is really an instance of jumping from the frying pan into the fire.

The much debated and criticized Superfund program has also been reviewed from a public choice perspective. Recognizing that Superfund seems to have much to do with administrative and litigation expenditures and less to do with cleaning up sites, J. A. Hird (1993) carefully examined a series of congressional votes on the initial 1980 legislation and the later 1986 amendment process. Exploring the notion that Superfund was simply a pork-barrel program used by politicians to funnel more cleanup funds to their states and districts, Hird found no evidence to support that proposition. Instead, the evidence suggests that Superfund was an environmental icon; voting patterns favoring Superfund were strongly influenced by the concentration of members in environmental groups in a politician's region, while negative influence came from the oil and chemical industry in that region. But the environmental influence to maintain the nonproducing program was so strong that politicians were unwilling to put their political careers at risk by opposing the program.

Other work on Superfund (Barnett 1985; McNeil, Foshee, and Burbee 1988) probed EPA's internal Superfund decision making, looking to see if, among other things, the agency assigned key importance to the protection of groundwater when choosing to list a site on the agency's priority listing. Barnett (1985) found that EPA decision making was strongly influenced by state regulatory efforts and surface water and air pollution issues but that threats to groundwater had no statistical power when it came to explaining agency choice.

McNeil, Foshee, and Burbee (1988) looked at EPA data to see if the Superfund taxes paid by chemical-using industries were significantly related to Superfund expenditures in the states where the tax receipts originated. Superfund supporters sometimes argued that the program was about collecting revenues in contaminated regions and applying the funds for cleanups in those regions. The research showed just the opposite. Taxes were collected in one region, where chemical use was high, and spent in other regions. On this basis, Superfund was a pork barrel.

Public choice scholars have even probed the political depths of the bureaucracy to see if lobbying activities and other incentives influence such things as EPA enforcement activities or U.S. Forest Service management of forests. Is it possible that lobbyist influence could somehow seep into the EPA bureaucracy and affect the number of penalty citations issued in the fight against global warming? Work by Mixon (1995) indicates that the answer is yes. Mixon examined data on urban-area carbon emission violations in regions experiencing rising ambient temperatures. Among other interesting findings, the results indicated that lobbyists per capita significantly reduced the magnitude of fines and the probability that EPA would issue carbon violation citations.

Focusing on bureaucratic incentives, Donald R. Leal (1993) examined the state and federal government management of similar forest lands in the northwestern states. Leal found a key difference in underlying incentives. The net revenues from state-managed forest lands are dedicated to public education, which means that citizens in general and teachers in particular closely monitor the gains when cutting rights are sold and roads and other necessary components of forest management are built and purchased. In general, the people who oversee state forests are long-standing citizens of the communities where they live. On the other hand, revenues from U.S. Forest Service operations do not redound fully to the states, are not dedicated to some highly visible functions, and therefore are not closely monitored. U.S. Forest Service personnel are generally moved from place to place and do not have generationally deep ties to the people in the communities where they reside.

On the basis of these incentives alone, public choice theory predicts different outcomes for similar forests. After examining data on operating costs, net revenues generated, and actions that reflect efforts to maximize net revenues, Leal (1993) found dramatic differences between state-operated and federally managed forests. Roads built for timber cutting in state land are crude, inexpensive, and less environmentally intrusive; similar roads in federal forests are more numerous, wider, and more permanent. Transportation systems and other operating costs are higher in federal forests. In short, far more net revenue is generated from state forests than from federal forests. In short, bureaucratic incentives matter.

Summary

Public choice and regulation theories tell us that the people who make and implement political decisions are just like all other people. They respond to the incentives contained in the institutions that form their decision-making environment. Politicians constantly sustain close scrutiny from those who may gain or suffer from their actions. The more tightly organized and better informed the interest group, the closer the group monitors political action. The less organized with less to gain or lose play a more passive role in the struggle. Politicians logically respond to the resulting payoffs; they produce what the political marketplace will pay for, which will seldom be the most efficient bundle of environmental protection.

By identifying potential gainers and losers, public choice scholars have been able to offer important insights on the construction, implementation, and enforcement of environmental rules. These insights help us understand why command-and-control regulation seems to trump the use of apparently more efficient performance standards and economic incentives. The theories explain why unusual coalitions tend to form when environmental rules are being developed and tell us that federal efforts to provide uniform approaches to diverse problems can generate immense gains to some interest groups, even when environmental outcomes are made worse.

The empirical literature supports many of these theoretical insights. A substantial body of evidence tells us that we do not always jump completely from the frying pan to the fire when we carry environmental problems to the national government. But although we do not always end up in the fire, the evidence suggests that the risk of being burned is substantial.

Final Thoughts

This chapter began with the observation that some environmental problems seem simpler to resolve than others. But for some reason, federal initiatives designed to solve even the simplest of problems have not successfully met legislative goals. In some cases, the shift to federal centralized control away from private law and decentralized control has even made some situations worse. In that sense, we jumped from the frying pan to the fire. The chapter then sought to explain why simple problems seem so hard to resolve efficiently and effectively. This leaves the uneasy impression that the more complex problems may never be solved, at least by centralized means.

The survey of some key elements of public choice literature and related empirical work highlighted difficulties to be expected when environmental decisions are made collectively. We all know that group decision making is more costly than individual decision making. And knowing this fact helps us to understand why community-reliant human beings make most life-sustaining decisions privately and somewhat reluctantly make others collectively (Ridley 1996). As Buchanan and Tullock (1962) explained years ago, collective choice involves two basic cost relationships. The more people who are involved in the process, the higher the cost of obtaining agreement; the greater the number required to decide (the larger the percentage defined by the voting rule), the higher will be the likely cost imposed on those holding a different opinion. Private decision making, on the other hand, requires unanimity. Agreement and minority-position costs are minimized.

A scan of history tells us that human beings have made environmental decisions at all levels—private, community, state, regional, and national. For centuries, simple problems, such as the discharge of pollution onto a neighbor's private land or into rivers imposing harm to private land, were handled by private law. Easily identified parties resolved the problem. When multiple parties or a larger public were involved, public officials brought action against polluters using the same private law. The wisdom of this approach had to do with two things. First, environmental problems were addressed quickly when damaged parties felt it was worth the cost. Private law contains a meaningful level of realism. Second, it was very costly to bring outside influence to bear in matters involving private law. Favor-seeking through the courts was never a burgeoning enterprise. Along these lines, it was impossible to obtain a court ruling in private matters that would apply to every plant nationwide in a given industry. Cartelization through the courts was impossible.

History tells us that in addition to common law courts and private law, communities, then states, and finally regions addressed environmental problems in meaningful ways. Although uniformity was lacking, the competition across groups brought recognition that costs and benefits matter. More often than not, solutions were designed to fit the problem at hand when the benefits to be obtained by relevant decision makers were greater than the costs of taking action. The benefits and costs tended to be internalized within and among the contracting parties and political groups; incentives were pushed in the direction of cost-effectiveness and away from the redistribution of wealth to far-flung places.

The lessons of public choice do not tell us that all political solutions are to be avoided. Indeed, politics cannot be avoided. Instead, the lessons tell us what to expect when the heaviest political hand of all, the federal government, enters the picture and responds to supporting interests. In brief, the dream of finding economically efficient solutions to real pollution problems at the level of the national government is just that—a dream. From this, it makes sense to conclude that centralized solutions to pollution problems should be reserved for those problems that truly involve the entire nation or most of it. Obviously, most environmental problems are local or regional, which suggests that we should seek to design institutions that fit the dimensions of the problem and, in doing so, seek to design and enforce environmental property rights that will encourage the push and tug of markets to provide real solutions to real problems.

REFERENCES

Ackerman, Bruce A., and William T. Hassler. 1981. *Clean Coal, Dirty Air.* New Haven: Yale University Press.

Anderson, Terry L., ed. 1997. *Breaking the Environmental Policy Gridlock.* Stanford, Cal.: Hoover Institution Press.

Anderson, Terry L., and Donald R. Leal. 1991. *Free Market Environmentalism.* San Francisco: Pacific Research Institute for Public Policy.

Anderson, Terry L., and P. J. Hill. 1980. *The Birth of a Transfer Society.* Stanford, Cal.: Hoover Institution Press.

Barnett, Harold C. 1985. The Allocation of Superfund, 1981–1983. *Land Economics* 61 (August): 255–262.

Becker, Gary S. 1983. A Theory of Competition Among Pressure Groups. *The Quarterly Journal of Economics* 118 (August): 371–399.

Brennan, Geoffrey, and Loren Lomasky. 1993. *Democracy & Decision.* New York: Cambridge University Press.

Buchanan, James M., and Gordon Tullock. 1962. *The Calculus of Consent.* Ann Arbor: University of Michigan Press.

Buchanan, James M., and Gordon Tullock. 1975. Polluters' "Profit" and Political Response. *American Economic Review* 65: 139–147.

Buchanan, James M., Robert D. Tollison, and Gordon Tullock. 1980. *Toward a Theory of the Rent-Seeking Society.* College Station: Texas A&M Press.

Ceplo, Karol, and Bruce Yandle. 1997. Western States and Environmental Federalism. In *Environmental Federalism,* edited by Terry Anderson and Peter H. Hill. Lanham, Md.: Rowman & Littlefield.

Coase, Ronald H. 1960. The Problem of Social Cost. *Journal of Law & Economics* 3: 1–44.

Crandall, Robert W., Howard K. Gruenspecht, Theodore E. Keeler, and Lave. 1986. *Regulating the Automobile.* Washington, D.C.: The Brookings Institution.

Downing, Paul B. 1984. *Environmental Economics and Policy.* Boston: Little, Brown.

Downs, Anthony. 1957. *An Economic Theory of Democracy.* New York: Harper and Row.

Greve, Michael S., and Fred L. Smith, Jr. 1992. *Environmental Politics: Public Costs, Private Rewards.* New York: Praeger.

Hird, J. A. 1993. Congressional Voting on Superfund: Self-Interest or Ideology? *Public Choice* 77: 333–357.

Leal, Donald R. 1993. Turning a Profit on Public Forests. PERC Policy Series, PS-4. Bozeman, Mon.: Political Economy Research Center.

Maloney, Michael T., and Gordon Brady. 1988. Capital Turnover and Marketable Pollution Permits. *Journal of Law & Economics* 31, no. 1: 203–226.

Maloney, Michael T., and Robert E. McCormick. 1982. A Positive Theory of Environmental Quality. *Journal of Law & Economics* 25: 99–124.

McChesney, Fred S. 1991. Rent Extraction and Interest-Group Organization in a Coasean Model of Regulation. *Journal of Legal Studies* 20: 73–90.

McChesney, Fred S. 1997. *Money for Nothing*. Cambridge: Harvard University Press.

McCormick, Robert E., and Robert D. Tollison. 1981. *Politicians, Legislation, and the Economy*. Boston: Martinus Nijhoff.

McNeil, Douglas W., Andrew W. Foshee, and Clark R. Burbee. 1988. Superfund Taxes and Expenditures: Regional Redistribution. *Review of Regional Studies* 18 (Winter): 4–9.

Meyer, Richard, and Bruce Yandle. 1987. The Political Economy of Acid Rain. *Cato Journal* 7 (Fall): 527–545.

Mixon, Franklin G. 1995. Public Choice and the EPA: Empirical Evidence on Carbon Emission Violations. *Public Choice* 83: 127–137.

Nelson, Robert H. 1993. Environmental Calvinism. In *Taking the Environmental Seriously*, edited by Roger E. Meiners and Bruce Yandle. Lanham, Md.: Rowman & Littlefield.

Olasky, Mavin N. 1987. *Corporate Public Relations*. Hillsdale, N.J.: Lawrence Erlbaum.

Pashigian, B. Peter. 1985. Environmental Regulation: Whose Interests Are Being Protected? *Economic Inquiry* 23 (October): 551–584.

Peltzman, Sam. 1976. Toward a More General Theory of Regulation. *Journal of Law & Economics* 19 (August): 211–240.

Pigou, A. C. 1920. *The Economics of Welfare*. London: Macmillan.

Quinn, Robert, and Bruce Yandle. 1986. Expenditures on Air Pollution Control under Federal Regulation. *Review of Regional Studies* 16 (Fall): 11–16.

Ridley, Matt. 1996. *The Origins of Virtue*. New York: Viking Press.

Stigler, George J. 1971. The Theory of Economic Regulation. *Bell Journal*, Spring: 3–21.

Turvey, Ralph. 1963. On Divergencies between Social Cost and Private Cost. *Economica* 30 (August): 309–313.

Yandle, Bruce. 1980. Fuel Efficiency by Government Mandate: A Cost-Benefit Analysis. *Policy Analysis* 6 (Summer): 291–301.

Yandle, Bruce. 1983. Bootleggers and Baptists: The Education of a Regulatory Economist. *Regulation*, May/June: 12–16.

Yandle, Bruce. 1997. *Common Sense and Common Law for the Environment*. Lanham, Md: Rowman & Littlefield.

Dean Lueck

3

The Law and Politics of Federal Wildlife Preservation

Introduction

In the United States, the federal government has a long history—roughly a century—of involvement in wildlife preservation, culminating with the Endangered Species Act of 1973 (ESA) and its progeny. For most of this history, the role of the federal government in wildlife preservation was relatively uncontroversial and largely irrelevant to most citizens. The ESA changed everything, making wildlife law a well-known and contentious battleground in law and politics for the last quarter of this century.[1]

Why is the federal government involved in wildlife preservation? What changes were invoked by the ESA in 1973 to bring about the dramatic changes in federal involvement? Why would a law passed with the overwhelming (virtually unanimous) support of the

1. For example, Yaffee (1982) notes, "While the passage of the ESA was uncontroversial, the history of its implementation is one of conflict and drama—a play with performances by the president, the Supreme Court, the attorney general, the secretary of interior, the secretary of commerce, and numerous congressional representatives, bureaucrats, and interest groups" (13). Even today, new legal battles are under way, and Congress is still in gridlock over reauthorizing the ESA since its appropriation authority expired in 1991. The ESA has continued to remain law via annual congressional appropriations.

Congress and the President generate such conflict?[2] How have various groups responded to the legal and political changes wrought by the ESA? This chapter brings the economics of property rights to bear on these questions, focusing in particular on the economics of owning land and wildlife. The framework allows a rationale for federal involvement in wildlife preservation and also offers an explanation for the contentious behavior (both private and political) that has emerged since the ESA.

This chapter argues that although there is an economic rationale for federal involvement in wildlife preservation based on transaction costs and incomplete property rights, the ESA marked a dramatic change in federal policy that led to conflicts on both private and public land. The ESA effectively placed property rights to wildlife habitat up for grabs and has led to extensive "claiming" activity within the constraints of the ESA and its administered regulations. For example, by invoking the ESA's protection of the northern spotted owl, environmentalists have been able to halt nearly all logging in old-growth Douglas fir stands in national forests in the Pacific Northwest. In a like manner, those adversely affected by claims made under the ESA (landowners and user groups on public lands) have used private and political actions to reclaim certain land rights. Landowners, for instance, have destroyed potential wildlife habitat in order to avoid costly land-use restrictions brought by the ESA. Landowners and public land user groups similarly have lobbied and litigated to mitigate adverse effects of the ESA. This claiming and reclaiming is directly the result of the ESA and was not a part of federal wildlife policies prior to 1973.

The study of federal wildlife preservation is important not only for the specific issues at stake but also because it illuminates many of the fundamental trade-offs in the political economy of environ-

2. The vote was 92–0 in the Senate and 390–12 in the House. President Nixon signed the ESA into law on December 28, 1973.

mental policy. Like all environmental problems, problems with wildlife preservation stem from imperfect property rights and high costs of private contractual solutions. By using voting rules rather than the unanimity required by contracting, government or political action has the advantage of lower contracting costs. But this action brings its own costs in terms of interest group rent-seeking and bureaucratic inefficiencies.[3] As this chapter shows, the regulations that define wildlife preservation are wrought with this same trade-off. Private contractual solutions have been limited but government action, especially since the ESA, has been filled with interest groups jockeying for advantage in a new regime. In the process, unusual coalitions have sometimes formed, vested interests have emerged, and groups have used private and political efforts to avoid costs associated with new regulations.

This chapter does not include a cost-benefit analysis of various wildlife preservation policies as that would be a monumental task requiring the collection of detailed data from landowners, government agencies, and wildlife "consumers."[4] Yet, the analysis in this chapter does give some insight into the distribution of the costs and benefits of various policies. The main finding is that the costs of protecting wildlife on private land are now borne primarily by a small group of landowners under the ESA, which was not true under pre-ESA preservation policy. On public land, the costs of preservation tend to be spread more widely, although when private investments in public lands become devalued because of preservation action, even these costs can be quite concentrated. The distribution of the benefits of species preservation is harder to determine. To the extent that species preservation is a public good, the benefits may be spread widely

3. See Adler (this volume) for an illustration of interest group behavior associated with environmental regulations. See Noll (1989) for a more general discussion of regulation.

4. Some of the basic issues are discussed in the recent symposia "Endangered Species Act," *Journal of Economic Perspectives* 12 (1998): 3–52.

across the populace. Closer scrutiny of many specific preservation cases, however, suggests that a smaller group of users often reaps a large fraction of the benefits. This view becomes clear once it is realized that species preservation policy is often about changing land use from commercial resource extraction to relatively passive preservation or recreation-based uses. For example, urban recreationists have benefited from the reduction in logging the Pacific Northwest, which resulted from protection of the northern spotted owl.

This chapter begins with a brief history of federal wildlife preservation. Next, an economic model of land use is developed to examine both the economic rationale for and methods of government involvement in wildlife preservation. Finally, the economic framework is used to explain various aspects of behavior by landowners, environmentalists, legislators, and federal agencies since the passage of the ESA. This behavior is contrasted with the behavior before the passage of the ESA.

The History of Federal Wildlife Preservation

Under the common law of property, wild animals were *ferae naturae*, "wild and untamable," meaning that generally no rights could exist in the live game stocks. The resulting common law rule of capture granted exclusive rights only to those who captured individual animals, usually by killing them. In the United States, because game populations tended to inhabit the properties of small and scattered landowners, *ferae naturae* often meant that game was treated as an open access resource.[5] Government intervention in wildlife began during the colonial period with seasonal restrictions on the taking of

5. During the early nineteenth century, some states even passed laws granting citizens "free access" to wildlife on undeveloped private land (Lund 1980). In *McKee v. Gratz* 260 U.S. 127 (1922), Justice Holmes noted the widespread custom of local open access to wildlife even on private land.

wild game (Lund 1980). The major thrust of government intervention in the nineteenth century was the expansion of state (and territorial) laws limiting the taking of wild game. Courts consistently upheld state authority to regulate the taking and trading of wildlife, ultimately articulating the "state ownership doctrine" in *Geer v. Connecticut* in 1896.[6] In *Geer*, Justice White argued that states have regulatory authority over game because of "its common ownership by all the citizens of the state." *Geer* and related rulings solidified state action and provided support for future regulations. Early game laws were enforced by local authorities, but by the turn of the century, states began to establish game agencies and to hire game wardens to enforce the game laws (Tober 1981). Today each state has a wildlife (or fish and game) agency vested with the authority to enforce laws regulating hunting, fishing, and trapping to manage state-controlled wildlife habitat and to conduct scientific research.

Federal Action before the ESA

The federal government did not become involved in wildlife protection until the Lacey Act of 1900,[7] which prohibited interstate commerce for wildlife killed in violation of state law (Yaffee 1982; Bean and Rowland 1997). The Lacey Act, arguably in response to the devastation of the passenger pigeon, also authorized the Secretary of Agriculture to provide for the "preservation, distribution, introduction, and restoration of game birds and other wild birds." The next major federal action, the Migratory Bird Treaty Act of 1918, ratified a 1916 treaty with Canada to protect and manage migratory birds and thus solidified the authority of federal involvement in wildlife.[8] The act was quickly challenged as an intrusion of federal authority

6. 161 U.S. 519 (1896).

7. The first federal legislation to protect wildlife was the Yellowstone Park Protection Act of 1894.

8. Mexico later joined the treaty, thus creating management jurisdiction encompassing the entire North American continent.

into state matters. It was equally quickly upheld by the Supreme Court in *Missouri v. Holland*.[9] Justice Holmes attacked the state ownership doctrine of *Geer* and wrote: "To put the claim of the State upon title is to lean upon a slender reed. Wild birds are not in the possession of anyone; and possession is the beginning of ownership" (434).

In addition to the regulation of interstate game trade and the taking of migratory waterfowl, the federal government has long been involved in establishing and managing wildlife refuges. The first national refuge was established by President Roosevelt at Pelican Island (Florida) in 1903.[10] In the early 1900s, refuges tended to be established on a case-by-case basis by both Congress and the President, usually for the protection of a particular species.[11] Soon the federal role became more systematic and independently funded. The Migratory Bird Hunting Stamp Act of 1934 required waterfowl hunters to purchase a federal "duck stamp" and generated millions of dollars for habitat acquisition, research, and management of migratory birds. The Pittman-Robertson Act of 1937 implemented a federal tax on hunting equipment and further generated revenues for wildlife. In both cases, significant fractions of these funds were distributed back to state game agencies for local implementation. Thus, by the middle of the twentieth century, the federal government had a well-established role in wildlife management, primarily vested in the U.S. Fish and Wildlife Service (FWS) in regulating wildlife trade, managing migratory waterfowl, conducting research, acquiring habitat, and overseeing a federal refuge system.[12]

9. 252 U.S. 416 (1920).

10. Earlier, in 1892, President Harrison prohibited hunting and fishing on Alaska's Afognak Island, essentially creating a refuge for the salmon fishery (Bean and Rowland 1997).

11. Examples include the National Bison Range in Montana, the National Elk Refuge in Wyoming, and the Charles Sheldon Antelope Range in Nevada. The bulk of the national refuges, however, have provided habitat for migratory waterfowl.

12. The FWS resides within the Department of Interior but has a history that goes back to 1871 under various names and organizations <<http://www.fws.gov/who/origin.html>>.

The 1966 Act. In 1964, two important events preceded the federal government's involvement in endangered species protection. First, the Land and Water Conservation Fund Act of 1964 established funds not only for land acquisition and development under recreational auspices, but also for acquisition "for any national area which may be authorized for the preservation of species of fish and wildlife that are threatened with extinction" (Yaffee 1982, 37).[13] Second, the initial federal endangered species list was developed by nine biologists making up the Committee on Rare and Endangered Species for the Interior Department's Bureau of Sport Fisheries and Wildlife (now FWS). The committee published the now famous *Redbook,* listing sixty-three vertebrate species deemed by FWS biologists to be endangered.[14]

Two other things happened in the 1960s that, in retrospect, seem crucial in generating federal endangered species legislation (Yaffee 1982). First, biologists with the FWS—after recently beginning to document species extinction and to learn about its technical causes—developed a strong interest in comprehensive legislation. Second, the modern environmental movement emerged with species protection high on its agenda. The result was the 1966 Endangered Species Preservation Act, which directed the secretary of the interior to establish a comprehensive program for protecting endangered species and which had several key features. First, it explicitly gave the secretary the ability to use conservation funds for protecting the habitat of endangered species by purchasing habitat, basically as part of the federal refuge system.[15] Second, it directed the secretary of

13. Revenue initially came from the sale of "excess federal property," federal motorboat fuel taxes, and Park Service entry fees. In 1968 Congress authorized general appropriations for this fund. The fund averaged $140 million in the first decade.

14. U.S. Department of Interior, *Redbook—Rare and Endangered Fish and Wildlife of the United States—Preliminary Draft* (Washington, D.C.: Bureau of Sport Fisheries and Wildlife, August 1964).

15. The funds were limited to $5 million annually with a limit of $750,000 for any single refuge.

the interior to publish in the *Federal Register* a list of native, vertebrate species threatened by extinction.[16] Third, the act prohibited the taking of endangered species, but only on federal wildlife refuges. Fourth, the act required that federal agencies consider the effects of their programs on endangered wildlife populations but only "to the extent practicable."

Compared with the 1973 ESA, the 1966 law was extremely limited.[17] The 1966 act had trivial restrictions on takings and trade; it had a limited fund for habitat acquisitions; it only considered native, vertebrate species; and it imposed only trivial constraints on other federal agencies. The 1966 act was drafted by Interior Department personnel and passed on a voice vote in both houses of Congress. In committee and full house hearings, there was no detectable opposition to the act.

The 1969 Act. Just three years later, the 1966 act was embellished with the passage of the 1969 Endangered Species Conservation Act. The 1969 act primarily addressed international aspects of endangered species protection (Bean and Rowland 1997). First, the act directed the secretary of the interior to develop a list of species threatened with worldwide extinction and to coordinate international efforts. It even called for an international conference on the topic.[18] Second, it increased the funds available for habitat and raised the per-area cap on expenditures from $750,000 to $2.5 million. Third, invertebrates were now included in "fish and game" species to be protected under the act. Fourth, the Lacey Act was extended to

16. At the time of the bill, FWS testified that only seventy-eight species (only mammals and birds) were considered endangered.

17. According to Yaffee (1982), the act was considered by many to be a "refuge" bill; indeed sections 4 and 5 formally established the National Wildlife Refuge System.

18. This ultimately led to the Convention on International Trade in Endangered Species (CITES).

cover amphibians, reptiles, mollusks, and crustaceans, mainly because of increasing evidence of alligator poaching in the Southeast.

In sum, the 1969 act did little to change the original 1966 law, and similarly it was passed on a voice vote in both houses. As with the first law, the draft legislation came from the Bureau of Sports Fisheries and Wildlife and initially sailed through Congress unopposed. Along the way, however, opposition emerged and reshaped the final law (Yaffee 1982). Members of the American fur industry noticed that the draft legislation would unilaterally restrict trade on internationally endangered species and noted that this would burden them relative to international competitors. Pressure from the fur industry modified the act to list a species only when it was endangered worldwide and to further limit the unilateral implementation of international sanctions. After this modification, the bill quickly became law without controversy.

1973 Endangered Species Act

The Endangered Species Act (ESA) of 1973 fundamentally changed the role of the federal government in wildlife issues. Not only did the ESA expand the federal authority beyond its traditional role of regulating trade and managing migratory species, it also dramatically changed the way in which endangered species would be managed. The initial draft of the ESA was introduced in 1972, and after a few iterations, it passed on voice votes in both houses of Congress. There was overwhelming support throughout the process and almost no opposition from any commercial or agency interests.[19]

19. Yaffee (1982) and Rohlf (1989) do note some contention between the Interior and Commerce Departments over jurisdiction. They also note some opposition to federal authority over resident species from state game agencies. The first issue was resolved by giving FWS (Interior) primary jurisdiction over the ESA but giving the National Marine Fisheries Service (Commerce) authority over certain marine species. The second issue was resolved through a grant program to states.

The Initial Structure of the ESA. First, the secretary of the interior was required to establish a list of species, subspecies, and/or isolated populations that were endangered or "threatened." These provisions extended the coverage to subspecies and populations and even protected species that had physical features similar to protected species. These provisions also extended protection to plants.[20] Any citizen who had evidence of endangerment could propose a listing, and the secretary would be required to respond to such a petition. Second, the act made it unlawful to take any endangered or threatened species whether on private or public land (section 9). More important, *take* was broadly defined to mean "harass, harm, pursue, hunt, shoot, wound, kill, trap, capture, or collect" an endangered species (section 3). Third, the act required federal agencies to review all their actions and to make certain they did not jeopardize any listed species or modify critical habitat (section 7). Unlike the 1966 act, the ESA did not allow agencies to consider endangered species only when practicable. Fourth, the act allowed citizen lawsuits to force the secretary to follow the law and allowed courts to award court costs for plaintiffs (section 11). Fifth, the ESA dramatically extended federal authority into the management of resident wildlife traditionally held by states.

Together these features of the ESA substantially increased the legal mandate to protect species beyond that of either the 1966 or the 1969 act. The most notable features were the expanded categories of potentially endangered species, the broad definition of *take* and its application to private land, the tight restrictions on the behavior of federal agencies, and the citizen lawsuit provision. The ESA also

20. There were some categories exempted from protection: insect pests, bacteria, viruses, and some species used by native Alaskans. The "threatened" category was also an addition and created a new category of protected species, which gives great discretion to the relevant agency as far as implementing protective policies (Bean and Rowland 1997, 200–202). In practice, endangered and threatened categories do not seem to have differential regulatory impacts.

prohibited trade in endangered or threatened species and established a program of cooperative state–federal grants to develop programs to protect species (section 6); divided management authority between the FWS (Interior Department) and the Marine Fisheries Service (Commerce Department); and established relatively severe penalties for violations (Yaffee 1982; Bean and Rowland 1997).[21]

Amendments, Court Decisions, and Regulations Define the ESA. Even though the ESA had strong language, it lay almost dormant for half a decade. From 1973 to 1978, the Fish and Wildlife Service moved very slowly to list species and promulgate regulations (Yaffee 1982). Over time, court decisions, administrative decisions, and congressional amendments defined the ESA's structure. The notorious snail darter case, *Tennessee Valley Authority (TVA) v. Hill*,[22] was the first important judicial decision to specify the reach of the ESA. In *TVA*, the court ruled that section 7 of the ESA required that the construction of a nearly completed federal dam be halted in order to save the habitat of an endangered minnow (the snail darter). In interpreting the ESA, the court issued its now famous mandate: "The plain intent of the statute was to halt and reverse the trend toward species extinction, whatever the cost" (184). In effect, *TVA* established the unilateral authority of the ESA to control the actions of federal agencies.

Just as section 7 was strongly defined by the courts, so was section 9, which made it unlawful for "any person subject to the jurisdiction of the United States" to take any endangered species. This provision clearly applied to activities on private land as well as on federal and other government land, yet like the section 7 provisions, little activity occurred under section 9 during the first years of the

21. The ESA still allowed for the acquisition of habitat via the Land and Water Conservation Fund. In this dimension, the ESA was similar to existing federal preservation law.

22. 437 U.S. 153 (1978).

ESA. The restrictions on taking an endangered species were treated like typical hunting or fishing restrictions on actually killing individual animals. The ESA left the details of defining the verbs in section 3 (*harm, harass,* and others) to the secretary of the interior. In 1975, the secretary defined *harm* as:

> [A]n act or omission which actually injures or kills wildlife, including acts which annoy it to such an extent as to significantly disrupt essential behavioral patterns, which include, but are not limited to, breeding, feeding, or sheltering; significant environmental modification or degradation which has such effects is included within the meaning of "harm."[23]

Although it was clear from the secretary's regulation that the ESA had the potential to restrict land use dramatically, the ESA was not used for such purposes for several years. This changed in 1979 with a federal decision in a case known as *Palila I.*[24] The Sierra Club and other environmental groups brought suit under the ESA charging that the state of Hawaii was taking an endangered bird—the palila—by maintaining a population of feral sheep and goats for sport hunting. Both trial and federal appellate courts agreed that the sheep and goats adversely affected the palila's nesting sites, constituting an unlawful taking under the ESA's definition of harm. The court ordered the sheep and goats to be removed from the area.[25] In the 1995 case of *Babbitt*

23. 40 Fed. Reg. 44412, 44416 (1975), current version at 50 C.F.R. §17.3 (1995). The regulations similarly define *harass.*

24. *Palila v. Hawaii Department of Land and Natural Resources* 471 F. Supp. 985 (D. Hawaii 1979), *aff'd,* 639 F2d 495 (1981). See Bean and Rowland (1997, chapter 7) and Rohlf (1989, 62–66). In an important later case, *Sierra Club v. Lyng* 694 F. Supp. 1260 (E.D. Texas 1988), the court relied on *Palila I* and found that logging on national forests harmed the red-cockaded woodpeckers.

25. In *Palila II* [*Palila v. Hawaii Department of Land and Natural Resources,* 649 F. Supp. 1070 (D. Hawaii 1986), *aff'd,* 852 F2d 1106 (9th Cir. 1988)] the court went further than *Palila I* to hold that harm applies to species, not just individuals, making habitat modification even more likely to fit the definition of *harm.*

v. Sweet Home,[26] this broad view of *take* to include habitat alteration and its direct authorization by the ESA was supported by the Supreme Court.[27]

In addition to judicial clarification of the ESA,[28] Congress has amended the act three times, in 1978, 1982, and 1988. The first set of amendments came on the heels of the *TVA* case. Many in Congress were surprised by the court's overwhelming support of the ESA that, in effect, forced federal agencies to comply with the ESA without considering the costs. The decision in *TVA* led Congress to enact the 1978 amendments that established a rigorous, formal process for exemptions under section 7.[29] These amendments also established the so-called "god committee," a seven-member cabinet-level committee designed to rule on ESA exemptions (Bean and Rowland 1997). Although the 1978 amendments passed easily by voice vote, there was lengthy, acrimonious debate, and a number of preliminary amendments were defeated.[30] Further amendments came in 1982

26. *Babbitt v. Sweet Home Chapter of Communities for a Greater Oregon* 515 U.S. 687 (1995).

27. Notably, "take" under the Migratory Bird Treaty Act does not include habitat destruction [(*Seattle Audubon Society v. Evans* 952 F2d 297 (9th Cir. 1991)].

28. There are, of course, other provisions of the ESA that have similarly evolved. The citizen lawsuit provision of the ESA (§11) is quite liberal and has been refined through the courts. The key case supporting an expansive view of standing for environmental groups is *Defenders of Wildlife v. Hodel* 851 F2d 1035 (8th Cir.), discussed in Rohlf (1989, 184–185). Recently, however, the Court unanimously interpreted the Endangered Species Act to permit lawsuits not only by people who think the government is doing too little to protect endangered species but also by those who think that federal regulation has gone too far. The decision, *Bennett v. Spear*, No. 95-813, opens the door to suits against federal regulators by business interests and affected property owners. Courts have also defined the listing process (§4) through a series of cases including a decision that forced the listing of the northern spotted owl (*Northern Spotted Owl v. Hodel* 716 F. Supp. 479, 483 W.D. Wash, 1988). (See Bean and Rowland 1997, 207–209 for a discussion.)

29. Endangered Species Act Amendments of 1978, Pub. L. No. 95-632 as codified at 16 U.S.C.

30. See 1978 *Congressional Quarterly Almanac* (1978, 707–711). Similar close votes on ESA amendments took place during 1982.

with an act to reauthorize the ESA for three years.[31] These amendments added exemptions to the ESA, including "experimental populations," and allowed "incidental" taking of an endangered species under section 10 of the act: To obtain an "incidental take permit," an applicant must submit a "habitat conservation plan" to the FWS.[32] The 1982 amendment also required that listing decisions be made solely on biological grounds and even prohibited economic factors from being considered. The final set of amendments came in 1988, after a three-year period in which the ESA was not reauthorized, with a five-year reauthorization of the ESA.[33] The 1988 amendments also increased civil and criminal penalties for ESA violations, established a monitoring system for listing, and protected species that were proposed but not yet listed.

The Current Reauthorization Gridlock. By the mid-1990s, a large part of the ESA's structure had been fleshed out by the amendments, regulations, and court decisions.[34] The most important features of the ESA are the primal duty of all federal agencies to alter their behavior in accordance with the ESA and the broad definition of *harm* that makes habitat modification a taking. Table 1 summarizes federal wildlife preservation law and shows the striking difference in approach before and after the ESA.

The reauthorization of the ESA in the 1988 amendments expired after fiscal year 1992, and since that time Congress has failed

31. Endangered Species Act Amendments of 1982, Pub. L. No. 97-304 codified at 16 U.S.C. §1539.

32. Bean and Rowland (1997, 234–235) argue that although these changes were originally designed to lessen the strength of the act, they actually have strengthened the act by giving greater leverage to the secretary of the interior.

33. Endangered Species Act Amendments of 1988, Pub. L. No. 100-478 codified at 16 USC §1533.

34. There are other, less-settled issues such as listing procedures and habitat conservation plan requirements.

to enact reauthorization legislation. Extremely contentious debate over the future of the ESA has prevented agreement, so Congress has simply appropriated funds on an annual basis. The crux of the contention has been the treatment of private landowners given the broad definition of *harm* as applied to section 9's prohibition on taking. Landowner groups are insistent that either this provision be loosened or the federal government must compensate landowners for lost value when certain uses are prohibited in order to protect habitat.

In the interim, numerous bills have been introduced to modify the ESA, and the FWS has implemented new policies that are less onerous for private landowners. The two recent policies implemented in the past few years are Safe Harbor and No Surprises. Safe Harbor was adopted in April 1995 and authorizes all incidental taking—while maintaining an initial baseline population—of a listed species that inhabits a landowner's property as the result of affirmative conservation efforts. This means, for example, that if a landowner's actions attract more members of a listed species, the landowner would be able to develop that land even if the population of the species was adversely affected as long as the population of a listed species remained above a baseline level agreed to by the FWS and the landowner. The Safe Harbor policy originated in North Carolina in response to evidence that landowners were destroying habitat in order to avoid possible regulations under section 9. No Surprises was established in 1994 and is similarly designed to ensure nonfederal landowners that land-use restrictions under section 9 will not be subject to change. No Surprises prohibits FWS from adding land-use restrictions or financial burdens on a landowner with an authorized habitat conservation plan.

In recent years there have been numerous attempts to amend the ESA. These efforts reflect the growth of interest groups that now reap benefits and incur costs from the ESA. Most introduced legislation has been hostile to the current ESA and has included provisions

TABLE 1 Summary of Federal Wildlife Legislation

Legislation	*Year*	*Take Restrictions*	*Trade Restrictions*	*Land Acquisition*	Land-use Restrictions		*Other Features*	*Vote/ Supporters*
					Private	*Public*		
Lacey Act	1900	No	Yes	No	No	No	Regulated interstate commerce in wildlife taken in violation of state law. Result of passenger pigeon extinction.	
Fur Seal Treaty	1911	Yes	Yes	No	No	No	Limited seal harvest among signing countries.	
Migratory Bird Treaty Act	1918	Yes	Yes	No	No	No	Prohibits taking of migratory birds in any way during closed seasons.	
Black Bass Act	1926	No	Yes	No	No	No	Extended Lacey Act to fish.	
Migratory Bird Conservation Act	1929	Yes	NA	Yes	No	No	Major source of authority for wildlife refuge acquisition.	
Migratory Bird Hunting Stamp Act	1934	NA	Yes	Yes	No	No	Provided funding for the land acquisition authorized in the 1929 act.	
Fish and Wildlife Coordination Act	1934	NA	NA	Yes	No	No	Authorized investigations into pollution effect on wildlife. Mandated consultation on dam construction.	
Pittman-Robertson Act	1937	NA	Yes	No	No	No		

Bald Eagle Protection Act	1940	Yes	Yes	No	No	No	Golden eagles protected in 1962 amendments. Allows some taking for livestock depredation and coal recovery. 1978 amendments extended taking to nests.	
Land and Water Conservation Fund Act (LWC)	1964	NA	NA	Yes	No	No	Non species-by-species habitat acquisition power allowed.	House: Voice Senate: 92–1 Conf. Rept.: Voice
Endangered Species Preservation Act	1966	No	No	Yes	No	Yes (weak)	Directed federal agencies to protect endangered species when “practicable.” Allowed use of land and water conservation funds for habitat acquisition for endangered species. Required secretary to publish list of endangered species.	Conservation groups Voice votes
Endangered Species Conservation Act	1969	Yes (ban)	Yes	Yes	No	No	Increased funding for habitat acquisition. Expansion of Lacey Act to include reptiles, amphibians, mollusks, and crustaceans as well as international endangered species. Authorized secretary to promulgate a list of species endangered throughout the world. Directed secretary to seek an international convention on endangered species.	Voice votes

TABLE 1 *(continued)*

Legislation	*Year*	*Take Restrictions*	*Trade Restrictions*	*Land Acquisition*	LAND-USE RESTRICTIONS		*Other Features*	*Vote/ Supporters*
					Private	*Public*		
Wild Free-Roaming Horses and Burros Act	1971	Yes (ban)	Yes	NA	NA	Yes	Directed federal agencies to protect wild horses and burros.	
Marine Mammal Protection Act	1972	Yes (ban)	Yes	NA	NA	NA	Moratorium on killing of ocean mammals or importation of products made from them.	House: 362–10 Senate: 88–2 Conf. Rept.:
Voice								
Endangered Species Act (ESA)	1973	Yes (ban)	Yes	Yes	Yes	Yes	Allowed citizen lawsuits. Expanded the list of species to include plants. Added “threatened” category. Broad definition of “take” to include harm. Strong compliance language for federal agencies.	House: 390–12 Senate: 92–0 House Conf.: 355–4
ESA Amendments	1978	Yes (ban)	Yes	Yes	Yes	Yes	Defined “critical habitat” and requires its designation when a species is listed. Allowed consideration of “economic impacts.” Established “god committee” and process for agency exemptions. Added a “self-defense”exemption.	Bipartisan support after contentious debate and several failed bills.

ESA Amendments	1982	Yes (ban)	Yes	Yes	Yes	Yes	Required listing decision to be made solely on biological grounds (ruled out economic factors). Added experimental populations and incidental taking.	
ESA Amendments	1988	Yes (ban)	Yes	Yes	Yes	Yes	Increased civil and criminal penalties. Created a monitoring system for listing.	Bipartisan support after contentious debate and several failed bills.
Safe Harbor Policy	1995	Baseline ban	NA	NA	Yes	NA	Allowed incidental taking of listed species as long as a baseline population is maintained.	NA
National Wildlife Refuge System Improvement Act	1997	Limited	NA	Yes	No	NA	An "organic act" to govern the national Wildlife Refuge System. Establishes hunting, fishing, wildlife observation, and photography as "priority public uses."	Bipartisan support Senate: 100–0 House: 419–1

NA = not applicable.

SOURCES: Bean and Rowland (1997), Rohlf (1989), Yaffee (1982), and various government documents.

that would make listing more difficult and require compensation for mandated changes in land use for private landowners.[35] Most recently, in February 1999, California Representative William Thomas introduced three bills to amend the ESA. Together these bills would dramatically alter the current policy by making it more difficult to list species, requiring compensation to landowners if ESA regulations diminish property values by more than 50 percent, and narrowing the definitions of *take* and *harm*.[36]

Property Rights and Wildlife Preservation

An economic model of wildlife preservation that focuses on land and habitat ownership illuminates the behavior of landowners, wildlife-environmental groups, politicians, and bureaucrats. The model begins by considering the allocation of land between wildlife habitat and other non-wildlife uses. Two basic types of government action can be, and have been, used to preserve wildlife (or enhance wildlife habitat): a pay-to-protect program, in which landowners are compensated for habitat provision; and an ESA-style land-use restriction that attempts to lock in existing habitat by penalizing landowners for adverse alterations. As the Coase Theorem (Coase 1960) implies, with zero transaction costs or well-defined property rights, either policy will generate the first-best allocation of land among wildlife and non-wildlife uses. In practice, however, these regimes will have dif-

35. There have also been numerous bills that require compensation for regulatory takings beyond the ESA. Less common are bills that would strengthen ESA enforcement. One such example is H.R. 2351 introduced by California Representative George Miller.

36. See Roger Platt for a discussion of the interest group politics behind ESA reauthorization ("Ships Passing in the Night: Current Prospects for Reauthorization of the Endangered Species Act," *Endangered Species Update* Nov/Dec. 1997, 3–7). Platt focuses on the Endangered Species Recovery Act of 1997 (S. 1180).

ferent effects precisely because property rights to wildlife and their habitat are costly to define and enforce.

For wildlife, these costs have their roots in two key sources. First, like any resource, land comprises many dimensions, including wildlife habitat.[37] Thus it is typically the case that an optimal property rights structure is a complex mix of ownership spread across private and public parties (Barzel 1997). Legal landowners, who control most of the dimension of land, tend to have better information than the FWS has about the habitat productivity and existing populations of listed species on their property, which further implies that the landowner has the ability to alter the habitat to avoid losses associated with land-use regulations such as the ESA. A second source of property rights enforcement costs arises within bureaucracies where ownership is often ill-specified. FWS bureaucrats have limited incentives and resources to fully enforce ESA land-use restrictions. At the same time, organized interest groups may be able to influence politicians and bureaucrats to alter the level of enforcement by directly affecting FWS budgets and policies.

The analysis proceeds to develop implications about land use and landowner behavior under the two systems. The model also examines how parties other than landowners (wildlife/environmental groups, politicians, and bureaucrats) will behave in response to a shift from pay-to-protect to ESA-style regulations. Each of these parties may respond in both private and political ways. Political behavior, in this case, is derivative of a major change in property rights with the enforcement of the ESA.[38] In effect, people can

37. This important multidimensional view of property rights has been stressed most often by Barzel (1997).

38. Related incentives issues are discussed in Epstein (1997), Hermalin (1995), Innes, Polasky, and Tschirhart (1998), Polasky and Doremus (1998), Stroup (1997), and Thompson (1997). Libecap (1989) and Kantor (1998) examine how political institutions affect changes in property rights.

use political institutions to claim and establish rights to land under the ESA.

The Land Allocation Problem with Wildlife

The problem of wildlife protection can be examined by focusing on the allocation of land for wildlife habitat and other non-wildlife uses (farming/ranching and suburban development). The allocation of land among these uses depends on the property rights to the land as defined by laws, contracts, or custom. The model assumes that there are only two competing uses for a plot of land and that ownership of wildlife can be established by controlling its habitat.[39]

The First-Best Outcome. Assume there is a total amount of land (L) that can be devoted to wildlife habitat (w) or non-wildlife use (x). When the marginal values of the two uses are exactly equal, the value of the land will be maximized. This first-best allocation of land is shown in figure 1. The horizontal axis measures the total amount of land, with w denoting the amount of land devoted to wildlife habitat and x the amount devoted to non-wildlife uses. V_w is the marginal value of land used for wildlife habitat, and V_x is the marginal value of land used for non-wildlife uses. It is assumed that $V_x = 0$ for some $x \leq L$, so that some fraction of the land simply has no value in non-wildlife use. In figure 1, the first-best allocation of land occurs at L^*, where the marginal values of wildlife and non-wildlife uses are equated. As drawn, the marginal value function for wildlife is relatively small, so the optimal allocation of land is overwhelmingly devoted to non-wildlife uses.

The Contracting Problem: Small Landowners and Wildlife Ownership. In order for L^* to be chosen by a landowner, the property

39. The model focuses on habitat provision and ignores the dynamics of harvesting under various property rights regimes.

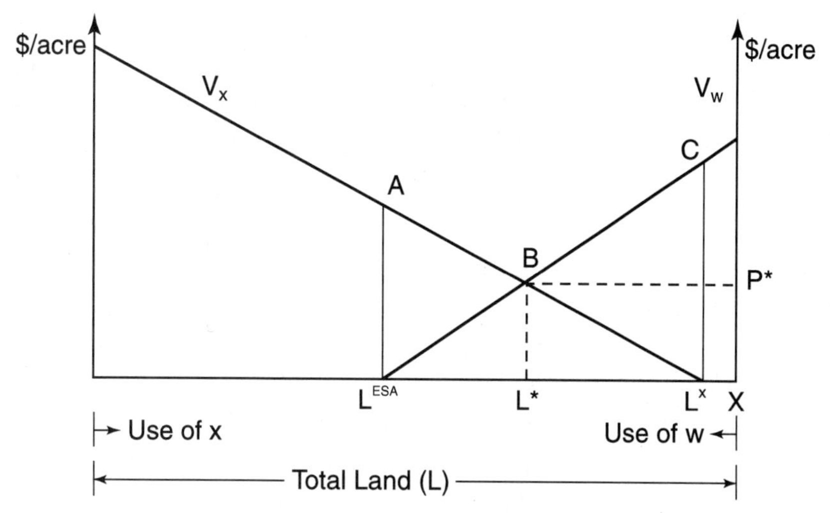

FIGURE 1 Optimal Land Allocation for Wildlife and Other Uses

rights to wildlife habitat must be perfectly defined so that the landowner can capture the full benefit from allocating land to wildlife uses. In general, however, land ownership patterns will be designed to accommodate non-wildlife use and will not be coincident with the habitat requirement of wild populations. This makes it costly—sometimes prohibitively so—for landowners to capture value from allocating land for wildlife habitat (Tobar 1981; Lueck 1989; Anderson 1999). Consider the extreme case in which the landowner cannot capture any value from wildlife habitat because his small holding essentially makes wildlife an open access resource.[40] Also assume that the landowner has no enforceable obligation to provide wildlife habitat and thus only cares about the alternative land use. His problem now becomes a simple choice of how much land to allocate to non-wildlife use in the absence of another profitable use. This choice is shown as L^x in figure 1. Land is

40. This is the worst case scenario because the landowner cannot claim any value from the wildlife.

"excessively" allocated toward non-wildlife uses but not exclusively so because the marginal value of land for non-wildlife use becomes zero before all wildlife habitat is converted.[41] The associated deadweight loss is given by the triangle BCL_x; this loss also represents the potential gains from a contract among a group of landowners that can effectively control the amount of habitat needed for the wildlife to thrive. In the case of public land ownership, the misallocation can be similar if the managing agency is subsidizing the non-wildlife land use or simply not recognizing wildlife uses.[42]

Consider a simple case in which ten identical, adjacent landowners control the amount of land needed to provide habitat for a potentially valuable wild population. In principle, a simple share contract, in which each landowner gets one-tenth of the total value of the wildlife, would generate the optimal allocation of land among the two uses. Because of large numbers or heterogeneous interests, contracting costs among landowners may make such a contract infeasible and cause the deadweight loss to remain (Libecap 1989; Lueck 1989).[43]

Collective Action to Provide Wildlife Habitat

A political organization such as a game department, however, might be able to enforce rights to the stock at lower costs because agreement among all landowners is not necessary for agency action. Indeed, this is the primary economic rationale for a game department

41. Such a scenario is common. For example, a rancher may inadvertently provide habitat for big game species simply because these species use habitat that is unsuitable ($V_x = 0$) for domestic livestock.

42. Indeed, this has been the claim of many environmentalist critiques of public land management.

43. If the wildlife were primarily valued for public goods such as aesthetics or biodiversity (rather than for private uses such as hunting), contracting costs would likely be even greater because landowners would find it even more costly to exclude consumers who value the wildlife for these reasons.

(Lueck 1989).[44] In the context of wildlife preservation, federal action has taken two forms.[45]

Before the ESA: Pay-to-Protect. Under legislation beginning with the Migratory Bird Treaty Act, federal preservation law typically had two policy components: (1) season closures or prohibitions on killing (the narrow definition of *take*) and (2) habitat acquisition through lease and purchase. Because the focus is on land use, the effect of season closures on wildlife is ignored. Under pay-to-protect, the government agency (FWS) identifies and purchases the most valuable wildlife habitat by operating in the land market and offering a price per acre (P) to the landowner for any land set aside as wildlife habitat. The landowner now faces a cost of allocating the land away from wildlife (the potential FWS payment). If the FWS can set the price correctly (P^*), the solution is identical to the first-best outcome as shown in figure 1.[46] Although it is unreasonable to suppose that the FWS can perfectly choose P^*, the FWS will be forced to purchase the least costly wildlife habitat of a given quality.[47] For example, the FWS can get more wildlife habitat by buying poor farmland than it could by purchasing prime urban real estate. Indeed, this is the same

44. Although the game department can mitigate the contracting problem, this regime is still imperfect. Two limits are worth noting. First, the game department cannot directly control agricultural and other uses of land that can affect the land's value as wildlife habitat. Second, the political institutions that allowed game departments also generate well-known collective choice problems.

45. Historically, most game departments have been state organizations that regulate access to resident game populations. State game departments have handled most wildlife issues, arguably because state agencies have enough jurisdictional authority to manage wildlife without generating excessive bureaucratic costs. Federal action emerged in two areas where state authority seems to have been a suboptimal jurisdiction: game trade and migratory waterfowl.

46. The first-best price must be equal to the marginal values of wildlife and non-wildlife uses at L^*.

47. See Swope, Benjamin, and Anderson (this volume) for an analysis of how such prices are determined and how landowners respond.

approach taken by land trusts and other private groups that preserve habitat by working within the real estate market.

ESA: Land-Use Regulations. The key change brought by the ESA was the broad definition of *taking* to include habitat modification. Thus, under the ESA, the prime policy becomes a restrictive land-use regulation. Also as interpreted by the Supreme Court in *TVA*, the ESA forbids consideration of the cost of preserving a species. This means that ESA regulation of habitat for a listed species forces all land with any positive habitat value (defined as $V_w \geq 0$) into wildlife use. As figure 1 shows, this means that the ESA requires the land-use allocation L^{ESA}. This allocation has a deadweight loss (DWL) associated with "excessive" habitat provision shown by the triangle ABL^{ESA}. Strictly speaking, the ESA cannot generate first-best land use unless it is not enforced.[48] Because landowners are not compensated, they bear the entire opportunity cost of allocating land toward wildlife preservation (L^x to L^{ESA}) and out of non-wildlife use. Given this cost, it is not surprising that landowners oppose ESA restrictions.

Claiming and Reclaiming Rights to Land under the ESA

The ESA alters the property rights of a landowner when an endangered species is present or when there is a positive probability that a species will inhabit the land. A pay-to-protect system, however, retains the same system of rights to land but generates a market for wildlife habitat. Under the ESA, the FWS essentially controls wildlife (at least for listed species) by virtue of its enforcement authority. Either the ESA or the pay-to-protect regime would generate the first-best allocation of land if the property rights were perfectly

48. In practice, it is likely that the ESA will not be fully enforced because the deadweight losses get large and because the gains for wildlife values get similarly low.

defined; yet it is the high cost of establishing rights to wildlife and their habitat that has led to the problem of wildlife preservation. So in the presence of imperfect rights these two regimes will generate different outcomes. The pre-ESA regime (pay-to-protect) will tend to provide too little wildlife habitat, but first-best can be approached through a program of habitat acquisition. The ESA regime can, in principle, lead to the protection of wildlife habitat, but this analysis ignores the behavior of various interest groups and their response to the incentives under the ESA.[49]

Claiming Land under the ESA. Once a species has been listed, the ESA is in force, so that land that provides habitat for a listed species (endangered or threatened) is governed by the regulations under section 9. A landowner thus finds that a portion of his or her rights to the use and income of the land are essentially transferred to the FWS and to those who can influence FWS through political or legal avenues. Because the ESA allows citizen lawsuits, environmental groups can sue for listing and implementation of the ESA and thus claim land by removing it from non-wildlife uses.[50] Also, because the ESA places no limits on the number of species to be listed or the number of acres to be affected and does not require that landowners be compensated for their losses, there is a weaker budget constraint than with a federal habitat acquisition program. In principle, a group can claim large areas by seeking the listing of a species that inhabits large areas and thus impeding those land-use actions that harm the species.

The ESA can also lead to land claiming on public lands. On public land, the ESA creates different incentives because land managers and land users do not have effective control over land use like

49. There are, of course, interest group forces at play under pay-to-protect systems (Swope, Benjamin, and Anderson, this volume).

50. Claiming could and does take place through debate over the definition of *critical habitat*.

a private landowner has (Nelson 1995). Property rights to public lands can take the form of long-term leases (cabins, ski areas), shorter-term use permits (timber-harvest contracts), or simply lengthy historical practice. For example, in the Pacific Northwest, timber companies have been purchasing and cutting public timber for nearly a century and likely had (prior to the ESA) the expectation that this practice would continue. So although some private rights to public lands do exist, they tend to be less clearly defined (compared with private lands) and subject to changes through political and administrative processes.[51] Historically, many public lands have been managed for single uses (timber, grazing) because of the ability of strong interest groups to control public agencies and because of the inability of public agencies to administer transfers of land rights. In this context, the ESA can provide a mechanism for environmentalists to attack what they view as pork-barrel projects that lower environmental quality.

Reclaiming Land: Preemption and Political Action. As the model shows, a private landowner will suffer uncompensated losses once the ESA is invoked on his or her property. Yet the landowner maintains important influence over the land by virtue of control over non-wildlife uses. As a result, the static model does not fully capture the behavior of landowners facing potential ESA restrictions. Because of the information advantage the landowner has over the FWS (who must enter and survey the land to enforce the ESA),

51. The presence or the possibility of an endangered species on public land can weaken and even dissolve other property claims to public lands, such as timber harvest rights or other actions that might alter the habitat for the listed species (road development, mineral extraction, grazing). If, for example, an endangered species is found in an area where public timber is harvested, the ESA may be used to place a moratorium on timber harvest and essentially transfer ownership of this land to the FWS or environmental groups pushing for the implementation of the ESA.

the landowner may be able to take action to prevent the administration of the ESA. If the ESA can be avoided, then the landowner has successfully reclaimed rights to wildlife habitat. Potentially, there are various means by which landowners can thwart the implementation of the ESA. First, if the species is already present but unknown to the FWS, landowners may simply kill all listed species inhabiting their property.[52] Second, if the species is not yet present but the potential for inhabitance is high, landowners may destroy habitat in order to preempt section 9 regulations. Preemptive habitat destruction might be active (bulldoze junipers that provide habitat for endangered warblers), or it might be passive (stop understory burning that maintains pine forest habitat for endangered woodpeckers).

The preemption decision can be examined using a two-period model (Lueck and Michael 1999) with two agents: a landowner (L) and a government agency (FWS) enforcing the ESA. The landowner can choose to maintain or destroy habitat in period 1. Destroying habitat has a one-time cost (C_D) and generates benefits (B_D) from development (timber harvest). C_D is the cost of early development, such as foregone revenue from harvesting timber before it is financially mature. The agency moves in period 2 and will detect the presence of an endangered species (ES) with probability $\alpha \varepsilon (0,1)$. If the habitat is destroyed in period 1, the probability that the agency finds an endangered species is zero. If the agency detects an endangered species, it regulates land use (under section 9) so that habitat cannot be altered. The agency can perfectly enforce this regulation. If an endangered species is detected, the firm loses all benefits from development in period 2 ($B_D = 0$). If, however, L waits until period 2 to develop, it faces no costs of development ($C_D = 0$). The landowner faces two sets of exogenous forces: market prices (which determine the magnitudes of the various benefits and costs)

52. This, of course, is a clear violation of the ESA's §9 and is known by the slogan, "Shoot, shovel, shut up."

and the probability of the agency detecting an endangered species in period 2.[53]

The decision tree in figure 2 illustrates the problem. Assume that the landowner chooses destroy or maintain in period 1 in order to maximize the expected value of the land. Thus the landowner will choose to destroy the habitat if the expected value of that option exceeds the value of habitat maintenance; that is, if the following condition holds: $[B_D - C_D] > (1 - \alpha)B_D$. The decision to destroy or maintain depends on the value of these parameters and leads to several straightforward comparative statics predictions. First, an increase in the probability that an endangered species will be found will lead to more habitat destruction.[54] Second, as the value of development increases, habitat destruction is more likely. Third, as the cost of development increases, habitat destruction is less likely.

Once the possibility of preemption is included in the model, the outcome under the ESA changes from that derived in the static land-use model. If preemption is chosen, there will be a decrease in the amount of wildlife habitat provided, even compared with that provided without the ESA. In figure 1, this outcome is shown as point X. This also implies that when preemption occurs, the population of the listed species will ultimately decline under the ESA because the amount of land allocated to wildlife habitat declines. The possibility of this behavior has led to criticism of the ESA by both landowners and environmentalists and is discussed later in this chapter. There are other implications that can be derived with minor adjustments to the model. First, if permits are necessary for de-

53. Although the model illustrates the basic incentives facing a landowner under the ESA, it is not comprehensive. For example, in this simple model, the FWS does *not* react to the landowner, nor does it get a payoff of its own.

54. The prediction also holds for other increases in α, such as increased detection and enforcement effort by FWS. Because the FWS is often forced into enforcement action by citizen lawsuits, it may well be appropriate to consider this probability as exogenous.

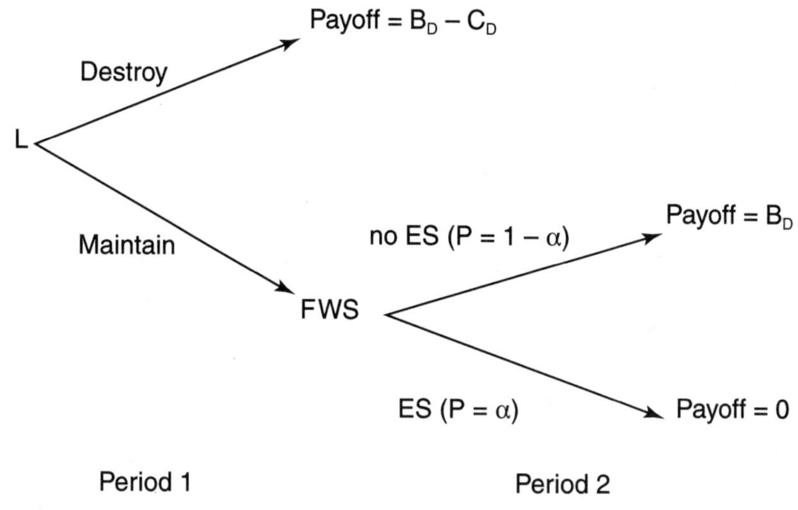

FIGURE 2 Decision Tree for Landowner under the ESA

velopment, the ability of FWS to detect listed species on the parcel prior to development will increase, and the likelihood of explicit preemption will decline.[55] In this case, the alternatives—killing listed species or using passive preemption—will become more attractive to landowners. Second, adding landowner compensation for providing habitat for listed species will decrease the expected payoff from preemption. Third, and somewhat paradoxically, increases in the probability of endangered species detection (in period 2) will increase the likelihood of preemption. On the other hand, if endangered species can be detected in period 1 (the landowner loses the information advantage), then preemption will be less likely and the outcome will be that described in the static model. Fourth, risk-averse landowners (perhaps the smaller, less wealthy landowner) will preempt more often than will risk-neutral landowners.

55. Such permits are found in some states for timber harvesting. Thompson (1997, 314–315) discusses these and related issues.

Landowners may also reclaim rights to habitat through political actions rather than through private preemption. Landowners may contract with each other to form interest groups and lobby for changes in the ESA or its implementation by the FWS. They can, for instance, use political means to reduce the penalties from ESA violations, limit the scope of these violations (limit the amount of critical habitat designated for a listed species), or reduce the probability of endangered species detection (reduce the budget of the FWS).

Behavior under the ESA

The property rights framework offers an explanation for the behavior of various parties since the ESA was enacted and implemented. The general implication is that the ESA altered rights to wildlife habitat and thus created incentives for environmental groups, private landowners, FWS (and National Marine Fisheries Service), public land management agencies, and politicians to claim these rights. This section examines some of this behavior to show how the property rights framework illuminates the behavior of these groups.[56]

The ESA as an Exogenous Transformation of Rights

The land-use model generates an economic rationale for government intervention in wildlife preservation. To the extent that the intervention is funded by wildlife users and compensates landowners for land-use changes, such collective action is likely to have broad support and little contention. Indeed the history of pre-ESA federal action seems to largely fit this description. Hunters and fishers—through federal duck stamps and federal taxes on sporting equip-

56. There are a few other empirical analyses of behavior under the ESA, but these studies have not focused on property rights. Ando (1997; 1999) examines how interest groups attempt to influence the process by which species are listed. Cain and Kaiser (1999) examine voting on the Tellico Dam exemption.

ment—essentially funded wildlife refuges and research programs. Most of these efforts are tied closely to migratory waterfowl where wildlife ownership is especially costly. Landowners would not have been in opposition to such pay-to-protect programs because they would be compensated for land-use changes.[57]

The contentious history of federal wildlife politics since the ESA, however, suggests a significant change in regimes. Like the ESA, its direct ancestors (the 1966 and 1969 acts) also passed virtually uncontested, but these acts did not substantially change federal policy (see table 1). For the most part they merely directed the secretary of the interior to maintain and publish a list of endangered species and encouraged federal agencies to manage with concern for these species. As implied by the lack of change in rights to habitat, there was almost no political contention after the acts were in force.[58] In this regard, the ESA of 1973 could hardly be more different.

It is contrary to the modern economic theory of politics to see highly divisive and costly legislation emerge from nearly unanimous political consensus. Not surprisingly, the various special theories of ESA political economy are only mildly compelling. The leading theory is that of symbolic legislation (Dwyer 1990) in which legislatures unanimously agree to pass vague laws that spread benefits widely (but thinly) and essentially have no expected costs. Dwyer (1990) argues that agencies will resist such legislation, but Yaffee (1982) seems to think they will like the discretion that vagueness affords. As initially written, the ESA suggested, if not promised, widespread benefits, but the lack of opposition in committees and in the full Congress suggested that the costs were trivial. Mann and Plummer (1995, chapter 6) offer a variation on this thesis, which places

57. Swope, Benjamin, and Anderson (this volume) find that they may even support such purchases.

58. Bean and Rowland (1997, 194–198) find no litigation over the 1966 act and only a few cases over the 1969 act.

more conscious effort on the part of the FWS bureaucrats and political appointees in the Nixon administration who wrote much of the law, inserting language that they hoped would go unseen only to have great impact later.[59]

The difficulty, of course, is trying to explain a single, albeit highly unusual, observation. For the purpose of this chapter, however, it is useful simply to take the ESA as an exogenous shift in federal wildlife law and accordingly a shift in property rights to wildlife habitat. Given the land-use model developed above, this allows an examination of private and public responses to this regime shift. Regardless of the original explanation of the ESA, there is little dispute that the ESA expanded under judicial and administrative evolution into something clearly unintended by Congress in 1973.[60] There are several bits of evidence that support this view. First, FWS did little to enforce the ESA until the court's *TVA* opinion forced them to do so. In both the academic and industry presses, there were few hints that the ESA would amount to much until the *TVA* decision made it clear that the ESA was important.[61] Second, even though all but

59. Mann and Plummer (1995, 155–161) argue that three insiders—E.U. Curtis Bohlen (under-Secretary of Interior), Lee M. Talbot (Council on Environmental Quality), and Frank M. Potter, Jr. (Senate committee counsel)—surreptitiously strengthened the final ESA bill by, among other things, deleting the "practicable" language in the original House and Senate versions. This, however, only explains the rather strong limits on federal agencies (§7) that came out of *TVA* and does little to explain the strong takings regulations (§9) that have emerged. Yaffee (1982) notes that FWS agents were key in writing the bill and that there was some mild opposition by the Safari Club International (a trophy hunting group) and the fur industry. Yaffee also argues that a strong, well-organized coalition of environmental groups was important but provides little evidence.

60. Bean and Rowland (1997, 199), however, claim that the broad reach of the ESA was intended from the start. Justice Powell's dissent, however, in *TVA* (208–210) argues that no one in Congress contemplated the possible consequences of the Act. Mann and Plummer (1995) and Yaffee (1982) also argue that Congress had no idea of the potential implications of the ESA.

61. In an obscure law review article, Lachenmier (1974) suggested possible severe impacts on federal agencies. Shortly thereafter Hutcherson (1976) suggested that the ESA might have a great impact on federal lands used for commercial

four of the states have endangered species acts, none have implemented the broad taking restrictions of the ESA's section 9 (Defenders of Wildlife 1998).[62] Third, the dramatic hostility to the ESA after *TVA* and again after the maturation of the taking restriction could not possibly have generated the near-unanimous support for the ESA had those effects been well anticipated.[63]

Interest Group Behavior

By changing the system of property rights to land, the ESA altered the incentives of many people and institutions, most notably environmentalists, private landowners, the FWS, public land agencies, and others. In the "other" category are scientists who can now generate research support by discovering populations of endangered species, consultants and lawyers who arbitrate the disputes, and politicians who have new opportunities to serve constituents supporting or opposing the ESA and its development. One striking development since the ESA is the nearly perfect alignment of political parties supporting (Democrats) and opposing (Republicans). The current polarization is so complete that it is hard to recall that the earliest legislation on wildlife preservation was overwhelmingly

---

forestry. Neither writer, however, anticipated restrictions on private land use. Yaffee (1982, 84) quotes an FWS employee in 1977 who saw the huge potential for section 7 to impact adversely economic and social development in the United States.

62. No other country has endangered species legislation with the strong taking language present in the ESA.

63. Rohlf (1989, 66–67) corroborates this: "[S]ince section 9 applies to all persons subject to United States jurisdiction, an expansive reading of section 9's taking restrictions carries tremendous implications for private land use. A wide array of activities on non-federal land could adversely impact the recovery of endangered species and thus be illegal under a broad interpretation of harm. The ESA's legislative history, however, gives no indication [that] Congress intended the statute to create sweeping controls on non-federal land use. On the contrary, the 1982 ESA amendments suggest that Congress was sympathetic to non-federal landowners whose actions may be restricted by section 9." According to Rohlf (1989, 69), FWS predicted an "explosion of litigation" after *Palila II*.

bipartisan and often led by Republicans. Although the effects of the ESA are widespread, this chapter focuses on the behavior of environmental groups, private landowners, and government agencies.

Environmental Groups. For environmentalists, the ESA offers a mechanism to affect land use by changing policy on public land, halting private development, and eliminating what are seen to be pork-barrel subsidies that allow certain public agencies to thrive at the expense of environmental quality. Environmental groups can claim rights to land by invoking the ESA to influence the behavior of federal agencies under section 7 and to arrest private development under section 9. As with nearly all of the federal environmental legislation passed in the 1970s, the ESA (section 11) contained a citizen lawsuit provision that made it cheap for environmentalists to force the FWS to enforce the ESA. In addition, the ESA authorizes courts to award costs of litigation, including expert witnesses, to any party to a suit brought under the citizen's suit provision.[64] Environmentalists have at least two ways to accomplish their goals under the ESA. First, environmentalists can force the FWS to act by showing that federal agencies or private land use harm listed species. Second, environmentalists can encourage the listing of new species that inhabit land for which environmentalists desire to change existing or planned land use. Environmentalists can both petition the FWS to list new species and sue the FWS for not acting swiftly.

The litigation evidence since the passage of the ESA indicates that environmentalists have successfully used the citizen lawsuit provision to invoke and strengthen the ESA.[65] The surprisingly strong

64. In *Ruckelshaus v. Sierra Club*, 463 U.S. 680 (1983), the court supported the awarding of court costs for the Clean Air Act and supported similar awards for lawsuits under the ESA. Rohlf (1989, 201–204) discusses the early law case.

65. Rohlf (1989) finds more than forty federal cases by 1988; Bean and Rowland (1997) discuss recent litigation. From 1973 to 1998, the *Environmental Law Reporter* (various issues) shows 24 cases reaching the Supreme Court, 360 reaching a federal appellate court, and 488 reaching a federal district court.

interpretation of section 7 by the Supreme Court in *TVA* resulted from a lawsuit brought by environmentalists interested in stopping the Tellico Dam. Environmentalists, beginning with the *TVA* case, have been successful in forcing federal agencies—including the Bureau of Reclamation, the Corps of Engineers, the Forest Service, the Bureau of Land Management, the Park Service, and the military services—to alter their land management to comply with the ESA. In the process, millions of acres of federal land have been de facto set aside as refuges for listed species. For example, obtaining "threatened" status for the northern spotted owl in 1992 has led to dramatic reductions in timber harvest on national forests.

Litigation has also expanded federal authority over interests formerly governed by the states and broadened the definition of *take*.[66] The net effect of this litigation is to give environmentalists a strong claim to wildlife habitat management on private lands. One strategy that seems to have developed is using lawsuits to force the listing of species that are widely distributed geographically so that the ESA can govern enormous expanses of land, both public and private (Thompson 1997, 312–324). The northern spotted owl is perhaps the ultimate success to date; critical habitat extends over millions of acres in all three Pacific Coast states. In July 1998, the National Wildlife Federation led a petition to force the FWS to list the black-tailed prairie dog, a rodent primarily known as a pest to livestock producers. If successful, this would invoke section 9 prohibitions on taking on at least 750,000 acres of land in eleven states on the Great Plains.[67] At this writing, the FWS has not acted on the petition and two groups (Predator Project and Biodiversity Legal Foundation) have sued to force the FWS to act. One piece of evidence in support of the strategy to list widespread species can be found in the

66. In particular, see *Palila I* and *Palila II* noted above.

67. There are also efforts under way to list the coho salmon, the bull trout, and the sage grouse, which could potentially affect millions of acres in the West.

press release given by the National Wildlife Federation (NWF) at the time of the petition. On July 31, 1998, NWF President Mark Van Patten stated "This is the best possible use of the Endangered Species Act, . . . If we can help the prairie dog, we'll be saving grasslands that benefit all sorts of wildlife, and people too."[68]

Landowners. For a private landowner, the ESA represents an uncompensated transfer of rights to their land. Accordingly, landowners have an incentive to reclaim these rights through both private and public action. The preemption model implied that a landowner can take action to destroy potential habitat as a mechanism of land reclaiming. Although there are numerous accounts of premature timber harvest and land clearing (Dolan 1992; Lambert and Smith 1994; Mann and Plummer 1995; Pendler 1995; Bean 1998), there is limited systematic analysis documenting the extent of such behavior.[69] One of the more closely documented cases—the red-cockaded woodpecker—is discussed in the next section.[70] Environmental groups, too, are becoming concerned that preemption is important and have even pressed to incorporate some relaxation of ESA takings prohibitions (Wilcove, Bean, Bonnie, and McMillan 1996).

Since the late 1980s and early 1990s, when the section 9 prohibitions on taking clearly became a part of the ESA, landowners have engaged in political action to mitigate the effects of the ESA. Effective political action, of course, requires the formation of well-defined

68. Quoted in "NWF Seeks Prairie Dog Listing: Action Will Save Wildlife and Grassland Habitat" <<http://www.nwf.org/grasslands/prairied.html>>. The petition also attacks government support of prairie dog eradication.

69. Evidence on the extent of the related landowner response—"shoot, shovel, and shut up"—is even more difficult to assess.

70. The *Wildlife Law News Quarterly* (Spring 1995) reports Pacific Lumber Company logging redwoods in order to avoid providing habitat for the marbled murrelets. Mann and Plummer (1995) discuss how landowners have bulldozed and overgrazed habitat in central Texas to rid their land of habitat for the golden-cheeked warbler.

interest groups. In some cases, existing groups, such as the American Farm Bureau Federation and the Forest Products Association, were ready to champion the causes of landowners affected by the ESA. In other cases, new organizations were formed to explicitly address the concerns of landowners with the ESA. Indeed, the emergence of the so-called property rights movement in the early 1990s came as a response to ESA regulations (Echeverria and Ely 1995). The property rights movement gained supporters in the Republican-led 104th Congress in 1994, which generated numerous bills to amend the ESA as well as anti-takings bills that would require compensation to landowners if some portion of land value was lost (typically 20 percent).[71] Although none of these bills became law and the ESA remains in limbo, the political pressure undoubtedly is part of the reason for the development of No Surprises and Safe Harbor policies.

The Fish and Wildlife Service and Public Land Agencies. The economic theory of bureaucracy suggests that the FWS will use the ESA to its advantage. Even so, under the ESA, the FWS faces competing forces so its behavior is difficult to predict. On one hand, the ESA offers opportunities to expand the reach and size of the agency beyond its traditional role. On the other hand, using the ESA for these new efforts means alienating long-lived constituents and risking political attack. Although it is clear that FWS bureaucrats were active in expanding the role of the agency by assisting in writing endangered species legislation, the agency was extremely cautious in enforcing the ESA before and often since *TVA*. For instance, FWS tried to narrow the scope of *harm* after *Palila I*, but was beaten back by environmentalists (Bean and Rowland 1997, 214).

71. Constitutional attacks on the ESA under the Fifth Amendment takings clause seem unlikely to succeed (Thompson 1997, 326–328). FWS is clearly aware of the legal requirements for a successful claim, especially because Executive Order 12,63, 3 C.F.R. sect 544 (1988) requires agencies to prepare Takings Implications Assessments (TIAs) for all contemplated regulations.

Even so, the FWS seems to have thrived since the ESA.[72] The total FWS budget, which was $160 million in 1974, increased to $1.006 billion by 1995. The budget for the FWS endangered species programs similarly increased from $3.2 million in 1972 to $87.9 million in 1995,[73] representing an increase in the share of the FWS budget devoted to endangered species from 2 percent in 1974 to 8.7 percent in 1995. Meanwhile the number of listed species rose from 109 species in 1973 to nearly 1,177 species in 1995, 702 of which are plants.[74] As expected, the FWS structure also has changed since the ESA. For example, there are now relatively more biologists working in the Office of Endangered Species (OES) than at regional offices and wildlife refuges. From its inception to the ESA, the FWS had primarily served a hunting/fishing constituency. Since the ESA, however, that emphasis has clearly diminished and shifted toward a nonhunting environmentalist constituent base. For example, several writers have reported the close ties between OES biologists and environmental groups (Yaffee 1982, 107–109). Chase (1995, 255–257) and others have noted that many of the lawsuits forcing FWS to list or define critical habitat have been "friendly" suits initiated by FWS biologists within OES. Another resulting change in FWS since the

72. The National Marine Fisheries Service administers the ESA for marine species. A similar analysis could be undertaken for this agency. Houck (1993) argues that the FWS and the National Marine Fisheries Service have great discretion in their administration of the ESA.

73. Even in real terms this represents more than a doubling of the FWS budget from $415.9 million in 1974 to $933.56 million in 1995 (both in 1992 dollars). In real terms, the endangered species program budget has increased tenfold from $8.32 million to $81.57 million over the same period. These data are from the annual United States Federal Budget (Office of Management and Budget, various years). The FY 2000 Clinton Administration budget proposes a record $1.58 billion for the FWS and $114.9 million for the endangered species program <<http://www.fws.gov/>> 1 Feb. 1999. The implicit GDP deflator was used to adjust for inflation. See the *Economic Report of the President*, February 1998 (Table B-3, 384).

74. This does not include listed foreign species. See <<http://www.fws.gov./r9endspp/boxscore.html>>.

ESA is the centralization of the agency bureaucracy because of the rising importance of endangered species. In the pre-ESA bureaucracy, the FWS was highly decentralized among its seven regional offices and hundreds of refuges. Today, the FWS is much more centralized because OES is headquartered in Washington, D.C. In short, the FWS has been transformed from an agency almost exclusively concerned with migratory birds and wildlife refuges to one with a strong focus on the administration and enforcement of the ESA.

Public land agencies have similarly been transformed by the ESA and its implementation. Since *TVA*, federal agencies have been forced to enhance the conservation and restoration of listed species, which has meant that land uses and land management decisions have changed. Timber harvest has been reduced on national forests, grazing has been limited on public ranges, water development projects have been eliminated or reduced in scale, and military bases have been modified to accommodate the habitat for listed species. Not surprisingly, these changes have led to substantial increases in agency expenditures on endangered species in order to study species and develop habitat conservation plans. Using federal data, Gordon, Lacey, and Streeter (1997) find that from 1989 to 1993 annual expenditures rose from $7.5 million to $38 million for the U.S. Forest Service (USFS), from $1.5 million to $14 million for the Bureau of Land Management (BLM), and from $5 million to $11 million for the Department of Defense.[75] Simultaneously public land use has

75. For example, Eglin Air Force Base in Florida and Fort Bragg Army Base in North Carolina are both home to numerous populations of the endangered red-cockaded woodpecker (RCW). Under the ESA, large amounts of these bases are off-limits to many training exercises. In addition, training costs have increased substantially as units must be relocated to other bases for many exercises. Required gunnery qualifications cost an additional $42,000 because it is now necessary to transport an attack helicopter battalion from Fort Bragg, North Carolina, to Fort Stewart, Georgia, so that RCW habitat at Fort Bragg can be protected (Snedden 1995). Military administrative resources have also been diverted into RCW management, developing guidelines, conducting research, and ensuring compliance with the ESA.

been diverted from revenue-generating activities, such as timber harvest, mineral extraction, and range leasing, toward wildlife and recreational uses that do not generate revenues.

Some Case Studies

Three case studies illustrate the effects of the ESA's property rights: the takeover of public land by environmentalists via ESA litigation, preemptive habitat destructions by private landowners, and the comparative record of wildlife restoration before and after the ESA.

Takeovers of Public Land by Environmentalists: The Northern Spotted Owl. The northern spotted owl, named for the white spots on its head and nape and its mottled belly, is a medium-size owl that inhabits the old-growth conifers of the Pacific Northwest, from northern California to British Columbia (Forsman and Meslow 1986).[76] The number of northern spotted owls has dwindled as old growth is harvested and converted into managed second-growth forests. Although it is not clear why the owls prefer old growth, it is likely that the old-growth forests provide owls with desirable prey, suitable perches, or protection from extreme weather. Adult owls tend to mate for life and occupy the same territory year after year. The home range for adult owls can vary from 1,000 to 8,000 acres, but because a mating pair does not always travel together, the combined home range for such a pair is much larger.

76. The northern spotted owl is one of three subspecies of the spotted owl. The other two are the California spotted owl and the Mexican spotted owl (Forsman and Meslow 1986). The marbled murrelet is a small seabird, a bit larger than a robin, which lives along the Pacific Coast, from Alaska to central California. Like the owl, the murrelet inhabits old-growth forest, including the giant redwoods of northern California. Along with the spotted owl, the marbled murrelet was enlisted in the litigation effort to preserve old-growth forest along the Pacific Coast, ultimately leading, among other things, to the acquisition of 44,000 acres for Redwood National Park (Chase 1995).

The owl has been studied since the 1970s but was not listed under the ESA as a threatened species until 1990. By the early 1980s, however, environmentalists began to pressure federal forest managers (the USFS and the BLM) to limit harvest of old-growth forests (Yaffee 1994; Chase 1995). In two lawsuits filed during the late 1980s, environmentalists challenged both the BLM and the USFS under a variety of federal environmental laws for failing to consider how proposed timber sales would affect the spotted owl.[77] Ultimately, the FWS was forced, in the 1988 case of *Northern Spotted Owl v. Hodel,* to list the spotted owl as a threatened species throughout its range. In 1990 the owl was officially listed as a threatened species.

As a result of these lawsuits and the settlements that followed, millions of acres of public lands in California, Oregon, and Washington were set aside as critical habitat for spotted owls, reducing the stock of potentially harvestable timber.[78] Nearly eleven million acres of federal land in California, Oregon, and Washington are now considered as critical habitat and off-limits to logging.[79] This acreage represents a substantial fraction (as much as 50 percent in Oregon and Washington) of public forests in these three states.[80] The evidence is

77. The key cases are *Portland Audubon Society v. Hodel* (the BLM case) and *Seattle Audubon Society v. Robertson* (the USFS case). Early in 1988, the 9th Circuit Court of Appeals, in *Portland Audubon,* temporarily enjoined the BLM from selling old-growth timber. Although this particular case was temporarily overturned upon appeal, the general trend of the litigation had been established.

78. This battle culminated with the so-called "forest summit" held in Portland, Oregon, by President Clinton in April 1993, which led to the policy recommended by the Forest Ecosystem Management Team (Yaffee 1994; Chase 1995).

79. These areas are designated as either "congressionally withdrawn," or "administratively withdrawn," depending on the origin of the action, and indicate areas for which timber harvest is prohibited (Forest Ecosystem Management 1993).

80. This fraction depends on how one defines federal forest lands. If only USFS and forested BLM lands are included, the fraction is about one-half for Oregon and Washington combined. These data do not include millions of acres of public land in national parks and wilderness areas where logging is already prohibited and, therefore, already committed to preserving old-growth forests.

clear that by invoking the ESA (and related environmental legislation), environmentalists have dramatically altered land uses on public forest land in the Pacific Coast states.

Given that a substantial proportion of public forests have been designated as spotted owl habitat under the ESA, it is not surprising that timber harvests from public lands dramatically declined in the 1990s. Figure 3 shows the annual timber harvest in the Pacific

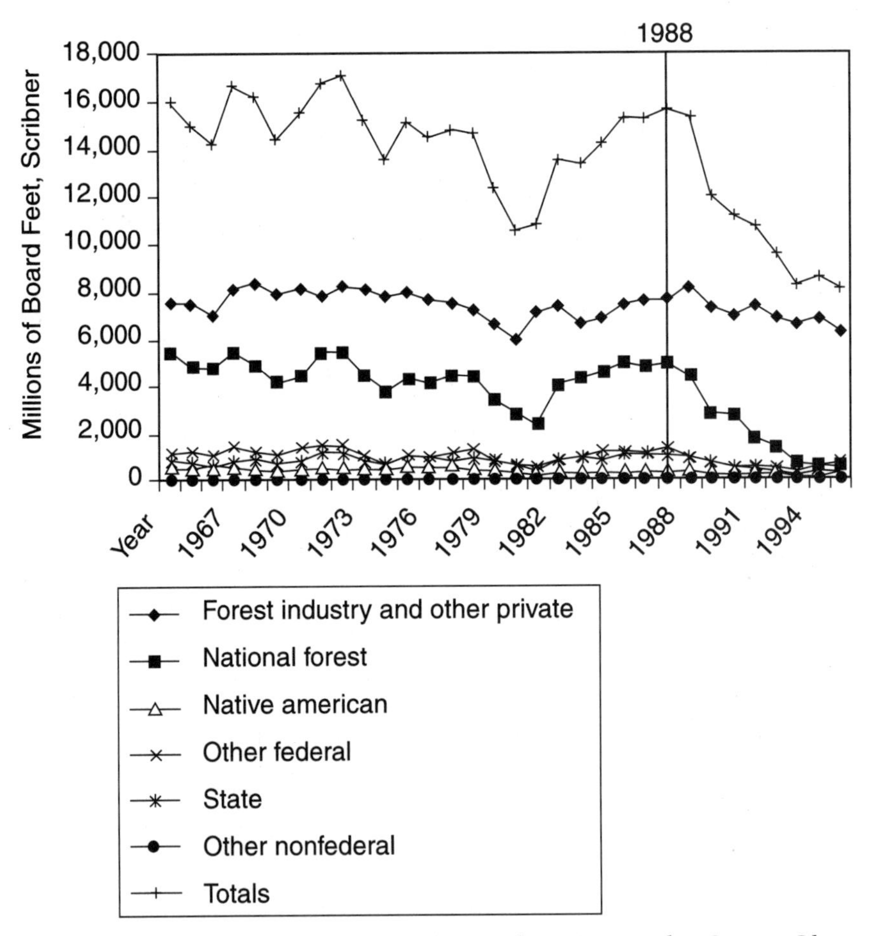

FIGURE 3 Washington and Oregon Timber Harvests by Owner Class, 1965–1996

Northwest from 1965 to 1996. The decline in harvest began in about 1988, when the first successful litigation—*Portland Audubon Society v. Hodel*—against federal timber policy was decided in a federal court. Figure 3 shows that the harvest decline is greatest for federal lands (labeled "national forest" and "other federal" in the figure) and almost nonexistent for private and state lands. Table 2 summarizes the data in figure 3 by showing the mean annual harvest for two periods according to various forest ownership classes.[81] Table 2 shows that annual harvest rates declined substantially on public forests but did not change appreciably on private industrial forests.[82] These effects are roughly consistent with the idea that environmentalists can affect public forest management by invoking the ESA. Of course, there are many other possible issues to examine to understand more fully the effect of spotted owl protection on land use and timber markets in the Pacific Northwest. Simple supply-and-demand analysis suggests that timber prices should have increased as owl acreage increased and that forest owners with few old-growth stocks may have benefited substantially from the reduction in the supply of old-growth timber. Indeed, the apparent lack of change in timber harvest in industrial forests (see table 2 and figure 3) suggests that private forest owners (who are also likely to have less old growth)

81. Acreage data come from the Spotted Owl Acreage from Forest Ecosystem Management: An Ecological, Economic and Social Assessment; Report of the Forest Ecosystem Management Assessment Team. 1993; Forest Service, National Marine Fisheries Service, BLM, Fish and Wildlife Service, National Park Service, Environmental Protection Agency. 1993. Pg. II-20, II-21. Timber harvest data come from two sources: a sole March 5, 1998, facsimile from the Washington Department of Natural Resources and the Oregon Department of Forestry's Annual Reports.

82. 1988 is not the only possible date to use, but this seems to be the beginning of major policy changes for spotted owl management. Murray and Wear (1998) also find that 1988 is a useful cutoff in their study of timber market integration. Figure 3 also shows that harvest rates seem to rise from 1982 to 1988, perhaps because firms were anticipating stringent owl regulations to limit future old-growth harvests.

TABLE 2 Mean Annual Timber Harvest in the Pacific Northwest before and after Spotted Owl Preservation

Place/Period	*Industry*	*USFS*	*BIA*	*BLM*	*State*	*Other Public*	*Total*
Oregon							
1978–88	3,259	2,982	112	889	228	30	7,500
1989–96	3,393	1,426	91	448	129	33	5,519
% change	+3.9	−52.2	−18.8	−50.4	−43.4	+10.0	−26.4
Washington							
1978–88	3,865	1,175	276	22	811	27	6,176
1989–96	3,716	485	212	10	549	25	4,996
% change	−3.9	−58.7	−23.2	−54.5	−32.3	−7.4	−19.1
Northwest							
1978–88	7,124	4,157	389	910	1,038	57	13,675
1989–96	7,109	1,911	302	457	678	58	10,515
% change	−0.01	−54.0	−22.4	−49.8	−34.7	+1.8	−23.1

All timber harvest numbers are mean annual harvest rates by owner class and are in millions of board feet, Scribner. (For Washington, BLM means "other federal" lands besides USFS.)

may have been such beneficiaries, which might be true for forest owners in other parts of the country.[83]

Preemptive Habitat Destruction on Private Land: The Red-Cockaded Woodpecker. The red-cockaded woodpecker (RCW) is a nonmigratory, territorial species that resides exclusively in longleaf pine ecosystems ranging from Virginia to Arkansas. The RCW was listed as an endangered species under the 1969 act, making it one of the longest listed species. RCWs live in social units called clans. Each clan has roughly nine birds and consists of a single breeding pair, the current year's offspring, and several helpers. Mating pairs reside in cavity trees—live mature pines that are excavated for nesting. An RCW clan requires 100 to 250 acres of mature pine forest for nesting and foraging (Hyde 1989; Kennedy, Costa, and Smathers 1996), and the FWS's foraging habitat guidelines for RCWs on private lands recommend parcels ranging between 60 and 300 acres (Kennedy, Costa, and Smathers 1996).

Even though most RCWs inhabit public lands in the Southeast, between 600 and 1,000 groups are on private lands owned by hundreds of different landowners (Costa 1992). The Environmental Defense Fund (Bonnie 1995) estimates the cost of foregone timber harvests from providing habitat for a single RCW colony (about 200 acres of mature pine forest) under the guidelines of the ESA to be as much as $196,107 ($981 per acre). These estimates indicate that a forest landowner has a large economic incentive to preemptively harvest timber if there is a reasonable chance that RCWs may locate on their land.

One North Carolina landowner, Ben Cone, has become famous for his confrontation with the FWS over habitat regulations (Stroup

83. This is consistent with Murray and Wear (1998), who find that after the ESA-based owl restrictions were in place, the U.S. timber market became more integrated, indicating that southern timber producers entered the northwest timber market.

1997). In 1991 the FWS implemented strict guidelines on timber harvest on portions of Cone's land that were inhabited by RCWs. In response, Cone increased his annual harvest on adjacent lands to roughly 10,000 tons of timber from just 919 tons over the previous eight years.[84]

Cone's behavior shows that the strong habitat restrictions of the ESA can prompt landowners to preemptively destroy RCW habitat and is consistent with the preemption model. Because of his well-publicized legal and political battles with the FWS, however, Cone may not be a representative landowner. A better way to test for the presence of preemptive timber harvesting would be to examine a large sample of forest landowners who face varying possibilities of being regulated under the ESA. Lueck and Michael (1999) do this using a detailed set of data on forest ownership and management coupled with detailed data on the location of known colonies of RCWs.

Lueck and Michael (1999) address two empirical questions: (1) how does the potential for ESA regulation affect the probability that a particular forest plot will be harvested, and (2) how does the potential for ESA regulation affect the age at which a forest stand will be harvested? Lueck and Michael use data on more than 1,000 individual forest plots from the U.S. Forest Service survey (data from 1984 and 1990) and from a North Carolina State University survey of more than 400 North Carolina forest landowners (data from 1997 and 1998). Their analysis is limited to privately owned plots in the Coastal Plain and Sandhills region of North Carolina, which consist of southern pine or a mixed forest of both hardwoods and pines. Lueck and Michael use these data to examine the effect of potential ESA regulations on the probability of harvest and the age of timber when it is harvested. Information on the location of RCW populations is used to construct measures of the probability (α in the pre-

84. Cone filed a suit but later settled. See *Cone v. United States* No. 95 Civ. 465 (Fed Cl. July 21, 1995).

emption model) that a forest plot will become inhabited by RCWs and thus subject to ESA restrictions on land use. RCW colony location data is taken from the North Carolina Natural Heritage Foundation to construct variables that measure the number of RCWs from five to twenty-five miles of each forest plot.[85] The basic prediction from the preemption model is that the closer a forest landowner is to known populations of RCWs, the more likely the landowner will take action to destroy the habitat for RCWs by prematurely cutting the pine forest. Controlling for other economic factors, such as timber prices and stand quality, Lueck and Michael consistently find that the closer a plot is to RCWs, the higher the probability that the plot will be harvested, even if the trees are younger than when trees are normally harvested. These estimates are robust to various specifications, samples, and measures of RCW colonization probabilities.

Using these estimates, Lueck and Michael (1999) determine how the proximity to RCWs affects the probability of harvest. For example, using U.S. Forest Service data for industrial landowners, the predicted probability of harvest is 40 percent for sites with an average number of RCWs within twenty-five miles to 62 percent for a site with high numbers of RCWs within twenty-five miles.[86] For nonindustrial forest owners, the increase in the probability of harvest from average to high-risk sites is smaller, only 10 percent. Lueck and Michael find that timber at high-risk sites is harvested nine years earlier than the average age of 47.9 years. The harvest age estimates using the 1997–98 survey data show that measures of RCW density within five and ten miles of a site are more important than measures

85. Lueck and Michael (1999) also incorporate information about the stand's age into these RCW measures, because RCWs will only inhabit mature pine stands.

86. *Average* is defined as sites with the mean number of RCWs and *high* is defined as sites with RCW numbers equivalent to the most dense populations in the data. See Lueck and Michael (1999) for details.

of populations within twenty-five miles. In addition, Lueck and Michael find that high-risk sites are predicted to harvest timber nearly seventeen years earlier than sites with no nearby RCWs. These findings are the first evidence of systematic preemptive habitat destruction and confirm both the preemption model and the dismay of some environmentalists who have noted that RCW populations have been declining on private land under the ESA (Wilcove et al. 1996).

Wildlife Restoration before and after the ESA. The history of modern wildlife preservation and restoration predates the ESA by at least a century. Often under open access exploitation in the presence of game markets, wildlife populations in the United States plummeted during the nineteenth and early twentieth centuries. Some species were extinguished (e.g., passenger pigeon), and many populations fell to dangerously low numbers. In perhaps the most alarming case, the population of bison was barely 2,000 by 1900, having fallen from numbers as high as 30 million in just fifty years (Garretson 1933). Similar, though less dramatic, stories of population decline occurred for numerous big game species, including deer, elk, and pronghorn antelope, and many birds, including wood ducks, turkey, and many species of plumed waterfowl. Entire regional populations were sometimes extinguished (e.g., elk in Arizona and New Mexico). The rise of season closures, bag limits, trade restrictions, wildlife refuges, and game departments came as many populations declined and reached their lowest levels (Lueck 1989). Today, however, nearly all of these species have recovered, and some are so populous as to be considered pests in many areas. Notably, the preservation and recovery of these wildlife came long before the enactment and implementation of the ESA.

The land-use and preemption models imply different outcomes for ESA and non-ESA-based policies. Wildlife restoration policy before the ESA used season closures and game trade restrictions to limit open access killing. Moreover, it used pay-to-protect methods to enhance wildlife habitat, by either purchasing or leasing land for refuges. Unlike the regulations inherent in the ESA, landowners were never penalized for altering habitat, thus the preemption incentive was completely absent. Under the ESA, the broad definition of *take,* which included harm to habitat, makes a crucial difference between the ESA and earlier policies.* Because of this definition, the ESA creates the incentive for preemption and also limits the potential for using the land market to allocate habitat. The main distinction between the two approaches is how each alters the incentives of landowners to provide and enhance habitat. Under a pre-ESA policy, the landowner has an incentive both to provide and to enhance habitat. Under the ESA, the landowner instead has an incentive to eliminate habitat. Thus, the ESA will be most successful where habitat development is not important or where the landowner's ability to manipulate habitat is limited.

The Record before the ESA. Many of the species driven to distressingly low numbers in the late nineteenth century have now recovered. For example, whitetail deer, estimated at twenty-five to fifty million in colonial America, fell to just one-half million by 1890, but are now estimated at fifteen to twenty-five million and growing.[87] The pronghorn antelope, present in large numbers throughout the Great Plains during the Lewis and Clark Expedition, had been reduced to 26,600 in the United States (30,320 in Canada) in 1924. By 1964, just forty years later, populations had increased more than tenfold in both the United States (365,160) and Canada (386,620) and have increased steadily, approaching 600,000 in the United States today (Van Wormer 1969; Gordon, Lacey, and Streeter 1997).

*It is also true that the ESA contains features of earlier protection policies such as trade restrictions and seasonal closures (the result of a ban on takings).

87. Richard Nelson. Deer Nation. *Sports Afield* (September 1998, 93).

Similar recoveries have occurred for bison, bighorn sheep, and elk (Gordon, Lacey, and Streeter 1997), as well as for many bird species. The bluebird, turkey, and wood duck have all experienced population recoveries at least as dramatic as the big game species noted above (Gordon, Lacey, and Streeter 1997).

In all of these cases of recovery, similar forces were at work. Season closures were enforced, and game trade was restricted. Habitat was often enhanced through refuges, especially for migratory waterfowl. Animals were live-captured in the wild and raised in captivity before being transplanted to depleted areas. The cooperation of private landowners to develop and protect habitat was important. For example, conservation groups built nesting boxes for wood ducks and bluebirds on private land. In New Mexico, landowners consented to the reintroduction of elk and pronghorn on the condition of being able to control hunting regulations once populations increased (Arha 1997). In most cases, there have been well-defined interest groups, such as Ducks Unlimited or the National Wild Turkey Federation, that have helped steer restoration by raising revenue and negotiating with wildlife agencies and landowners.

The Record under the ESA. The ESA has only been in effect since 1973, so its success at species restoration is difficult to fully assess. Yet the evidence thus far does not suggest any dramatic recoveries like those that occurred before the ESA. Of the more than 1,100 domestic species that have been listed as endangered or threatened, only twenty-four have been "delisted," as of February 1997.* Of these, seven were delisted because they were extinct, and nine because of "data error," indicating that the original listing was based on mistaken population estimates. The remaining eight species were

*As this chapter was going to press, the bald eagle and the peregrine falcon have both been delisted. In both cases the prohibition of certain toxic pesticides is cited as responsible for the recovery, rather than specific protection under the ESA.

considered "recovered." Gordon, Lacey, and Streeter (1997) examined FWS reports and contend that none of these eight recoveries is the result of the ESA.[88] For example, the "alligator probably should never have been listed" (Gordon, Lacey, and Streeter 1997, 383) because its population was severely underestimated at the time of listing. Similarly, the improving status of the bald eagle is now mostly attributed to the ban on DDT and enforcement against poaching, neither of which are unique ESA-based policies. Even dismissing the criticism of Gordon, Lacey, and Streeter (1997), the ESA's success record is still quite limited compared with some of the impressive restorations that occurred without the ESA. No dramatic species recovery can be claimed; indeed such long-listed species as the red-cockaded woodpecker (twenty-nine years) have declining populations.

Conclusion

Just twenty-five years ago, President Nixon signed the Endangered Species Act into law, setting in motion dramatic changes in the way land is used and the way land-use decisions are made. Celebrating the twenty-fifth anniversary of the act, many environmentalists have noted and lauded the striking changes it spawned. Interior Secretary Bruce Babbitt calls it "the most visionary environmental law that has ever been passed." National Wildlife Federation president Mark Van Patten says, "It's been the catalyst for a profound change in how we view and treat the land." Meanwhile, property rights organizations and their political representatives have decried the ESA. California Representative Richard Pombo sees the reach of the ESA as "de facto

88. The sources used by Gordon, Lacey, and Streeter (1997) include FWS biannual reports, annual species spending reports, individual species recovery plans, and all *Federal Register* notices to delist or reclassify species.

control of private property."[89] All students of the ESA recognize that it was a major shift in federal wildlife law, dramatically altering the property rights to habitat that sustains endangered species. Moreover, in the past twenty-five years, there have been so many adjustments to and investments in the ESA property regime that strong vested interests have been established. Thus the gridlock over reauthorization is not a surprise.

Even so, the current dissatisfaction with the ESA among landowners and environmentalists suggests that some of the incentive problems with the current ESA are becoming increasingly important. While property owners tend to be uniformly opposed to the ESA (unless they are sure they can avoid its force), the ESA has been a double-edged sword for environmental groups. On one hand, the ESA has allowed environmentalists to have great sway in the use and management of public lands and to attack large-scale federal development projects.[90] On the other hand, habitat is being destroyed and species are losing ground on private land because of the ESA. The combined force of landowners and environmentalists seems to be generating pressure to change the ESA, especially as it affects private landowners.

Two lessons can be drawn from this study of federal wildlife preservation policy. First, a focus on the property rights to land clarifies the issues and the motives of various groups in supporting or opposing various policies. Specific attention to the incentives of landowners, both private and public, is crucial in understanding the

89. All are quoted in H. Josef Hebert, "How Well Has It Worked?: 25 Years of the Endangered Species Act," Dec. 27, 1998, at <<http://www.abcnews.go.com/sections/science/DailyNews/esa981226.html>>.

90. In remarks celebrating the twenty-fifth anniversary of the ESA, Michael Bean (chair of the Environmental Defense Fund's Wildlife Program) notes the ESA "has sparked long-overdue changes in the management of our Federal forests. It has helped bring an end to the era of pork-barrel dam building." He is remarkably silent on the ESA's species recovery record. See "The 25th Anniversary of the Endangered Species Act" EDF Column, Vol XXX, No. 1, January 1999 at <<http://www.edf.org/pubs/EDF-letter/1999/Jan/j_endsp.html>>.

performance of various wildlife preservation policies. Second, because of the discretion of agencies and the courts' deference to them, the passage of seemingly benign legislation can evolve into a set of institutions largely unintended. Along the way the institutions may become quite permanent, regardless of their merits, as vested interests also evolve to take advantage of the new regime.

REFERENCES

Anderson, Terry L. 1999. Viewing Wildlife Through Coase-Colored Glasses. In *Who Owns the Environment?* edited by Peter J. Hill and Roger E. Meiners. Lanham, Md.: Rowman and Littlefield.

Ando, Amy Whritenour. 1997. Interest Group Behavior and the Endangered Species Act. RFF Discussion paper 97–44 (July).

Ando, Amy Whritenour. 1999. Waiting to Be Protected Under the Endangered Species Act: The Political Economy of Regulatory Delay. *Journal of Law and Economics* 42 (April): 29–60.

Arha, Kaushalendra. 1997. Wildlife Conservation on Western Private Lands: Improving Conservation Policies and Incentives. Ph.D. dissertation, University of California, Berkeley.

Barzel, Yoram. 1997. *Economic Analysis of Property Rights*. 2nd ed. New York: Cambridge University Press.

Bean, Michael J. 1998. The Endangered Species Act and Private Land: Four Lessons Learned from the Past Quarter Century. *Environmental Law Reporter* 28 (December): 10701–10702.

Bean, Michael J., and Melanie J. Rowland. 1997. *The Evolution of National Wildlife Law*. 3rd ed. Westport, Conn.: Praeger.

Bonnie, Robert. 1995. An Analysis to Determine Opportunity Costs of Red-Cockaded Woodpecker Habitat Protection on Private Lands in the Sandhills of North Carolina. In *Incentives for Endangered Species Conservation: Opportunities in the Sandhills of North Carolina*. New York: Environmental Defense Fund.

Cain, Louis, and Brooks Kaiser. 1999. Economics, Politics, and the ESA. Manuscript, Department of Economics, Northwestern University.

Chase, Alston. 1995. *In a Dark Wood.* New York: Houghton Mifflin.

Coase, Ronald H. 1960. The Problem of Social Cost. *Journal of Law and Economics* 3: 1–44.

Costa, R. 1992. Challenges for Recovery. Presented at Proceedings of the Sandhills Red-Cockaded Woodpecker Conference, 28–30 September, at Fort Bragg, N.C.

Defenders of Wildlife. 1998. State Endangered Species Acts: Past, Present, and Future. Washington, D.C.: Center for Wildlife Law.

Dolan, Maureen. 1992. Nature at Risk in a Quiet War. *Los Angeles Times,* 20 December, 1A.

Dwyer, John P. 1990. The Pathology of Symbolic Legislation. *Ecology Law Quarterly* 17: 233–316.

Echeverria, John D., and Raymond B. Ely, eds. 1995. *The Property Rights Movement.* Lanham, Md.: Rowman & Littlefield.

Economic Report of the President. 1998. Washington, D.C.: U.S. Government Printing Office.

Endangered Species Act. 1998. Symposium. *Journal of Economic Perspectives* 12: 3–52.

Epstein, Richard. 1997. *Babbitt v. Sweet Home:* The Law and Economics of Habitat Preservation. *Supreme Court Economic Review* 5: 1–57.

Forsman, Eric, and E. Charles Meslow. 1986. The Spotted Owl. *Audubon Wildlife Report,* pp. 743–761.

Garretson, Martin S. 1933. *The American Bison.* New York: The New York Zoological Society.

General Accounting Office (GAO). 1994. Endangered Species Act: Information on Species Protection on Nonfederal Lands. GAO/RCED-95-16 (December). Washington, D.C.: U.S. Government Printing Office.

Gordon, Robert E., Jr., James K. Lacey, and James R. Streeter. 1997. Conservation under the Endangered Species Act. *Environment International* 23: 359–417.

Hermalin, Benjamin E. 1995. An Economic Analysis of Takings. *Journal of Law, Economics, and Organization* 11: 64–86.

Houck, Oliver A. 1993. The Endangered Species Act and Its Implementation by the U.S. Departments of Interior and Commerce. *University of Colorado Law Review* 64: 277–370.

Hutcherson, Kate. 1976. Endangered Species: The Law and the Land. *Journal of Forestry* (January): 31–34.

Hyde, W. F. 1989. Marginal Costs of Managing Endangered Species: The Case of the Red-Cockaded Woodpecker. *Journal of Agricultural Economics Research* 41: 12–19.

Innes, Robert, Stephen Polasky, and John Tschirhart. 1998. Takings, Compensation, and Endangered Species Protection on Private Lands. *Journal of Economic Perspectives* 12: 35–52.

Kantor, Shawn E. 1998. *Politics and Property Rights.* Chicago: University of Chicago Press.

Kennedy, E. T., Ralph Costa, and W. M. Smathers, Jr. 1996. New Directions for Red-Cockaded Woodpecker Habitat Conservation: Economic Incentives. *Journal of Forestry* (April): 22–26.

Lachenmier, Rudy R. 1974. The Endangered Species Act of 1973: Preservation or Pandemonium? *Environmental Law* 5: 29–83.

Lambert, Thomas, and Robert J. Smith. 1994. The Endangered Species Act: Time for a Change. Policy Study No. 116, March, Center for the Study of American Business.

Libecap, Gary D. 1989. *Contracting for Property Rights.* New York: Cambridge University Press.

Lueck, Dean. 1989. The Economic Nature of Wildlife Law. *Journal of Legal Studies* 18: 291–323.

Lueck, Dean. 1998. Wildlife Law. In *The New Palgrave Dictionary of Economics and the Law*, edited by Peter Newman. Vol. 3. London: Macmillan, pp. 696–701.

Lueck, Dean, and Jeffrey Michael. 1999. Preemptive Habitat Destruction under the Endangered Species Act. Unpublished manuscript.

Lund, Thomas A. 1980. *American Wildlife Law*. Berkeley: University of California Press.

Mann, Charles C., and Mark L. Plummer. 1995. *Noah's Choice: The Future of Endangered Species*. New York: Alfred A. Knopf.

Murray, Brian C., and David N. Wear. 1998. Federal Timber Restrictions and Interregional Arbitrage in U.S. Lumber. *Land Economics* February, pp. 76–91.

Nelson, Robert H. 1995. *Public Lands and Private Rights*. Lanham, Md.: Rowman and Littlefield.

Noll, Roger G. 1989. Economic Perspectives on the Politics of Regulation. In *Handbook of Industrial Organization*, edited by Richard Schmalensee and Robert D. Willig. Vol. 2. New York: North Holland.

Pendler, William Perry. 1995. *War on the West*. Washington, D.C.: Regnery.

Platt, Roger. 1997. Ships Passing in the Night: Current Prospects for Reauthorization of the Endangered Species Act. Endangered Species Update, November/December, pp. 3–7.

Polasky, Stephen, and Holly Doremus. When the Truth Hurts: Endangered Species Policy on Private Land with Imperfect Information. *Journal of Environmental Economics and Management* 35: 22–47.

Rohlf, Daniel J. 1989. *The Endangered Species Act: A Guide to Its Protections and Implementation*. Stanford, Cal.: Stanford Environmental Law Society.

Snedden, B. A. 1995. Trained and Ready while Protecting Our Environment. In *Red-Cockaded Woodpecker Recovery, Ecology, and Management*, edited by D. L. Kulhavy, R. G. Hooper, and R. Costa. Nacogdoches, Tex.: Stephen Austin State University, Center for Applied Studies in Forestry, pp. 36–41.

Stroup, Richard L. 1997. The Economics of Compensating Property Owners. *Contemporary Policy Issues* 15: 55–65.

Thompson, H. Barton, Jr. 1997. The Endangered Species Act: A Case Study in Takings and Incentives. *Stanford Law Review* 49: 305–380.

Tober, James A. 1981. *Who Owns the Wildlife?* Westport, Conn.: Greenwood Press.

U.S. Department of Interior. 1964. *Redbook—Rare and Endangered Fish and Wildlife of the United States—Preliminary Draft.* Washington, D.C.: Bureau of Sport Fisheries and Wildlife.

U.S. Forest Service, National Marine Fisheries Service, Bureau of Land Management, Fish and Wildlife Service, National Park Service, Environmental Protection Agency. 1993. Forest Ecosystem Management: An Ecological, Economic and Social Assessment; Report of the Forest Ecosystem Management Assessment Team. Washington, D.C.

Van Wormer, Joe. 1969. *The World of the Pronghorn.* Philadelphia: Lippincott.

Wilcove, D. S., M. J. Bean, R. Bonnie, and M. McMillan. 1996. *Rebuilding the Ark: Toward a More Effective Endangered Species Act on Private Lands.* New York: Environmental Defense Fund.

Yaffee, Steven Lewis. 1982. *Prohibitive Policy: Implementing the Federal Endangered Species Act.* Cambridge: MIT Press.

Yaffee, Steven Lewis. 1994. *The Wisdom of the Owl: Policy Lessons for a New Century.* Washington, D.C.: Island Press.

Kurtis J. Swope, Daniel K. Benjamin, and Terry L. Anderson

Bucks for Ducks or Money for Nothin'?

The Political Economy of the Federal Duck Stamp Program

Economists generally advocate user fees that present demanders with prices that reflect marginal costs. User fees are a way of improving the incentives faced by demanders, especially with politically supplied goods, where the lack of prices encourages greater quantity demanded. Applications of user fees include mail services, garbage collection, municipal water, hunting licenses, and, recently, recreation on public lands. In each case, demanders face a cost for the good or service that gives them an incentive to consider alternatives and reduces political pressures that result when the quantity demanded exceeds the quantity supplied.

But the general support from economists for user fees has not focused sufficiently on the supply-side effects of user fees. As in the case of the recent Fee Demonstration Program for federal lands, which was implemented by Congress in 1996, policy analysts routinely presume that allowing agencies to keep 80 percent of fee revenues to spend on the service for which they are collected will improve the signal between private demanders and political suppliers. This presumption, however, ignores the gaping crevasse that can develop between fee collection and fee expenditure. In particular, if fees paid by the user can be captured by another special interest group, such as bureaucrats administering the affected program or other private individuals, the person paying the piper may not be calling the tune. Fees may simply create a pot of money, the value of which is dissipated as competing interests attempt to establish claims on it.

This pot of money may provide the impetus for a "bootlegger-and-Baptist" connection (Yandle 1983), fostering general tax funding well beyond what users would be willing to pay. If so, fees for recreation on public lands, higher fees for water use, or proposed taxes on backpacking and camping equipment for the purpose of purchasing or leasing endangered species habitat may not produce the desired result and, therefore, may yield examples of user fee failures.

Finally, most contemporary discussions of user fees typically address programs in isolation from their interaction with other policies and events. In fact, the existence of important interactions between a particular program and ongoing economic events, or between the program and other government programs, can play a key role in determining the viability of implementing user fees. Similarly, a failure to take account of these interactions can invalidate any attempt to assess the success or failure of a user fee.

This chapter examines one of the oldest user fee experiments in the environmental arena—the Federal Duck Stamp Program. This program was created in 1934 as a wildlife conservation program, with the stated purpose of supporting migratory waterfowl populations in the United States through the purchase and protection of waterfowl habitat. Initially, funding for the program came solely from a user fee in the form of duck stamps purchased by waterfowl hunters. During the past forty years, however, other sources of revenue have been added. According to the U.S. Fish and Wildlife Service (FWS), the agency in charge of administering the program, the Duck Stamp Program has "become one of the most popular and successful conservation programs ever initiated" (FWS 1988, 1).

The history of the Duck Stamp Program reveals that it has been more expensive and less effective at conserving waterfowl habitat than might be suggested by the FWS. Many of the program's early years were plagued by lack of funds. Moreover, available funds were initially diverted to non–land acquisition activities; very little habitat was actually purchased. More recently, the rising cost of suitable land for waterfowl habitat has greatly increased the cost of habitat protection and reduced the amount of habitat purchased. As a result, duck populations in the United States were at near-record low levels as recently as the late 1980s.

The rising cost of waterfowl habitat can be traced, at least in part, to U.S. agricultural policy. Farm programs change the expected returns to land used in agriculture and, therefore, can significantly alter the pattern of land allocation, both within agriculture and between agricultural and nonagricultural activities. Real farmland prices in the United States fell during the 1920s and 1930s, rose steadily during the 1950s and 1960s, and then skyrocketed from 1971 to 1982. Farmland prices then dipped in the mid-1980s before resuming their upward trend. During the past fifty years, the movements in farmland prices have been strongly influenced by federal crop price support programs and, in turn, have influenced the effectiveness of the Duck Stamp Program.[1]

The principal thrust of this chapter is to explain the observed pattern of purchases and leases of land under the Duck Stamp Program. There are two strands to this investigation. One is an understanding of the determinants of the program's funding levels; the other is an investigation of the links among farm programs, farmland prices, and purchases of waterfowl habitat. We demonstrate that although farm interests played a role in reinvigorating the Duck Stamp Program at a key junction, those same interests have proved to be a major impediment to habitat acquisition. One key message that emerges from our study is that the efforts of duck hunters to

1. See Alston (1986), Burt (1986), Robinson, Lins, and Venkatarman (1985), and Floyd (1965).

preserve waterfowl habitat have been repeatedly thwarted by the efforts of bureaucrats and politicians pursuing other objectives. In addition to providing a better understanding of the sometimes unanticipated interactions between federal programs, our findings also help explain why the ostensible beneficiaries of proposed user fee programs so often oppose the establishment of those programs.

Background and History of the Federal Duck Stamp Program

Origin and Early Years, 1929–1958

Although earlier legislation addressed the issue of migratory bird protection in the United States, the Federal Duck Stamp Program has its origins in the Migratory Bird Conservation Act, passed by Congress in 1929. The 1929 act established the Migratory Bird Conservation Commission (MBCC) and gave it authority to approve purchases of land containing sensitive migratory waterfowl habitat for the National Wildlife Refuge System. The act also authorized specific funds to be appropriated annually for the land acquisitions. The amount actually appropriated and made available for land acquisition each year, however, was far below the amounts originally authorized. During the first seven years of the program, $4,875,000 was authorized, but apparently due to budgetary difficulties occasioned by the Great Depression, Congress actually appropriated only $1,215,050 (MBCC 1936, 3). A great deal of land was surveyed with the appropriated funds, but very little was purchased. The 1932 MBCC report stated, "Inasmuch as the market value of lands continued to decrease and many landowners were disposed to liquidate their holdings, thus creating a buyer's market such as has not prevailed for years, progress in making desirable purchases was limited only by the funds available" (3). The lack of funds led the commission to note the following year that, "From the standpoint of accomplishments and benefit to the migratory birds, this was a serious matter, because of the urgent need of more refuges and the low prices at which suitable areas, many of inferior agricultural land, could be acquired" (MBCC 1933, 1).

Because the 1929 legislation provided no source of permanent funding, the Migratory Bird Hunting Stamp Act was passed in 1934. The stated purpose of the law was:

> To supplement and support the Migratory Bird Conservation Act by providing funds for the acquisition of areas for use as migratory-bird sanctuaries, refuges, and breeding grounds, for developing and administering such areas, for the protection of certain migratory birds, for the enforcement of the Migratory Bird Treaty Act and regulations thereunder, and for other purposes. (Public Law 124, 1934)

The law required all waterfowl hunters in the United States over age sixteen to purchase and carry a current federal migratory bird hunting stamp (or duck stamp) in addition to a state hunting license. The official name of the stamp was later changed to the federal migratory bird hunting and conservation stamp. The price of a stamp was set at $1, and revenue from stamp sales was deposited into a special fund known as the Migratory Bird Conservation Fund (MBCF), to be used in accordance with the Migratory Bird Conservation Act. In 1949, Congress raised the price of a stamp to $2 at the request of sports enthusiasts and conservationists to raise additional funds for the program.

Most of the revenue generated from duck stamp sales from 1934 to 1958 was expended for development, administration, and enforcement activities, with very little land acquisition taking place. For example, stamp sales during the first hunting year yielded $635,344 for the program. The 1935 report of the MBCC stated, "Of this amount $436,810 has been allotted for administration, development, and improvement of bird refuges. The balance, $198,534, has been expended for the enforcement and administration of this act.

None has been used for land acquisitions" (2). The report was similar the following years: Of the $54 million generated from stamp sales between 1934 and 1958, approximately 15 percent went toward land acquisition (Senate 1958).[2]

Years of Transition, 1958–1961

Two important pieces of legislation, one in 1958 and another in 1961, brought fundamental changes to the Federal Duck Stamp Program. Together the legislation increased annual expenditures for land purchases nearly tenfold over previous years, from a $1.6 million estimate of funds available for land acquisition in 1959 to almost $16 million for that purpose by 1964. Several factors prompted these changes.

The 1934 Duck Stamp Act was amended in 1958 to require 100 percent of duck stamp revenues (less post office printing and distribution expenses) to be used by the FWS directly for land acquisition activities. All remaining expenses of the program, including those associated with development, administration, and enforcement, were to be financed from general appropriations. The same amendment raised the price of a stamp to $3 and allowed the secretary of the interior to open portions of some refuges to public hunting, thus relaxing hunting prohibitions on refuge lands.

The second major change in funding for land acquisitions came in 1961 when Congress passed the Wetlands Loan Act, which authorized an interest-free loan of $105 million, available between 1962 and 1976, for acquisition of waterfowl habitat in accordance with the Migratory Bird Conservation Act. Repayment of the loan was to begin in 1976, with three-fourths of annual duck stamp receipts being paid to the U.S. Treasury.

2. According to a report to the Senate Subcommittee by the assistant secretary of the interior on March 20, 1958, $49,431,000 had been received by the FWS to date from duck stamp revenue. Only $7,449,908 was spent on land acquisition, with the remainder used for enforcement, research, maintenance, development, engineering, administration, and special studies (Senate 1958).

These significant changes in funding for the Duck Stamp Program appear to have been motivated on several levels. Hunters and conservationists argued that the intent of the original Duck Stamp Act was to provide additional funds for land acquisition but that the majority of funds were being wrongly diverted for development, administrative, and enforcement expenses. During congressional hearings on the subject of amending the Duck Stamp Act, Charles H. Callison, conservation director of the National Wildlife Federation, stated:

> First, the sportsmen and other conservationists of America feel the duck-stamp revenues have not been used as was intended by Congress and by the duck hunters who willingly supported this tax upon themselves. The hunters understood the primary purpose of the duck stamp was to supply funds to acquire lands for the Federal migratory-bird-refuge system.
>
> Secondly, we feel the wetlands-acquisition program must be speeded up on a crash basis to assure the future of waterfowl resources. The remaining areas of waterfowl habitat are disappearing too rapidly—through drainage, pollution, siltation, filling in, and other factors. (Senate 1958, 86)

According to this view, the alleged diversion of funds from acquisitions to administration could only be remedied by earmarking a larger portion of funds for direct land purchases.

The claim that duck stamp revenue was being diverted from its intended use raises interesting questions regarding the general issue of how user fees are to be spent. In this case, were duck hunters, the primary beneficiaries of the program, expected to finance all expenses associated with acquiring and maintaining waterfowl habitat? Or were the user fees intended to cover land acquisition costs only? The wording of the original Duck Stamp Act clearly authorized use of duck stamp revenue for development, administration, and enforcement expenses, in addition to land acquisition costs, but it did not specify in what proportions the monies were to be allocated.

Callison's testimony clearly suggests that hunters and conservationists believed that the choices made by the FWS had been inconsistent with congressional intentions and that far too few funds had been devoted to acquisition. But if duck stamp receipts were being inappropriately spent, why did it take twenty-five years for the problem to be addressed, when a full report of program expenditures was available every year since 1929?

It is possible that the chief motivation for the 1958 and 1961 amendments to the Duck Stamp Program was to rectify administrative errors or misdeeds on the part of the FWS. A more compelling explanation for the 1958 and 1961 increases in funding for land acquisition, however, centers around the effect of farm income support programs on land use and land prices. The farm programs had two major consequences relevant to the Duck Stamp Program: (1) wetlands were being cleared and drained at a rate far greater than they were being acquired and protected; and (2) land prices were being driven up by crop price supports, making suitable wildlife habitat much more expensive to acquire and protect.

The agricultural acts of the late 1940s initiated flexible price supports and changed the method of calculating parity farm commodity prices. This, in turn, led to substantial, politically embarrassing crop surpluses and pressure to increase controls on production. The Agricultural Act of 1954 reestablished flexible price supports and authorized commodity set-asides. The U.S. Department of Agriculture (USDA) followed with an increased emphasis on rural development that continued from the mid-1950s to the early 1970s. Farmers could increase the support payments they received by converting marginal lands (wetlands) into cropland, thereby increasing their base acreage. From the perspective of farmers, as long as the land could be used to satisfy set-aside requirements, it was inconsequential that much of the land was inferior for actual commodity production or was prone to flooding. To be considered as a set-aside to fulfill acreage restriction requirements, an acre had to be legitimate cropland, which meant clearing, draining, and even cultivating the land. So that is what farmers did.

Drainage of wetlands for agriculture was at historically high levels from the mid-1950s to the mid-1970s. Wetland losses from tile-and-open ditch drainage averaged an estimated 550,000 acres per year during this period. Much of the drainage activities were subsidized by the USDA's Agricultural Conservation Program (Dahl 1990). Wetlands in the northern plains were particularly hard hit because of the high participation rate in the wheat farm programs and the fairly low cost of draining prairie potholes in the area. In a statement included in 1957 U.S. Senate hearings on the Duck Stamp Program, the National Wildlife Federation reported that, "During the past 15 years farm drainage, much of it induced by Federal subsidies, has eliminated a million acres of high-quality nesting habitat in the prairie-marsh region of the Dakotas and Minnesota" (Senate 1958, 90). The effect of this drainage on duck populations was becoming clearer by the late 1950s as their numbers fell.

Compounding the problem of subsidized wetland conversion were the rapidly rising costs of land suitable for waterfowl habitat. The following discussion between Wisconsin Congressman Henry Reuss, cosponsor of the wetlands loan bill, and Washington Senator Thomas Pelly, member of the Subcommittee on Fisheries and Wildlife Conservation, at a Senate hearing on May 11, 1961, highlights the problem:

MR. PELLY. You mentioned that the price of these wetlands had been going up. Could you state for the record in any detail as to the amount percentagewise that the cost has been increasing?

MR. REUSS. I would prefer to supply that and I will, but I can tell in general terms. . . . I would be quite confident, however, that if I were to say that in the last 10 years the prices of wetlands have doubled, I would not be far from wrong.

MR. PELLY. That would be about the same percentage that farm lands have gone up.

MR. REUSS. Exactly. (Senate 1961, 132)

Again, the rise in the cost of wetlands can be traced, in part, to farm income support programs. Wetlands are often, by nature, marginal land for production of agricultural commodities. Price supports, set-asides, and drainage subsidies all raise the profitability of marginal farmland to the landowner, thereby driving up the price of such land. Even if the landowner chooses not to drain and clear the land, the option value of the land, and thus the price at which the landowner would be willing to sell it, will be higher. Duck stamp revenue alone was insufficient to achieve the land acquisitions necessary to offset the toll that farm programs were taking on the nation's wetlands, especially given the rising cost of remaining wetlands.

Accelerated purchases of habitat under the Duck Stamp Program were probably also attractive because they supplemented acreage control programs. Daniel H. Janzen, director of the FWS Bureau of Sport Fisheries and Wildlife, made the following comment during congressional hearings concerning the Wetlands Loan Act of 1961:

> This program will have broad impact on the national economy and the benefits will be reaped by a broad base of the taxpaying public. Some of these benefits are: (1) Every acre purchased will be an acre taken out of potential agricultural production at a time when the Federal Government is spending vast sums trying to cope with the surplus agricultural crop program. . . . (Senate 1961, 137)

The 1958 amendment to the Duck Stamp Act also authorized the "acquisition by gift, devise, purchase, or exchange of, small wetland and pothole areas, interests therein, and rights-of-way to provide access thereto" (MBCC 1961, 3). These "small wetland and pothole areas," designated Waterfowl Production Areas (WPAs), are located primarily in North Dakota, South Dakota, and Minnesota and contain "nearly all of the top quality waterfowl production habitat" (MBCC 1961, 3). Purchases and leases of WPAs, which are generally much smaller than wildlife refuges, sometimes consisting of thirty or fewer acres of wetland, need not be approved by the MBCC. Thus, the procedure for acquiring such lands was administratively simplified.

Although only about 10 percent of total duck-nesting habitat is located in the Canadian and U.S. prairie pothole area, the region produces from one-third to one-half of all ducks in North America (USDA 1986, 21). These small pothole wetlands of the northern plains are critical waterfowl habitat because, for breeding, ducks prefer small ponds and marshes to large lakes. The flip side of the story, however, is that although this area certainly contains vital breeding habitat for ducks and other migratory waterfowl, the wheat industry located in the same region was consistently being plagued by crop surpluses, resulting from the price support programs. Thus, accelerated purchases of wetlands under the Duck Stamp Program also served as a substitute for acreage restriction programs being conducted by the USDA.

Recent Developments, 1962–Present

In 1976 the period of the wetlands loan was extended to 1983, and the total permitted indebtedness increased to $200 million. At about the same time, the FWS developed a national priority list for waterfowl habitat acquisition. At the top of this list were the WPAs in the prairie pothole region, which constituted more than half of the acres targeted for acquisition for 1977 to 1986. The WPA program resulted in a large concentration of purchases in the upper Midwest, thereby transforming the character of the program's acquisitions. Table 1 shows the ten states with the largest number of land acquisitions in 1996 and in 1960. Only one of the three prairie pothole states (North Dakota) was among the top ten states in 1960; by 1996, all three of these states were among the top five.

TABLE 1 States with Leading Waterfowl Habitat Acquisitions, 1996 and 1960

1996	*Cumulative Acres**	*Total Program Acres (in percent)*	*1960*	*Cumulative Acres*	*Total Program Acres (in percent)*
N. Dakota	1,105,533.3	25%	Oregon	47,780.5	16%
S. Dakota	880,014.5	20	Texas	36,024.6	12
Georgia	356,970.1	8	Georgia	34,042.1	11
Minnesota	302,709.2	7	Florida	26,474.3	9
Texas	289,829.6	6	Wisconsin	20,677.8	7
California	146,640.6	3	N. Dakota	14,649.2	5
Oregon	132,110.5	3	Washington	14,586.0	5
Montana	112,928.0	3	New Jersey	12,854.5	4
Florida	88,305.6	2	Colorado	10,782.4	4
Louisiana	87,162.3	2	Virginia	9,834.3	3

*Includes acquisition by purchase and by lease

SOURCE: Migratory Bird Conservation Commission (1960; 1996).

The price of the duck stamp increased to $5 in 1973 and to $7.50 in 1980. After a second extension of the wetlands loan in 1983, the Emergency Wetlands Resources Act of November 10, 1986, canceled all repayment obligations on the loan. The act also provided for increases in the price of a duck stamp to $10 in 1987, $12.50 in 1989, and $15 in 1991, where it remains as of 1998. Table 2 gives both the nominal and real (inflation-adjusted) price of a duck stamp for selected years.

Program Funding

The Federal Duck Stamp Program is a market-oriented conservation initiative. Instead of imposing regulations on what landowners may or may not do with their property, the program purchases or leases land containing wildlife habitat at fair market value, and the beneficiaries of the program, mainly waterfowl hunters, pay for the habitat. The amount of habitat protected is determined by the

TABLE 2 Duck Stamp Prices for Selected Years

Year	*Nominal Price ($)*	*Real Price (1992 dollars)*
1940	$ 1.00	$ 9.79
1950	2.00	11.23
1960	3.00	12.93
1973	5.00	14.48
1980	7.50	12.64
1988	10.00	11.65
1990	12.50	13.42
1992	15.00	15.00

Note: Minimum real price = $5.53 in 1949. Maximum real price = $15 in 1992.

SOURCES: Duck stamp prices from U.S. Fish and Wildlife Service, Harvest Surveys Office, fax transmission, 7 pp.; GDP deflator (1992 = 100) from Budget of the United States Government, Fiscal Year 1998, Historical Tables.

demand, as measured by the level of available funds, and by the supply, which is a function of the price of habitat.

Duck Stamp Sales

Wetland purchases under the Migratory Bird Conservation Act of 1929 were originally financed by general federal tax revenue. Although wetlands are valued today for a variety of purposes, at the time the act passed they were primarily valued as duck and other migratory waterfowl habitat. Therefore, the primary beneficiaries of the program were duck hunters and bird watchers. When, because of the Great Depression, program funds for habitat purchases fell short of the amounts originally authorized, it was natural to turn to duck hunters and bird watchers as a source of permanent funding. The Migratory Bird Hunting Stamp Act of 1934 was supported by hunters who wanted to protect waterfowl habitat. In the words of Charles H. Callison, hunters "willingly supported this tax upon themselves" (Senate 1958, 86).

Because the success or failure of the program at achieving its objective depends importantly on the number of stamps sold, it is worth examining the determinants of duck stamp sales. The hunter's decision to purchase or not to purchase a duck stamp can be reduced to a simple utility maximization problem, wherein the hunter chooses to purchase zero stamps or one stamp and spends the remaining income on other goods.[3]

Several factors are likely to influence the number of duck stamps sold. For example, the abundance of ducks contributes to the success of duck hunters and affects their decision to purchase stamps. Although hunters cannot know with certainty how many

3. This assumes that the marginal utility of duck stamps falls to zero after the purchase of the first stamp, an assumption that can easily be dropped if the hunter has other motives for purchasing a stamp. Some duck stamps are also purchased by stamp collectors. The largest fraction of total stamp sales by the post office philatelic unit and by stamp and art shops was nearly 7.7 percent in 1991–92.

ducks will migrate through a region of the country in a year, they can predict this number by looking at the previous year's populations. Indeed, the simple correlation between duck populations from one year to the next is $r = 0.69$. Thus, holding other factors constant, the increase in the number of ducks in a given year should increase the likelihood that a hunter will purchase a duck stamp the following year.

Although the income of individuals may influence their decision to hunt ducks, the direction of this influence is unclear. If hunting is a normal good, then the pure income effect should be positive. But rising incomes are normally associated with a rising value of time, so higher income raises the implicit cost of duck hunting. Hence, an increase in consumer income could cause either an increase or a decrease in the observed purchases of duck stamps.

The relationship between the demand for duck stamps and current income is further complicated by two additional factors. First, as with other consumption goods, purchases of duck stamps should be driven by permanent income, which is unobservable and which may be poorly proxied by current income. Second, the past forty years have witnessed an explosion of alternative recreational opportunities that compete with the leisure time of duck hunters. Two measures of recreational spending are used to account for both of these factors—one designed to control for the secular rise in competing leisure activities and the other intended to control for significant changes in permanent income.

To control for the incomes and leisure activities of potential hunters, data on real recreational spending in the United States during our sample period were collected and decomposed into two parts. First, the natural log of this spending was regressed on a time trend. The predicted values from this regression represent the upward secular trend in alternative leisure activities. We expect this component of recreational spending to have a negative effect on duck stamp purchases, reflecting the competition for duck hunters' dollars. From this regression, we also used the residuals—which tend to mimic the business cycle, rising in times of economic expansion and falling in recessions. We regard these residuals as measuring the role of changes in income on recreational spending of all types, duck hunting included. Hence, we expect this variable to have a measured positive effect on duck stamp purchases.

Yet another factor influencing the demand for stamps may come from members of conservation organizations who purchase duck stamps for nonhunting reasons. In testimony during Senate hearings concerning the 1958 amendment to the Duck Stamp Act, an Audubon Society representative argued that "if they were sure all this money was going for acquisition, which the bill makes mandatory, a great many of their members would buy duck stamps with no intention of going hunting, but only to help preserve the waterfowl areas" (Senate 1958, 85). Although there are no data on the proportion of duck stamps sold to hunters and nonhunters, the nonhunting demand for stamps could be significant. We proxy the nonhunting demand for stamps with membership in conservation organizations.

Assuming hunters have similar preferences and aggregating across hunters and nonhunters, the total number of duck stamps sold in a given year should be a function of the real price of a duck stamp, the number of ducks the previous year, average leisure time available for hunting, membership in conservation organizations, and the incomes and other leisure alternatives of potential hunters. Using ordinary least squares, the natural log of number of duck stamps sold in the United States (*stamp*) was regressed on the following variables: the log of the real stamp price (*price*), the log of the previous year's estimate of breeding ducks (*ducks*), the log of membership in the Audubon Society (*audubon*), and the two components of recreation—the predicted or secular log of recreational spending (*secular*) and the residual or cyclical log of recreational spending (*cyclical*). The results are given in table 3.

TABLE 3 Regression Results for Duck Stamp Sales, 1959–1994 (absolute t-statistics in parentheses)

$$\text{Log(stamp)} = \underset{(5.81)}{11.06} - \underset{(5.03)}{0.47}\,\text{Log(price)} + \underset{(6.16)}{0.70}\,\text{Log(ducks)}$$

$$+ \underset{(3.13)}{0.17}\,\text{Log(audubon)} - \underset{(3.01)}{0.40}\,\text{secular} + \underset{(2.71)}{0.73}\,\text{cyclical}$$

$F(5,30) = 40.6$ $\qquad R^2 = 0.87$ $\qquad$ D.W. = 2.10

SOURCES: Duck stamp sales and prices from U.S. Fish and Wildlife Service, Harvest Surveys Office, fax transmission, 7 pp.; duck breeding populations from U.S. Fish and Wildlife Service, electronic mail transmission, 1 p.; Audubon Society membership from Audubon Society, electronic mail transmission, 1 p.; personal income and personal consumption expenditures on recreation from *Historical Statistics of the United States: Colonial Times to 1970, Part 1*, U.S. Department of Commerce, 1976; and *Statistical Abstract of the United States*, U.S. Department of Commerce, various years.

The coefficients on the real stamp price and on lagged duck population estimates both have the expected signs and are statistically significant. Because all variables are measured as natural logarithms, the estimated coefficients are elasticities. Hence, the results imply that the demand for stamps is inelastic: a 10 percent increase in the real price of a stamp induces a 4.7 percent decrease in the number of stamps sold per year. Moreover, a 10 percent rise in the duck breeding population in one year appears to induce a 7 percent rise in sales of duck stamps in the next year. Because stamp sales are so strongly responsive to the estimated breeding population of ducks, we infer that this factor is indeed a good measure of the health of the U.S. duck population. We will return to this matter when we analyze other sources of funding for habitat purchase.

The positive link between Audubon Society membership and stamp sales is consistent with the arguments that members of conservation groups are purchasing duck stamps. We have no way of knowing if these results reflect actual stamp purchases by Audubon members or if Audubon membership is simply correlated with purchases by other individuals who wish to preserve habitat or want to add to their philatelic collections.

It also appears that the secular growth of other recreational activities has cut into duck hunting and, thus, into stamp sales, presumably reflecting the fact that other recreational activities are a substitute for hunting. Finally, the positive coefficient on the cyclical component of recreational spending suggests that duck stamp sales follow the same pro-cyclical pattern followed by other consumption spending.

Wetlands Loans and Other Funding

With the passage of the Wetlands Loan Act in 1961, duck stamp receipts were merged with loan appropriations, which were subject to a $20-million-per-year limit. Duck stamp receipts and loan appropriations were also supplemented with additional funds classified as "other receipts" in the MBCF records. Other receipts prior to 1986 consisted primarily of revenue from small land sales by the FWS. These other funds were relatively insignificant until the passage of the Emergency Wetlands Resources Act of 1986, which canceled repayment of the wetlands loan and supplemented duck stamp receipts with revenue generated from import duties on arms and ammunition and from entrance fees to wildlife refuges. In recent years, other receipts have been approximately equal to duck stamp receipts. For example, duck stamp receipts in 1993 totaled just over $22 million whereas other receipts were approximately $20 million.

The fact that duck stamp revenue was diverted largely to non–land acquisition activities prior to 1958 is one explanation for the congressional decision to supplement duck stamp revenue with additional funds. At the time, wetlands were being converted faster than quality habitat could be purchased and developed. Habitat loss and lack of purchases began to be reflected in duck populations, which plummeted to record lows in the late 1950s and early 1960s. Farmland prices were also rising steadily during this time, largely due to agricultural policies that raised crop prices and, thus, increased the demand for farmland. Rising land values threatened to cause a further decline in habitat purchases, given the funds available. Confronted with unhappy hunters, policy makers were forced either to cut the farm programs that were contributing to wetland conversion and higher farmland prices or to accelerate habitat acquisition by turning to taxpayers for additional funds. That policy makers chose the latter over the former should not be surprising.

Once the decision was made to supplement duck stamp receipts with other revenue, the question that remained was, how many additional funds should be deposited into the fund each year? Although never binding, a $20-million-per-year cap was placed on appropriations from the wetlands loan beginning in 1962. There are several factors that would be expected to influence the level of additional funds (loan appropriations and other sources) that supplement duck stamp receipts each year. These factors are as follows:

1. The business cycle influences federal discretionary funding. When unemployment is high, the federal budget deficit increases as tax revenue falls and transfer payments increase. This generates an incentive to reduce the deficit by decreasing funding for many programs. When unemployment is low, the resulting rise in tax revenues and decline in transfer payments make more money available for nonstabilization activities, such as wildlife conservation programs. Hence, we include the overall U.S. unemployment rate (*unemployment*) in our estimating equation.

2. Much of the additional funding after 1961 came from loan fund borrowing. As the outstanding balance rose, we would expect this to put downward pressure on additional borrowing and thus downward pressure on nonstamp spending. To test this hypothesis, we include in the equation the real outstanding (*cumulative*) amount of Wetlands Act borrowing as of the end of the prior year (*loan balance*).

3. To control for the role of income in influencing the demand for environmental amenities, we include total real personal income

(*income*) as an element determining the amount of nonstamp funding for the program.

4. Based on our findings from estimating the demand for duck stamps, we would expect that the size of the duck population might influence nonstamp funding for habitat acquisition. Specifically, we would expect managers of the program to base borrowing decisions on this factor, borrowing more when the duck population was low and borrowing less when the population was larger and presumably healthier. To test this hypothesis, we include the size of last year's duck population (*ducks*) in the equation.

5. Finally, we expect that managers of the program would take into account the real price of habitat when making their purchase decisions. Thus, we include the real per-acre value of farmland (*land price*) in our equation. Note that the effect of price on expenditures, and hence on nonstamp funding, will depend on the acquiring agency's elasticity of demand. If demand for habitat is inelastic (elastic), a rise in farm values will cause a rise (fall) in expenditures and hence in nonstamp funding. If demand is approximately unit elastic, the estimated effect of *land price* on funding will be approximately zero.

Table 4 shows the results of our estimates of the influence of these factors on the determination of nonstamp funding for the program after 1962. The dependent variable is obtained by subtracting real duck stamp receipts from real total funds available. All variables, except the unemployment rate, are measured as natural logarithms.

There are several points worth noting about these estimates. First, the effects of the unemployment rate, the outstanding loan balance, and real personal income are all as expected: a higher unemployment rate or loan balance tends to decrease nonstamp funding, while a rise in real income increases it. Second, habitat acquisition appears to be a luxury good, because the estimated income elasticity of demand is consistently greater than unity. Third,

TABLE 4 Estimates of the Determinants of Nonstamp Funding for Wetland Acquisition, 1963–1994 (absolute t-statistics in parentheses)

Dependent variable: Natural log of nonstamp funding, in 1992 dollars

Independent variables	1	2	3
Unemployment	−0.31	−0.34	−0.32
	(4.86)	(5.02)	(3.74)
Log(loan balance)	−0.60	−0.93	−0.87
	(2.06)	(2.38)	(2.04)
Log(income)	1.51	2.47	2.40
	(3.63)	(2.41)	(2.26)
Log(breed)		1.11	1.23
		(1.24)	(1.29)
Log(land price)			−0.23
			(0.41)
F-stat	13.22	10.50	8.17
R^2	0.60	0.62	0.62
D.W.	1.77	1.94	1.97

SOURCES: Unemployment from *Economic Report of the President*, 1997; loan balance and duck breeding populations from U.S. Fish & Wildlife Service, Division of Realty, fax transmission, 1 p.; personal income from *Historical Statistics of the United States: Colonial Times to 1970, Part 1*, U.S. Dept. of Commerce, 1976; and *Statistical Abstract of the United States*, U.S. Dept. of Commerce, various years; land prices from U.S. Department of Agriculture, *Agricultural Statistics*, various issues.

there appears to be no statistically significant effect of duck breeding populations on nonstamp funding for duck habitat acquisition, which suggests that FWS managers are not responding in any systematic way to the size of duck populations when making their aggregate habitat acquisitions.[4] One interpretation of this finding is that the health of waterfowl populations has little to do with decisions regarding the acquisition of land that is nominally to be used

4. If anything, the positive point estimate suggests a perverse effect, with funding being cut when duck populations fell, thereby exacerbating the decline.

to protect the habitat of those species. Fourth, we interpret the lack of any apparent effect of farm values on funding to reflect a demand for habitat that is at least approximately unit elastic. It appears that funding levels are determined independently of market conditions, leaving program managers to purchase as many acres as they can, given the prices they find. Finally, although the results are not shown explicitly in table 4, we have examined the possible linkage between duck stamp sales receipts and other funding provided for the program. Including either the current or the lagged value of (the log of) real duck stamp receipts in the funding equations has no statistically significant effect and leaves the estimated effects of the other variables substantively unaffected. This suggests that the 1961 legislation (and its successors) that established the supplemental funding successfully insulated the supplemental funding from current or recent funding provided by duck hunters. Although we do not know which provisions of the legislation accomplished this result, this is a finding that may be of interest to those proposing designs for user fee programs elsewhere.

The Effect of Farm Programs on Habitat Acquisition

Farm Programs and Farmland Prices

Many studies have examined the factors influencing farmland values. Among these factors are rents to farmland, inflation, farm income, nonagricultural demand for land, tax rates, government payments, alternative investment opportunities, credit subsidies, input prices, and crop yields. For our purposes, the farm programs that have had the most important effects on farmland prices are (1) price supports and (2) subsidies to the conversions of wetlands to farmland.

Price supports—minimum prices guaranteed by the government—for crops increase the demand for farmland and, thus, tend to push farmland prices up. But price supports also cause a surplus of the crop to be produced. Consumers will purchase less of the commodity at the higher price, whereas producers will supply more. The government is forced either to purchase the excess quantity at the higher price or to require producers to cut production. Because it is costly to store or dispose of crop surpluses, price supports are generally accompanied by output controls. In the case of wheat and corn, output controls have taken the form of restrictions on the number of acres a farmer is permitted to plant in order to be eligible for government price-support payments.

Although the value of land in production rises with the increase in rents generated by higher output prices, the value of idled acres falls to (approximately) zero because no output can be produced on these acres. If no compensation is paid for idled acres, the overall effect of acreage restrictions on land prices is ambiguous (Hallberg 1992, 167). To induce enough farmers to participate in the program, however, the government usually compensates farmers for idled acres at a rate well above zero. If farmers are compensated for idled acres at the full rental value of land in production, then the overall effect is an unambiguous rise in farmland values (Hallberg 1992, 167).

Floyd (1965) has examined the theoretical effects of support prices on farmland values under various output control scenarios. In his analysis, Floyd reached the following conclusion:

> Provided that (a) the elasticity of supply of [farm]land is very low, (b) the share of land in total [farm] revenue is less than the share of the other inputs, and (c) the elasticity of demand [for agricultural products] is less than the elasticity of substitution [between land and labor], the return to land will . . . rise by a smaller amount [from support prices] when acreage is controlled than when it is not. These conditions are likely to be satisfied with respect to U.S. agriculture. (154)

Floyd's results suggest that if reasonable conditions on the parameters in his model are satisfied, the price of farmland will unambiguously rise when price supports and acreage restrictions are used.

Nevertheless, the price of land will rise by less when acreage restrictions are used in addition to price supports than when they are not.

Using a reasonable range of estimates for the parameters in his model, Floyd predicts that if no output controls are used, a 10 percent government-induced increase in output price will generate a 15 percent to 30 percent increase in the price of land used to produce that commodity. If marketing restrictions are used and marketing quotas are tied to the land, a 55 percent to 65 percent increase in land values is likely. If acreage restrictions are used and enough acreage is idled to eliminate any crop surplus, an increase in land values of 6 percent to 14 percent is reasonable (Floyd 1965, 156). The less acreage idled and the greater the compensation rate on idled acres, the more farmland values should rise.

Data on the market and support prices of several commodities were obtained from various issues of *Agricultural Statistics*, compiled by the USDA. Real prices were generated using the gross domestic product (GDP) deflator, with 1992 as the base year. The effect of price supports on land prices is estimated for wheat and corn because these are two important program crops grown in the Midwest and the northern plains, where a significant amount of duck habitat is located.

Between 1940 and 1995, the real support price on wheat was 23.5 percent higher than the market price of wheat, on average. Acreage restrictions have been the dominant output control method on wheat production. Using Floyd's predictions of the effect of a 10 percent higher support price, and assuming the relationship between support prices and farmland prices is linear in the relevant range, a 23.5 percent increase in the price of wheat would generate a 14 percent to 32 percent increase in the price of land used for wheat, depending on the extent of acreage restrictions and the compensation rate on idled acres. The persistence of surplus production in the wheat industry indicates that less acreage has been idled than assumed in Floyd's model, which implies that the true increase in farmland values generated by the support price program on wheat is likely to be significantly higher than the 14 percent lower bound.

Between 1940 and 1995, the real support price on corn was 11 percent higher than the market price of corn, on average. Acreage restrictions have also been the dominant output control method on corn production. Using Floyd's predictions, an 11 percent increase in the price of corn would generate a 7 percent to 15 percent increase in the price of land used for corn, again depending on the extent of acreage restrictions and the rate of compensation on idled acres.

The discussion thus far has assumed that all land is equally productive and that the expected rent that can be earned from farming is the same for all acres of land. Of course, this is not entirely accurate. Even within a region that produces only a single crop, some soil may be drier or wetter than average and, therefore, more or less productive as cropland. A distinction between land quality will help us evaluate the effect of farm programs on the protection of waterfowl habitat.

In many cases, the productivity of low-quality land can be increased through drainage and tiling investments. The farmer will be willing to invest in conversion only if the net return from conversion is positive. If the conversion costs are greater than the present discounted value of rents from a high-quality acre, no conversion will take place. Furthermore, the price of low-quality acres will effectively be zero because no positive rents could be earned from farming those acres, which implies that the price of a parcel of land containing low-quality acres should be lower than parcels containing only high-quality acres.

Clearly, however, if the rents to high-quality land are sufficiently great, then conversion of low-quality land will take place and the value of the converted land will rise. The incentive to convert can be stimulated by price supports, which raise the rents to high-quality land, or by drainage subsidies, which reduce the cost of conversion.

In many areas, government programs in the past have subsidized the cost of drainage projects through direct cost-sharing programs or by allowing tax credits for drainage costs. Once an acre of wetland is converted, its selling price will rise from zero to an amount equal to high-quality land. If the area is to be restored to waterfowl habitat, not only must the higher price be paid to purchase the area, but an additional restoration cost must also be incurred.

Conversion is sufficient, but not necessary, for the price of a wetland to rise. Farmers are likely to enroll their least-productive land in acreage restriction programs first. To generate the decrease in output desired by the government, the compensation rate on idled acres must rise enough to induce farmers to enroll more-productive land in the program. As the compensation rate increases, the least-productive acres receive the greatest increase in rent because these areas would generate little or no rent in the absence of the programs (Hallberg 1992, 168). Wetlands that formerly would have been sold to the Duck Stamp Program at a low price now command a price that equals the present discounted value of rental payments under acreage restriction programs.

Heimlich and Langner (USDA 1986) have studied the economics of wetland conversion and the effects of farm programs on wetland conversion. They report that, of the nation's remaining wetlands in 1982, the prairie pothole region of the northern plains had the most total acres with high or medium conversion potential—62,000 acres with high conversion potential and 2.5 million acres with medium conversion potential (USDA 1986, 22).

Abstracting from changes in conversion costs, Heimlich and Langner estimate that in 1985 price supports on wheat alone increased the number of wetland acres that would have been profitable to plant from 5.1 million acres to 6.4 million acres, an increase of 25 percent. Because wheat is a primary agricultural commodity in the critical duck-producing wetlands of the prairie pothole area, government price supports increase the cost of purchasing habitat in the area by artificially raising the expected return from farming the region's wetlands. Including all program crops in the United States, Heimlich and Langner report that an additional 4.7 million wetland acres would have been profitable to plant because of government price supports (USDA 1986, 11). The numbers are significant when compared with total wetland purchases under the Duck Stamp Program. It has taken the program more than sixty years to purchase four million acres of wetlands.

Heimlich and Langner do not investigate the actual magnitude of the effect of tax rules on the conversion of wetlands. They do, however, list several provisions of the Internal Revenue Code that effectively subsidize land clearing and drainage costs. These provisions include the deductibility of land clearing, drainage, and shaping costs; depreciation under the accelerated cost recovery system; deduction of interest payments on debt financing of clearing and drainage; investment tax credit equal to 10 percent of depreciable investments associated with clearing and drainage; and exclusion of 60 percent of long-term capital gains from the sale of improved farmland. All of these provisions encourage the conversion of wetlands to agriculture and increase the cost at which wetlands can be protected as wildlife habitat.

Farmland Prices and Habitat Purchase Prices

Because the Duck Stamp Program provides funds for purchasing wetlands duck habitat, it might be thought that there would be only a tenuous connection between the prices paid for this habitat and the price of prime farmland. In fact, for much of the period under consideration, the FWS was competing head-to-head with the USDA, paying productive farmland prices and receiving in return wetlands duck habitat.

To be eligible to receive price support payments, farmers had to set aside a certain percentage of their base acreage without any additional compensation on those set-aside acres. If farmers sold or leased one of their set-aside acres to the Duck Stamp Program, they had to withdraw an additional acre from production in order to satisfy the set-aside requirement. Thus, even though farmers were delivering wetlands to the Duck Stamp Program, they would insist on compensation equal to what they were earning on the additional land they had to remove from production. Thus, the Duck Stamp Program was paying top dollar for farmland that was probably marginal at best for agriculture. This was solely a product of set-aside programs that substantially increased the value to the farmer of marginal land.

The link between farmland prices and the prices paid by the Duck Stamp Program is evident in the data that we have for a subsample of our period, reported in summary form in table 5. During 1962 to 1977 data on WPA purchase prices and lease rates show that the bulk of these purchases and leases were for land located in the prairie pothole region of the upper Midwest. Therefore we constructed an area-weighted average of farmland prices for the Dakotas and Minnesota.

Two points are clear from table 5. First, purchases of wetlands duck habitat cost an amount per acre that is roughly equal to that of prime farmland in the upper Midwest. Second, both the purchase prices and the lease rates paid by the FWS were highly correlated

TABLE 5 Farmland Prices and Pothole Prices, 1962–1977

	Average Price per Acre (1992 dollars)	*Correlation with Upper Midwest Farmland Price*
Upper Midwest farmland price	$341.14	—
Pothole purchase price	360.50	$0.912
Pothole lease rate	79.11	0.935

SOURCES: Upper Midwest farmland prices from U.S. Department of Agriculture, *Agricultural Statistics*, various issues; pothole purchase price and lease rate from U.S. Congress. House. Merchant Marine and Fisheries Committee. House Report No. 95-1518, Aug. 18, 1978, p. 7. *Cong. Record*, vol. 124 (1978).

with movements in prime farmland prices during this period. Given these facts, we infer that the average price of farmland is a suitable proxy for the cost to FWS of duck habitat.

Determinants of Habitat Purchases

The FWS has the responsibility of using duck stamp receipts and revenue from other sources to purchase habitat from landowners. Assuming that purchases in any particular region under the Duck Stamp Program are small relative to the total amount of land in use, then the program will not affect land prices. The supply of habitat to the program will be perfectly elastic at the market price of land, and we can use the observed price of farmland as an exogenous variable in the equation for estimating habitat demand.

Purchases and leases of habitat in any given region are limited only by the price of habitat and by the total level of funds available. Reports from the MBCC and Senate hearings on Duck Stamp Act amendments indicate that the majority of people who privately own wetlands suitable for waterfowl habitat are farmers. The relevant land market to consider, then, is the market for farm real estate. The variable used to represent land prices is the value of real farmland. In the empirical analysis, the real level of funding available is also included as an explanatory variable for habitat purchases and serves as a demand shift parameter. Finally, because both the price of farmland and the level of funding are subject to substantial year-to-year fluctuations, we allow for the possibility that the response of FWS to a temporary change in either may differ from its response to a permanent change. Hence, we include the lagged value of the dependent variable in the equations we estimate, which enables us to estimate both the short- and long-run responses to changes in the other exogenous variables.

Land is protected under the Duck Stamp Program in two forms and under two classifications. Land can be protected through direct purchase or by lease. Acquisitions are classified either as migratory bird refuge (*MBR*) or waterfowl production area (*WPA*). To facilitate the empirical analysis, the two land purchase types are combined into one variable, *purchases* = *MBR purchases* + WPA *purchases*. The same is done with leases, such that *leases* = *MBR leases* + *WPA leases*. The data used and empirical results are reported in the next section.

Data on total acres of waterfowl habitat purchased and leased with funds from the Migratory Bird Conservation Fund were obtained from MBCC annual reports. Data on average U.S. farmland values were obtained from USDA statistical tables. Data on total Migratory Bird Conservation Funds were obtained from the FWS Division of Realty records. We assume that both purchases and leases depend positively on real total funding for the program (*total fund*) from both stamp sales and nonstamp funds and negatively on the real price of farmland (*land price*). Finally, because both land prices and funding are subject to substantial year-to-year fluctuations, we include the lagged value of the dependent variable in estimating each equation to allow for the possibility that the responses to temporary and permanent changes in prices and funding may be different.[5]

Measuring all variables as natural logarithms yields the estimates shown in table 6 and also enables us to express the results in terms of elasticities, as shown in table 7. From these results, it is evident that leases of habitat by FWS are more responsive to changes in both prices and budgets than are purchases and that these findings are true for both the short term (a given fiscal year) and the long term. The findings suggest that FWS is making core purchases of habitat and then using habitat leases as the vehicle for absorbing shocks to farmland prices or to its budget.

5. FWS could alter purchases for a given level of funding by carrying over (not using) funds from years with large populations so that they could be spent on habitat in years when populations were low.

TABLE 6 Purchases and Leases of Waterfowl Habitat, 1962–1964
(absolute t-statistics in parentheses)

$$\underset{}{\text{Log(purchase)}} = \underset{(0.65)}{3.02} + \underset{(2.84)}{0.47\ \text{Log(purchase)}_{t-1}} - \underset{(1.75)}{0.50\ \text{Log(land price)}} + \underset{(1.23)}{0.33\ \text{Log(total fund)}}$$

$R^2 = 0.68$ $F(3, 27) = 19.34$ D.W. = 2.24

$$\text{Log(lease)} = \underset{(0.22)}{-1.35} + \underset{(4.96)}{0.59\ \text{Log(lease)}_{t-1}} - \underset{(2.15)}{0.63\ \text{Log(land price)}} + \underset{(1.71)}{0.55\ \text{Log(total fund)}}$$

$R^2 = 0.72$ $F(3, 27) = 23.24$ D.W. = 2.05

SOURCES: Purchases and leases from *Annual Report of the Migratory Bird Conservation Commission*, 1929–1996 reports; land price from U.S. Department of Agriculture, *Agricultural Statistics*, various issues; total fund from U.S. Fish and Wildlife Service, Division of Realty, fax transmission, 1 p.

TABLE 7 Estimated Short-Run and Long-Run Price and Budget Elasticities

	Short-Run		*Long-Run*	
	Purchase	*Lease*	*Purchase*	*Lease*
Price elasticities	−0.50	−0.63	−0.94	−1.54
Budget elasticities	0.33	0.55	0.62	1.34

SOURCE: Computed from estimates in table 6.

The Effects on Habitat Purchases and Leases

One other noteworthy result, not shown explicitly in tables 6 and 7, concerns the effect of duck populations on FWS purchase and lease decisions. A principal motive for introducing taxpayer-financed funding in 1961 was not merely to expand the total level of funding, but also to permit the FWS to break the positive feedback loop that existed between duck populations and stamp purchases. In our discussion of the determination of funding levels, we noted that the size of the duck population had no significant effect on nonstamp funding. Including duck populations in the equations of tables 6 and 7 also has no effect on purchases or leases, given the level of funding. Taken together, these results imply that there is still no mechanism in place for breaking the feedback loop from duck populations to funding, a loop that tends to destabilize the health of the U.S. waterfowl population. In this dimension, the legislative changes of 1961 appear to have failed in their objective.

Thus far, we have established several key facts about the link between agricultural programs and the Duck Stamp Program. First, according to the research done by others, agricultural programs have had a substantial upward effect on farmland prices. This effect has been associated with increases in the cost of the land available for waterfowl habitat acquisition. Moreover, because these cost increases have not been met with budgetary supplements, they have, on balance, caused a reduction in the acquisition of habitat. The purpose of this section is to illustrate the magnitude of these effects.

Table 8 gives the results of a simulation in which the real level of Duck Stamp Program funds is held constant and real farmland values are increased. Predicted values for total habitat purchases and leases are generated using the regression results from table 6. Funding for the program is held constant at $43.7 million, its actual average real level from 1962 to 1994. Several levels of farmland prices are considered in column 1. The first of these is $400 per acre, the likely upper bound on the value of farmland that would be observed without price supports.[6] In addition, we show (1) $550 per acre, reflecting roughly the median effect of wheat price supports during our sample period; (2) $650 per acre, a level of land prices that would be expected given wheat price supports during the mid-1980s; and (3) $850 per acre, reflecting the peak effect of price supports, such as during 1968 to 1971. Given the assumed level of real expenditures, the demand for habitat enables us to deduce the long-run levels of habitat purchases and leases associated with each hypothetical acreage price (shown in columns 2 and 3). Finally, in column 4 we show the proportion of duck stamp funds that are being distributed to farmers as economic rents.

6. For example, during the formative years of the modernized Duck Stamp Program, support prices for both wheat and corn were close to market prices, and as shown in the table below, real farmland values were just below $400 per acre.

Crop Support Prices and Land Prices, 1960–1962

Year	*Wheat Support Price*	*Wheat Market Price*	*Corn Support Price*	*Corn Market Price*	*Real Farmland Price*
1960	1.78	1.74	1.06	1.00	370.53
1961	1.79	1.83	1.20	1.10	363.79
1962	2.00	2.04	1.20	1.12	376.88

TABLE 8 The Effects of Price Support Programs on Habitat Purchases and Leases

Farmland Value	*Habitat Purchases (acres)*	*Habitat Leases (acres)*	*Farmers' Rents as a Share of Program Expenditures (in percent)*
$400	59,870	66,200	0%
550	44,370	40,590	27
650	37,900	31,400	39
850	29,420	20,790	53

SOURCES: Computed from estimates in table 6; wheat and corn market and support prices from U.S. Department of Agriculture, *Agricultural Statistics*, various issues.

In this simulation, a budget-fixed $150 increase in real farmland values (from $400 to $550) would cause habitat purchases to fall by approximately 15,500 acres per year; leases would decline more than 25,000 acres. Furthermore, 27 percent of total expenditures for that year would simply be rents transferred from the individuals funding the program to landowners. An additional $100 increase in farm values (to $650) would cause purchases to fall by an extra 6,500 acres per year and leases would drop another 9,000 acres, with 39 percent of expenditures being transferred as rents. Finally, at $850 per acre, when wheat price supports were having their maximum effects, purchases would be at less than half the levels observed at $400 per acre, leases would be down by two-thirds, and rents would climb to 53 percent of total expenditures. During the thirty-plus years spanned by our estimates, habitat purchases would likely be reduced by about 500,000 acres, with leases being reduced by some 750,000 acres.

The Role of Wetland Conversions

Wetland conversion and higher real farmland values also have some less direct, though no less interesting, long-run effects on the conservation of waterfowl habitat in the United States. In our empirical analysis, the level of the duck breeding population is treated as an exogenous variable, which implies that total stamp sales and, therefore, duck stamp revenue are determined solely by exogenous variables. Nevertheless, wetland conversion certainly reduces total wetland acres for duck production, and rising land prices reduce the amount of habitat that is purchased and developed for wildlife use. Less habitat means fewer ducks. According to the duck stamp demand results in table 3, fewer ducks mean fewer duck stamp revenues the following year, which, of course, results in a decrease in available funds and even fewer purchases in the long run. Although the complex dynamics and lack of sufficient data on total wetlands, wetland conversion, and the production rates of ducks make it impossible to incorporate this explicitly in our models, these potential effects are worth keeping in mind when considering the long-run implications of any policy changes.

Evidence of such a downward-spiraling scenario in habitat purchases can be found in congressional hearings on the topic of Duck Stamp Program funding from May 11, 1961. Wisconsin Congressman Lester Johnson stated:

> As every duck hunter knows, waterfowl hunting has grown poorer in recent years, and fewer hunters have taken to the field. As a result duck stamp sales have lagged. . . . Mr. Chairman, with fewer duck stamps being sold, less money has been available for the purchase of new refuges. This, in turn, has resulted in poorer hunting, fewer hunters, smaller duck stamp receipts and a further lag in the acquisition program. (Senate 1961, 134)

The result of these hearings was the $105 million wetlands loan to the program for the purpose of speeding up the purchases of duck habitat. The argument was that increased spending would lead to more ducks, more hunters, more duck stamp sales, and more funds to repay the loan in the future.

Despite this funding, drainage of wetlands for agriculture reached a peak from the mid-1950s to the mid-1970s. Wetland losses from tile-and-open ditch drainage averaged an estimated 550,000 acres per year during this period, much of which was, ironically, subsidized by the so-called Agricultural Conservation Program (Dahl 1990). Therefore, the accelerated wetland protection efforts that began in 1958 were probably more than offset by increased wetland conversion, at least in terms of the net change in total wetland acres. Under these circumstances, it is easy to understand the reaction of the sports enthusiasts and wildlife conservationists who were financing the habitat protection efforts. The vice president of the Wildlife Institute submitted the following statement to Congress: "Conservationists are appalled by this ridiculous situation that finds one Federal agency paying for the destruction of wetlands while another is charged with the responsibility of securing and restoring them for a wildlife program in which the Federal Government has a primary responsibility" (Senate 1961, 142). Our results do nothing to diminish the conclusion that what the duck stamp hand of the federal government was doing to enhance waterfowl habitat conservation, the agricultural policy hand of that same government was more than offsetting through wetland conversion.

Conclusions

The Duck Stamp Program is one of the earliest examples of a user fee program for producing environmental amenities with public good characteristics; it, thus, has lessons for how other user fee programs might work. The Duck Stamp Program was instigated by waterfowl hunters willing to pay for duck habitat as a means of increasing the number of ducks. These hunters are willing to provide a steady source of funds for financing habitat conservation as long as they observe a positive supply response to their expenditures. When duck populations decline, however, whether due to natural forces such as droughts or political forces such as farm programs, duck stamp sales lag, causing a decrease in habitat purchases. Of course, the amount that users are willing to pay is always limited by the price, as evidenced by the responsiveness of duck stamp sales to changes in the real price of duck stamps.

The Duck Stamp Program also provides an excellent example of how a well-intentioned program for applying market forces to public good provision can be captured by political forces. Sometimes these forces are within the government itself: until Congress stepped in and explicitly forbade it, the FWS used duck stamp proceeds chiefly to fund activities other than habitat acquisition. Other times these forces originate among the private citizens affected by the programs: when duck hunters concluded that they were not getting what they thought they were paying for, they turned to Congress to increase funding for the program.

Policy analysts must consider the interface between well-intentioned user fee programs and other governmental policies. Increased wetland conversion and rising land values resulted from farm programs. Because these programs raised the opportunity cost of land containing wildlife habitat by increasing the returns to agricultural production, they also raised the cost of habitat conservation under the Duck Stamp Program.

Herein is a bootlegger-and-Baptist story in which duck hunters and farmers joined forces to increase tax funding for habitat purchases. As long as tax funding was forthcoming, the duck hunters could get what they wanted, albeit at a higher cost to the taxpayer. But it was the farmers who were the real beneficiaries; their marginal lands were made more valuable by the farm programs and were purchased at a higher price by the Duck Stamp Program. Ironically, this story ended with less habitat conservation and more wetlands drained for agricultural production, and now we regulate wetland use, forcing private landowners rather than users or taxpayers to pay for past sins.

Three lessons follow from the duck stamp experience. First, user fees can provide a marketlike solution for the provision of environmental amenities. Second, good intentions are not enough; if user fees are to be successful in providing environmental amenities, their proceeds must be insulated from competing claimants. During the first twenty-five years of the Duck Stamp Program, most of the fees were spent on administrative expenses rather than habitat acquisition. Third, user fee programs appear to be subject to the same political forces found elsewhere. When duck hunters did not get what they thought they were paying for, they turned to politics to increase funding for the program. Unfortunately, the Duck Stamp Program shows that the insulation of market solutions from political forces is easier said than done.

REFERENCES

Alston, J. M. 1986. An Analysis of Growth of U.S. Farmland Prices, 1963–82. *American Journal of Agricultural Economics* 68, no. 1: 1–9.

Burt, O. R. 1986. Econometric Modeling of the Capitalization Formula for Farmland Prices. *American Journal of Agricultural Economics* 68, no. 1: 10–26.

Dahl, T. E. 1990. *Wetlands-Losses in the United States, 1780s to 1980s.* Washington, D.C.: Fish and Wildlife Service Report to Congress.

Floyd, John E. 1965. The Effects of Farm Price Supports on the Returns to Land and Labor in Agriculture. *Journal of Political Economy* 73, no. 2: 148–158.

Hallberg, M. C. 1992. *Policy for American Agriculture: Choices and Consequences.* Ames: Iowa State University Press.

President. *1997 Economic Report.* Washington, D.C.: Government Printing Office.

Robison, L. J., D. A. Lins, and R. Venkataraman. 1985. Cash Rents and Land Values in U.S. Agriculture. *American Journal of Agricultural Economics* 67, no. 4: 794–805.

U.S. Department of Agriculture. Various years. *Agricultural Statistics.*

———. 1986. *Swampbusting: Wetland Conversion and Farm Programs,* by Ralph E. Heimlich and Linda L. Langner. Economic Research Service, Economic Report No. 551.

U.S. Department of Commerce. 1976. *Historical Statistics of the United States, Colonial Times to the Present, Part 1.* Washington, D.C.: Government Printing Office.

———. Various years. *Statistical Abstract of the United States.* Washington, D.C.: Government Printing Office.

U.S. Fish and Wildlife Service (FWS). 1988. *The Duck Stamp Collection.* Washington, D.C.: Government Printing Office.

U.S. Migratory Bird Conservation Commission (MBCC). *Annual Report for Fiscal Year 1932.* Washington, D.C.: Government Printing Office, 1933.

———. *Annual Report for Fiscal Year 1933.* Washington, D.C.: Government Printing Office, 1934.

———. *Annual Report for Fiscal Year 1935.* Washington, D.C.: Government Printing Office, 1936.

———. *Annual Report for Fiscal Year 1936.* Washington, D.C.: Government Printing Office, 1937.

———. *Annual Report for Fiscal Year 1961.* Washington, D.C.: Government Printing Office, 1962.

U.S. Public Law 124. 73d Cong., 2d session, 16 March 1934. *Migratory Bird Hunting Stamp Act. U.S. Statutes at Large* 48.

U.S. Senate. 1958. Subcommittee of the Committee on Interstate and Foreign Commerce. *Fish and Wildlife Legislation:* Hearings before the Committee on Interstate and Foreign Commerce. 85th Cong., 2d sess.

———. 1961. Subcommittee on Fisheries and Wildlife Conservation. *Miscellaneous Fish and Wildlife Legislation:* Hearings. 87th Cong., 1st Sess.

Yandle, Bruce. 1983. Bootleggers and Baptists: The Education of a Regulatory Economist. *Regulation* (May/June): 12–16.

Elizabeth Brubaker **5**

Unnatural Disaster

How Politics Destroyed Canada's Atlantic Groundfisheries

On July 2, 1992, Canada's fisheries minister banned fishing for cod off the northeastern coast of Newfoundland and off the southern half of Labrador. The northern cod stock, once one of the richest in the world, had collapsed.

The moratorium on northern cod marked the beginning of an unprecedented disaster for virtually all of Canada's Atlantic groundfisheries—the fisheries for species that feed near the ocean floor. In 1993, there were dramatic reductions in the allowable catches of cod in the northern part of the Gulf of St. Lawrence and closures of the cod fisheries off Newfoundland's southern coast and Nova Scotia's eastern coast, as well as in the southern Gulf of St. Lawrence. With the following years came further reductions and new moratoriums, not only on cod but also on redfish (ocean perch), white hake, American plaice, turbot (Greenland halibut), and witch flounder.

Despite the fishing bans, many stocks continued to decline, setting new historical lows year after year. Cod populations dropped to one one-hundredth of their former sizes. In 1997, fishing for twenty-two stocks remained prohibited; most other groundfish stocks supported only severely limited fishing (DFO 1997, 79–82). In 1998, the Fisheries Resource Conservation Council (FRCC), which is responsible for advising the fisheries minister on catch levels, expressed "surprise," "alarm," and "dismay" over the status of several stocks and projected further declines, even in the absence of any fishery (FRCC 1998b, 5–12). The council warned, "The outlook as described by scientists is even more bleak than at the beginning of the moratorium" (FRCC 1998a, 5). Some scientists worried that the worst-hit stocks might never fully recover.

The collapse of the Atlantic groundfish was more than an ecological disaster—it was also an economic disaster. Groundfish landings in the 1980s had an average landed value of $345 million[1] and a processed value of considerably more (Cashin 1993, Appendix Table 2-1). According to Gus Etchegary, former chair of the Fisheries Council of Canada and former president of Newfoundland's largest fishing and processing company, if catches off Newfoundland and Labrador had not declined in the previous twenty-five years, by 1997 they would have had an annual export value of $3 billion (Commons 1998a, 950–955).

Fishery closures, which threw 40,000 fishermen and fish processors out of work, created social and economic chaos throughout Atlantic Canada, where half of the region's 1,300 fishing communities depend entirely on the fisheries for their existence (Auditor General 1997, 14-9). In the words of Earle McCurdy, president of the Fish, Food, and Allied Workers union, "What we have is not an adjustment problem, but the most wrenching societal upheaval since the Great Depression. Our communities are in crisis. The people of the fishery are in turmoil" (quoted in Harris 1998, i).

The moratoriums hit Newfoundland especially hard. The province has always depended on cod fishing. Cod inspired its first settlements, posts where English merchants salted and dried cod before shipping it to Europe. For centuries, fishing was Newfoundland's only major industry, and it has remained the province's most important primary industry. Many communities have known nothing but fishing and fish processing, and many are prepared for noth-

1. Unless otherwise stated, figures are in Canadian dollars.

ing else. Of the province's fishermen, 83 percent have not graduated from secondary school, and more than 37 percent have not attended any secondary school at all (Auditor General 1997, 14-10). Former Fisheries Minister John Crosbie described Newfoundland's special relationship with cod:

> Through the centuries, the northern cod was the economic foundation for the settlement and growth of communities along the east coast of Newfoundland and the coast of Labrador. Without the abundant fish stocks, there would have been no Newfoundland—as a British colony, a British dominion, or, after 1949, a province of Canada. . . . Cod was the reason why Newfoundland was settled; it permitted our people to survive. (Crosbie 1997, 375–376)

The fact that the destruction of this critically important resource could have been avoided makes it even more tragic. The collapse of the groundfisheries resulted from the wrong people controlling the resource. Politicians, pursuing their short-term interest in putting voters to work, subsidized the expansion of the fisheries and set catch levels exceeding those recommended by their own scientists. If instead, fishermen, fishing companies, and fishing communities with exclusive, permanent rights to the stocks had controlled the resource, the groundfish collapse would, in all likelihood, never have occurred. Their financial interest in the long-term health of the stocks, and their confidence that reducing their own catches wouldn't simply provide an opportunity for other fishermen to benefit, would have compelled those with fisheries rights to conserve.

Nature Overthrown

For five centuries, the area now known as Canada's Atlantic Coast offered some of the world's best fishing. John Cabot's son reported that, upon arriving in Newfoundland in 1497, the explorers found "a great abundance of that kind of fish which the savages call baccalaos"—what we call Atlantic cod (quoted in Matthiessen 1959, 26). Cabot's crew returned to Britain with tales of a sea "swarming with fish, which could be taken not only with the net but in baskets let down with a stone, so that it sinks in the water" (quoted in Kirby 1982, 7). The fish were as large as they were plentiful: Cabot likely found five- and six-foot-long cod weighing up to 200 pounds (McKibben 1998, 60).

Throughout the following centuries, fishermen sailed from Portugal, France, Spain, and England to catch between 100,000 and 200,000 tonnes (metric tons) of cod a year (McKibben 1998, 62). The ocean remained bountiful; one seventeenth-century discourse on Newfoundland reported cod so dense "that we heardlie have been able to row a boate through them" (quoted in Harris 1998, 43). All assumed that the cod stocks were boundless. And indeed, given the technological limitations of the fleets, they probably were. An 1883 report on fisheries for the British Government asserted that "The cod fishery . . . and probably all of the great sea fisheries are inexhaustible. Nothing we can do can seriously affect the numbers of fish" (quoted in Iles 1980, 6). Two years later, the Canadian Ministry of Agriculture predicted, "Unless the order of nature is overthrown, for centuries to come our fisheries will continue to be fertile" (quoted in Kurlansky 1977, 32).

Overthrowing nature's order proved surprisingly easy. In the 1950s, western Europeans intensified fishing in the northwest Atlantic, followed by eastern Europeans in the next decade. The introduction of high-powered factory trawlers—which operated in all seasons and weathers, located fish on their spawning grounds with sonar equipment, dragged huge nets to scoop vast quantities of the fish from the seabed, and then filleted and froze the fish in onboard processing plants—made possible dramatic increases in catches. Cod catches grew from an annual average of 500,000 tonnes in the first half of the twentieth century to 1,475,000 tonnes in 1968 (FRCC 1997, 9). That year the catch of northern cod alone reached

810,000 tonnes (FRCC 1996a, Annex 2). With two hundred factory trawlers plying the waters off Newfoundland, it took only the fifteen years from 1960 to 1975 for fishermen to catch as many northern cod as they had in the 250 years following Cabot's arrival in Newfoundland (Harris 1998, 63–64).

The glory days of high cod catches would soon end. By 1978, catches had declined to 404,000 tonnes. Many hoped that Canada's establishment, in 1977, of a two hundred mile exclusive economic zone excluding many foreign boats from rich fishing grounds would allow stocks to recover. But chasing foreign boats from Canadian waters did little for the stocks, because Canadian boats soon took the place of the foreign boats. After a brief recovery in the 1980s, cod catches plummeted. They fell from 508,000 tonnes in 1982, to 475,000 tonnes in 1986, to 461,000 tonnes in 1988, to 384,000 tonnes in 1990, and to 183,000 tonnes in 1992 (Cashin 1993, 26). In 1996, four years after the imposition of the first moratorium, fishermen caught only 13,000 tonnes of cod (FRCC 1997, 13).

Other groundfish catches fared as badly. From a peak of 2,829,000 tonnes in 1965 (Dept. Environ. 1976, 29), groundfish catches fell to 819,000 tonnes in 1977, rebounded somewhat in the following decade, and then collapsed (FRCC 1997, 9). In 1996, catches remained below 200,000 tonnes.

Laying Blame

Canada's fisheries managers tried desperately to blame the groundfish collapse on forces beyond their control. Colder water temperatures, they suggested, had driven the cod away, while increasing seal populations had eaten both cod and its favorite food, capelin. It has become increasingly clear, however, that such environmental factors played only minor roles in the destruction of the stocks. The real problem, scientists now widely agree, was that the politicians and bureaucrats running Canada's Atlantic fisheries permitted—and even encouraged—overfishing.

Following the collapse of the northern cod stock, scientists published numerous papers documenting the unambiguous role of overfishing. "Cold water and other environmental factors have been suggested as the underlying cause of the observed declines, but the data now emerging show that overfishing has been the prime agent" concluded one researcher (quoted in FRCC 1996a, Annex 8). Others stated, "Our analysis suggest[s] that even if natural mortality has been higher in recent years, that overfishing was responsible for the collapse in this population before 1991" (quoted in FRCC 1996a, Annex 8). With study after study, it became increasingly indisputable that "the northern cod stock had been overfished to commercial extinction" (Steele, Andersen, and Green 1992, 37).

Scientists reached the same conclusions about other Atlantic groundfish stocks. In a study of the southern Gulf of St. Lawrence cod, for example, researchers noted the low abundance of mature fish and examined the causes of the increased mortality of these fish. They concluded that "the most likely cause is increased exploitation in the late 1980s and early 1990s. . . . [I]t is unlikely that Grey seal predation was the main cause of this trend in mortality. . . . [I]t is also unlikely that unfavourable environmental conditions are primarily responsible for this pattern" (quoted in Hutchings, Walters, and Haedrich 1997, 1202–1203).

Fisheries managers fought hard against such conclusions. Long after their arguments had been discredited, official documents continued to stress environmental factors. In its overview of the causes of stock collapses, the 1995 report of the Department of Fisheries and Oceans (DFO) on the status of Newfoundland's groundfish stocks barely mentioned overfishing, focusing instead on environmental change. Given that research on overfishing not only had been published, but also had been presented at stock assessment meetings, it is evident that the report's focus resulted from explicit bias rather than mere ignorance (Hutchings, Walters, and Haedrich 1997, 1202).

Well into 1996, the government's Fisheries Resource Conservation Council remained reluctant to single out overfishing, instead attributing Atlantic stock collapses to a combination of environmental, managerial, scientific, and political factors. Even the council's inaptly named *Learning from History* stressed nature's effects on fish stocks, leading one member to list the scientific evidence pointing to the primary role of overfishing and to express his disappointment in "the report's inability or reluctance to address the causes of the collapse of the Northern cod stock" (FRCC 1996a, Annex 8). Frustration at the apparent bias toward environmental causes prompted the FRCC to attach to the report a preface in the form of a letter stating that "environmental changes cannot be seen as the principal cause of the collapse of the Northern cod, and certainly should not be used to overshadow the central fact of over-fishing" (FRCC 1996a).

The government's bias led it not only to ignore evidence of overfishing, but also to actively conceal it. DFO's 1995 report on the status of groundfish stocks in the Gulf of St. Lawrence excluded information on overfishing after a senior bureaucrat challenged its appropriateness. After reading the draft report's conclusion that "It is unlikely that seal predation or environmental conditions are responsible for these trends in total mortality," the assistant deputy minister fired off a memo asking not only if evidence could support this statement, but also whether it was consistent with the department's previous statements on seals. Not surprisingly, the statement blaming overfishing disappeared from the report's final version (Hutchings, Walters, and Haedrich 1997, 1203).

This rewrite was not an isolated incident: the DFO routinely suppressed politically inconvenient research into the causes of the cod decline. An internal government report, based on meetings in

1992 with almost every member of the DFO's Science Branch, charged that "Scientific information surrounding the northern cod moratorium, specifically the role of the environment, was gruesomely mangled and corrupted to meet political ends," (DFO 1993, 55). It noted that the department routinely gagged its scientists, leaving communication with the public to ill-informed spokespersons. "Management is fostering an attitude of scientific deception, misinformation and obfuscation in presenting and defending the science that the department undertakes and the results it achieves," the report said. "It appears that science is too much integrated into the politics of the department. . . . It has become far too convenient for resource managers and others to publicly state that their decisions were based on scientific advice when this is clearly not the case" (DFO 1993, 34, 44, 54).

The federal government's attitude toward scientific evidence is reflected in its suppression of Ransom Myers's research. Myers, who worked for the DFO between 1984 and 1997 and who has been called "the best fish scientist in Canada" by his peers (quoted in Cameron 1998), was one of its first scientists to challenge the official view of the cod collapse. In 1994, he co-authored an article that stated, unambiguously, "We reject hypotheses that attribute the collapse of the northern cod to environmental change. . . . We conclude that the collapse of the northern cod can be attributed solely to overexploitation" (quoted in Harris 1998, 196).

Once the government got wise to the threat posed by Myers, it did its best to silence him. In one instance, it forbade him and two colleagues to distribute written copies of a paper that minimized the effects on young cod of increased seal populations to an international conference on marine mammals. One of the co-authors recalled, "Because of the politically sensitive nature of the work and because our conclusions were at odds with recent statements by the minister and government spokespersons regarding the influence of seals in the collapse and recovery of northern cod, we were not permitted to distribute copies of our work to our fellow scientists" (Commons 1997a, 945–950). When a member of Parliament requested a copy of the report, then-Fisheries Minister Brian Tobin denied that it existed (Thorne 1997). Later questioned about his denial, Tobin replied that scientists could be petulant, pompous prima donnas and suggested firing them: "Take all of these scientists if they feel constrained working within government and make them free" (quoted in Canadian Press 1997b).

In another case, the threat of departmental intimidation persuaded a colleague to withdraw an article, co-authored with Myers, maintaining that harp seals had not caused the cod collapse (Harris 1998, 297). Senior bureaucrats also harassed Myers's adviser and the director of his laboratory in their efforts to suppress his politically undesirable research (Commons 1997b, 945–950). Myers pointed out that the department "seemed to have a notion that you could sit in Ottawa and *make up* reality. If you could enforce a scientific consensus, that would *become* reality" (quoted in Cameron 1998).

When, in 1995, Myers told Canada's national newspaper that "what happened to the fish stocks had nothing to do with the environment, nothing to do with seals. It is simply overfishing," DFO formally reprimanded him:

> Your comments, as presented by the media, did not give a balanced perspective on the issue of the status of the cod stocks and were inconsistent with the June 1995 Newfoundland Stock Status Report. . . . Your . . . disregard for both departmental policy on communication with the media and the professional opinions of your colleagues warrant the disciplinary action of a written reprimand. In the future, you are expected to respect both the system of primary spokespersons and peer conclusions on matters within your area of expertise. (quoted in Hutchings, Walters, and Haedrich 1997, 1203)

Myers was lucky to get off so easy. He later recalled that the assistant deputy minister of science had wanted to fire him, but that his science director had bargained the assistant deputy minister down to a reprimand (Commons 1997b, 1050–1055).

Even Myers's departure from the DFO did not spare him the department's wrath. In 1997, after he told the *Ottawa Citizen* about the bureaucracy's efforts to suppress his research into the role of seals in the cod stock collapse, two senior bureaucrats sued both the paper and the scientist for libel (Strauss 1997b). David Schindler, a scientist who worked with the DFO for twenty-two years, called the lawsuit "the worst form of intimidation" (quoted in Harris 1998, 299). But the suppression and intimidation hardly surprised him: "It's almost a tradition in the Canadian civil service to act this way" (quoted in Harris 1998, 299). Tradition or not, Myers refused to be cowed. He told a government committee, "I believe it is simply a suit to get me to shut up. . . . This is not a private suit. This is a suit by bureaucrats who are doing it on government time and who are using government resources to harass citizens whose opinions they don't like" (Commons 1997b, 950–955).

Myers pointed out that he has not been the DFO's only target. When, in 1992, Gordon Mertz said in an interview that everyone knew that the cod fishery would collapse because of overfishing and not cold water, he was required to write a letter admitting that he was wrong. Not one to pull his punches, Myers described the incident as "Stalinist behaviour" (Commons 1997b, 950–955).

It is hardly surprising that senior bureaucrats would find offensive the research of Myers and his colleagues that held their institution's own failures—rather than nature—responsible for the collapse of the cod. It is likewise to be expected that politicians would shy away from suggestions that they, who ultimately approved each year's catch levels, must be held accountable for the disastrous overfishing of the Atlantic groundfish stocks. And sure enough, politicians proved reluctant to accept responsibility for the collapse. The government's news release announcing the moratorium on northern cod claimed that the stock's decline was "due primarily to ecological factors" (DFO 1992). The previous day, then-Fisheries Minister John Crosbie had shouted at hecklers that there was no point in taking their frustration out on him because he "hadn't removed the 'goddamned fish' from the sea" (Crosbie 1997, 387). In his memoirs, Crosbie offered a weak defense: "There wasn't much I or anyone else could do" (Crosbie 1997, 372).

Although it is true that the federal government could not bring the fish back, it is equally true that the blame for the disappearance of the fish must be laid at the government's feet. The government has long had jurisdiction over inland fishing and, since 1977, has controlled fishing within two hundred miles of Canada's shores. Economists have described the tidal fishery as "among the most closely regulated of industries in Canada and comparable industrial democracies" (Scott and Neher 1981, 2). Canada's Fisheries Act grants the federal fisheries minister absolute discretion over the issuing of fishing licenses and empowers his agents to prohibit fishing in designated areas. Over the decades, the Fisheries Act and other fishing regulations have governed almost every detail of the fishery—from the number and size of boats fishing, to the type of gear used, to the amount of drinking water fishing boats must carry. Tragically, successive governments abused their virtually complete power over the fisheries, managing them not for long-term biological or economic sustainability, but for short-term political gain.

How Many Jobs?

In his paper on the history of fisheries management, DFO's T. D. Iles spelled out four kinds of questions that can be asked of a fishery: the biological question (how many fish?); the economic question (how many dollars?); the social question (how many jobs?); and the political question (how many votes?) (Iles 1980, 3). The politicians and bureaucrats managing Canada's Atlantic fisheries have too often asked only the social and political questions. The inevitable answers to these questions have spelled doom for what was once a great biological and economic resource.

Putting to work as many fishermen and fish processors as possible has long been a goal of Canada's fisheries managers. In 1970, the government's *Economic Policy for the Fisheries* spelled out its primary objective of maximizing employment in the commercial fishery (Auditor General 1997, 14-16). Six years later, the Department of the Environment's *Policy for Canada's Commercial Fisheries* again stressed the social elements of the fishery. In what it called a major policy shift, it said that federal fisheries management would be guided not by the traditional notion of maximum sustainable yield but by the principle of "the best use of society's resources," or the sum of net social benefits, including "occupational opportunity" (Dept. Environ. 1976, 53). The government would base allowable catches "on economic and social requirements . . . rather than on the biological-yield capability of a fish stock" (Dept. Environ. 1976, Appendix 1, 3). Although the policy gave a nod to the goal of minimizing dependence on paternalistic government, it proposed programs to stabilize and supplement fishermen's incomes (Dept. Environ. 1976, 65, Appendix 1, 1). The policy summarized the government's position with a startling announcement: "Although commercial fishing has long been a highly regulated activity in Canada, the object of regulation has, with rare exception, been protection of the renewable resource. In other words, fishing has been regulated in the interest of the fish. In the future it is to be regulated in the interest of the people who depend on the fishing industry" (Dept. Environ. 1976, 5).

A 1980 ministerial speech elaborated on the federal position: "The allocation of fish must come from a mixture of reasons: not just what is 'economical' but also the survival of communities, the preservation of a way of life, . . . the reasonable well-being of fishermen and plant workers, and so on" (quoted in Iles 1980, 4). The following year, a DFO discussion paper, *Policy for Canada's Atlantic Fisheries in the 1980s*, confirmed that Canada based catch limits not only on what it thought the fishery could bear but also on "the economic needs of coastal fishing communities" (DFO 1981, 23).

As questions arose about the economic viability of policies maximizing employment, the government paid lip service to balancing social concerns with economic reality. The resulting policies often seemed schizophrenic, with contradictory policies appearing within a single document. In the 1980s, the Atlantic Fisheries Restructuring Act adopted both economic viability and employment maximization as policy objectives for the Atlantic fisheries, giving the former priority over the latter. More recently, the government has ostensibly made conservation a primary objective. Its actions, however, have belied its conflicting priorities: Too often, short-term jobs—and the votes they bring—continue to come first.

Fishing for Subsidies

In their quest to put constituents to work, successive governments devised dozens of assistance programs for fishermen and fish processors. Federal support for the Atlantic fisheries dates at least as far back as 1930, to the formation of the United Maritime Fishermen and the funding of its cooperative processing and marketing efforts (Alexander 1997, 24, 40, 83). Subsidies increased over the years, generally in response to periodic crises in the industry. Subsidies skyrocketed after 1977, as federal and provincial governments alike pushed the fishing industry to take advantage of the new opportunities presented by the extension of Canada's fisheries jurisdiction to two hundred miles. One bureaucrat recalled, "It was a gold rush kind of mentality," while his colleague suggested that the new two hundred mile limit created a "bonanza attitude. It was El Dorado again" (quoted in Finlayson 1994, 26). Fisheries biologist Richard

Haedrich elaborated: "The idea was that the streets were paved with fish and that now that the Europeans were gone it would come to the Canadians" (quoted in McKibben 1998, 64).

In those heady days, provincial loan boards showered fishermen with loans at concessionary interest rates to help them buy bigger boats and more-sophisticated gear. Between 1977 and 1982, fishermen's indebtedness to the boards increased by 400 percent to $219.4 million. Provincial officials apparently gave little thought to the likelihood of repayment of their 7,917 outstanding loans. By 1982, almost half of the loans made to Newfoundland's fishermen were overdue (Kirby 1982, 76–77).

Loans provided just one of many kinds of assistance. Governments made cash grants to fishermen and fish processors. They created tax exemptions for fuel and equipment. They acquired equity in insolvent processing companies. They subsidized workers with various unemployment programs. They purchased canned fish for international food aid. Public expenditures on management, surveillance, enforcement, infrastructure, and programs ranging from vessel insurance to bait service added to the tab. By one estimate, public expenditures on the Atlantic fisheries reached $8 billion during the 1980s (Harris 1998, 78).[2]

Newfoundland attracted the most assistance. All told, between 1981 and 1990, federal and provincial net outlays for Newfoundland's fisheries amounted to $2.934 billion—far in excess of the

2. Other countries are no strangers to the patterns so familiar to Atlantic Canadians. Since the French began subsidizing their fisheries in 1815, governments have actively promoted both increases in the numbers of fishermen and advances in the technology they use (Kurlansky 1997, 118). One study concludes that governments around the world subsidize their fisheries to the tune of U.S.$21 billion a year ("Loaves and Fishes" 1998, 13). The World Wildlife Fund estimates annual subsidies to the world's fishing industry to be between U.S.$16 billion and U.S$32 billion (Mittelstaedt 1998). Another estimate puts the annual subsidy figure at U.S.$54 billion, a considerable sum, given that the industry produces only U.S.$70 billion of fish each year (Harris 1998, 325).

value of the catch. The most generous subsidies took the form of unemployment insurance (UI) benefits, which, after netting out premiums, amounted to $1.647 billion during that period (Schrank, Skoda, Parsons, and Roy 1995, 362, 367). During the 1980s, Newfoundland's fishermen relied on UI for an ever-increasing portion of their income. By 1990, they were receiving $1.60 in benefits for every dollar they earned in the fishery, up from $0.96 in 1981 (Auditor General 1997, 14-11).

Unemployment insurance (renamed employment insurance in 1997) supported generations of Atlantic fishermen and processors. Introduced in the mid-1950s, the program became progressively more generous; it simultaneously evolved from an insurance program to a permanent income-transfer program. In 1971, six weeks of fishing bought five weeks of benefits; by 1976, eight weeks of fishing bought twenty-seven weeks of benefits (Schrank et al. 1995, 368). Although eligibility requirements became somewhat stricter in the 1990s, for many years plant workers had to work only ten weeks to qualify for forty-two weeks of benefits (May and Hollett 1995, 55).

Unemployment benefits, particularly for those who were already financially secure, became quite ample. In 1992, the average UI benefit for fishing families in Atlantic Canada was $12,219—a far cry from the days of the Great Depression, when Newfoundland was still a British colony and unemployed fishermen received allowances of six cents a day (Kurlansky 1997, 178). In 1992, fishing families with incomes at or above $80,000 received on average $16,668 from UI; benefits for this wealthiest group of recipients comprised 9 percent of the total benefits paid to fishing families (May and Hollett 1995, 66–67).

By the early 1980s, UI was widely taken for granted as a natural part of fishermen's incomes. The 1982 Task Force on Atlantic Fisheries, in recommending objectives to guide Atlantic fisheries policy, said that "employment in the Atlantic fishing industry should be maximized subject to the constraint that those employed receive a reasonable income as a result of fishery-related activities, including fishery-related income transfer payments" (Kirby 1982, 186). The task force called the UI program vital to the achievement of this objective and rejected the notion that the sums transferred through it should be reduced (Kirby 1982, 312).

In fact, some have suggested that fishermen now consider UI itself, rather than fish, as a resource—indeed, another part of Canada's natural resources—to be tapped (Burke and Brander 1996, 12). As former fisheries minister John Crosbie explained:

> The way of life of the outports of Newfoundland has been centred on the fishery from the earliest days, but the nature of people's dependency has changed. In recent years, their economic survival has depended less on the fish they caught than on their ability to qualify for financial-support programs. Federal unemployment insurance is the lifeblood of rural Newfoundland. (Crosbie 1997, 384)

Unemployment Insurance to Ensure Unemployment

Lifeblood or not, it is hard to imagine that anything could have so effectively threatened rural Newfoundland's fishing communities as did their reliance on unemployment insurance. The perverse effects of UI have become tragically clear: It created a dependence that it could not sustain, leaving tens of thousands of fishermen, processors, and their families wondering how they will survive in the coming years.

Unemployment insurance encouraged people to remain in communities that lacked any promise of a viable future. More insidiously, the program prompted young people to quit school. Although forgoing education seemed like a rational occupational choice—youths could earn more in the UI-supplemented fishery, which required no formal education, than they could working in many year-round jobs—the decision left them ill-equipped for other jobs when the fishery collapsed (May and Hollett 1995, 43–45). The UI program also subtly eroded the work ethic of Atlantic Canadians and threatened the pride that accompanies self-sufficiency.

Unemployment insurance's most egregious legacy was its contribution to overcapacity in the fishing industry—overcapacity that eventually led to the collapse of the groundfish stocks. The program lured workers into an industry that could not support them. In Newfoundland, the seven years following the introduction of UI saw a 33 percent increase in the number of inshore fishermen, even as the average fisherman's catch fell by 50 percent (Harris 1998, 67–68). And again, during the fifteen years following 1972's changes to the UI system, the number of fishermen doubled and the number of fish processors almost tripled. John Crosbie explained the numbers: "They weren't catching or processing any more fish. What they were doing was spreading the work around so that everyone could qualify for UI" (Crosbie 1997, 385).

Indeed, the goal of enabling more workers to qualify for UI drove much of the fishery expansion of the 1970s and 1980s. Shortly before his retirement, Newfoundland Premier Clyde Wells described the complicity of provincial governments, the federal government, industry, and the workers themselves:

> To some degree both governments encouraged the use of the fisheries to create qualification for unemployment insurance. . . . They [the people on the UI system] were induced! They were shown methods by governments as to how to do it! In some cases fish plants and make-work projects would hire workers for a certain number of weeks and then lay off those workers and hire others, so that they'd all have qualification for unemployment insurance. This was done with the approbation and knowledge of both the federal and provincial governments. (quoted in Harris 1998, 176)

According to Wells, putting people on UI "was the easier way to cope with the political problem of unemployment" (quoted in Harris

1998, 176). For the provinces, which feared having to support the unemployed with welfare, the federally funded UI program was also the economically attractive alternative.

As the number of workers in the fishing industry increased, so, thanks to other subsidies, did the capacity of their boats and plants. The 1993 Task Force on Incomes and Adjustment in the Atlantic Fishery summed up the problem: "Too many harvesters use too many boats with too much gear trying to supply too many processing plants by finding and catching too few fish" (Cashin 1993, 14). The artificially inflated workforce, with its artificially inflated investments, pressured politicians to maintain artificially inflated catch limits. Regardless of the state of the fish stocks, there were loans to repay and UI benefits to qualify for. The politicians complied, perpetuating a vicious circle that only the collapse of the fishery could break.

The unintended but ultimately tragic consequences of Canada's most generous fisheries subsidies were fittingly described in a study of the UI "trap" in Atlantic Canada:

> The 1956 introduction of UI fishing benefits probably seemed the act of a caring, sharing society. We believe, however, that . . . by encouraging many rural Atlantic Canadians to enter and remain in the fish-harvesting industry, UI has contributed to its overcapacity and hence to the destruction of the groundfisheries stock. . . . In other words, UI has played an active role in the current tragedy of the oceans. (May and Hollett 1995, 62)

Intensifying the tragedy was its foreseeability. The overcapacity that eventually killed the Atlantic groundfishing industry was hardly a new, or unrecognized, problem. Even as governments pushed expansion in the 1970s, cooler heads warned that too many fishermen chased too few fish. As early as 1970, a federal cabinet memorandum described a fishing industry that was overcapitalized by a ratio of more than two to one; it estimated that Canada's commercial catch could be harvested by 40 percent of the boats, half as much gear, and half the number of fishermen (Auditor General 1997, 14-15).

The Department of the Environment's 1976 *Policy for Canada's Commercial Fisheries* acknowledged the overcapacity problem in both the catching and processing sectors. But no sooner had the department warned that the long-term viability of the industry depended on getting rid of this structural defect than did it start backpedaling. Any change that occurred would have to be gradual and would have to present acceptable alternative opportunities. "Where adverse social side-effects such as reduced employment opportunities can be kept within acceptable limits, restructuring should proceed. Where damage to the community would outweigh advantages in the short run the changes must be postponed" (Dept. Environ. 1976, 56). How the department proposed to reduce capacity without eliminating jobs it did not say.

To be sure, the government of the day faced enormous pressures to expand, given the boom mentality that followed the declaration of the two hundred mile limit. Pressures came not only from fishermen and fish processors, some of whom even took out newspaper advertisements promoting fleet expansion, but also from provincial governments that worked up ambitious fishery development plans costing hundreds of millions of dollars (Kirby 1982, 19–21). And so, despite repeated warnings of the dangers of overcapacity, the industry, assisted by the government, grew apace. Between 1974 and 1981, the number of licensed fishermen in Atlantic Canada increased by 45 percent, to approximately 53,500, while the number of processing facilities increased by 35 percent, to 700 (Kirby 1982, 31).[3]

3. A comparison of the Icelandic and Canadian fisheries suggests that by the late 1970s something was terribly amiss. Although Atlantic Canadians landed and processed only 82 percent of the amount of fish caught by Icelanders, Canadian fishermen far outnumbered Icelandic fishermen. There were ten Canadian fishermen for every Icelandic fisherman and two Canadian plant workers for every

In 1981, yet another federal department—this time the DFO—warned of overcapacity and promised a major policy shift. The government would no longer base fisheries management on the "expansionist development philosophy" of the previous decade. It would harmonize assistance programs "to provide a better match between available resources and harvesting and processing capacity" (DFO 1981, iv–v). Despite the promising words, nothing changed. Nor did change follow the warning, issued by the Task Force on Atlantic Fisheries the following year, that if the government did not deal effectively with the incentives to expand, "overcapacity will forever plague the fishery and rob it of vitality" (Kirby 1982, 32). And still no change followed the 1989 Scotia-Fundy Groundfish Task Force's conclusion that "excessive harvesting capacity was a major obstacle to a turnaround in the fishery, and that overcapacity and overinvestment had to be reduced as quickly as possible" (Auditor General 1997, 14-18).

By the time the 1993 Task Force on Incomes and Adjustment in the Atlantic Fishery issued its predictable warnings about overcapacity, it was too late. The groundfish stocks had collapsed. Decades of subsidies, amounting to billions of dollars, had created only a false economy based on a resource that no longer existed. Governments had paid people to destroy the fishery.[4]

Icelandic worker (Schrank et al. 1995, 358–359). Although not directly comparable because of differences in the species caught and the quality and value of the product, these figures suggest considerable inefficiencies in the Atlantic Canadian fishery.

4. The world over, subsidies have resulted in fleets technologically capable of, and economically bound to pursue, increasingly unsustainable catches. The World Wildlife Fund estimates that "two-thirds of the world's fishing fleet could be eliminated without affecting sustainable fish harvests" (Mittelstaedt 1998). Two former senior managers in the United Nations Food and Agriculture Organization's Fisheries Department calculate that the world's industrial fishing capacity increased by 22 percent between 1992 and 1997 (Fitzpatrick and Newton 1998). Many stocks will doubtless be unable to withstand the additional pressures created by this new capacity. The Food and Agriculture Organization reports that at the

The Fruits of Canadian Citizenship

Ironically, the collapse of the Atlantic groundfishery did not mean that the government could stop spending money. On the contrary, the federal government has already spent more than $4 billion on Atlantic groundfish programs for the 1990s and shows no signs of slowing down (Auditor General 1977, 14-22; Anderssen 1998b). Upon closing the northern cod fishery in July 1992, John Crosbie announced an interim assistance program that would provide fishermen and plant workers with benefits of $225 a week for ten weeks. Newfoundland Premier Clyde Wells immediately wrote to the prime minister, protesting a level of compensation "that for many is less than welfare. That, Prime Minister, cannot be the fruits of Canadian citizenship in this province or any other" (quoted in Harris 1998, 164). Within two weeks, the Canadian government announced a new deal, the Northern Cod Adjustment and Recovery Program, which would provide benefits of up to $406 a week.

The bulk of federal spending in the 1990s has gone to The Atlantic Groundfish Strategy (TAGS). That $1.9-billion program initially included retraining, license buyback, and early retirement elements, with the goal of reducing capacity by 50 percent. But with more than 40,000—rather than the anticipated 26,500—people eligible for the program, and with a budget insufficient to support these

---

beginning of the 1990s, about 69 percent of the world's conventional species were fully fished or overfished: 44 percent of the world's marine stocks were fully to heavily exploited, 16 percent were overexploited, 6 percent were depleted, and 3 percent were very slowly recovering from overfishing (UN Food and Agriculture Organization 1995, 8). In the United States, the National Marine Fisheries Service estimates that at least ninety-six species—nearly one-third of the U.S. marine fish stocks—are either overfished or nearing that condition ("One-Third of Marine Species" 1997). As conventional, high-value stocks decline, fishermen are turning their attention to species lower on the food chain, often jeopardizing both their economic returns and the earlier targeted species' chances of recovery (McGinn 1998).

numbers, the government soon reallocated TAGS funds from capacity reduction to income support (Auditor General 1997, 15-10). Not surprisingly, given its revised mandate, TAGS miserably failed to wean people from the industry. Even leaving the program did not signify independence. In a peculiar twist, as their TAGS benefits ran out, recipients could return to the UI program: The government decided in 1997 that drawing TAGS benefits should be considered a "labour force attachment" for the purpose of qualifying for UI (Harrigan 1998, 14). As the program neared its close, almost 25,000 fishermen and processors continued to draw benefits; the great majority expected to see a follow-up assistance program when TAGS expired (Harrigan 1998, 5, 7). The government was not to disappoint them. In June 1998, it approved a new $550-million assistance package for East Coast fishermen (Greenspon 1998). Within days, amid howls of protest over its stinginess, it upped the promised assistance to $730 million (Anderssen 1998b).

The Atlantic Groundfish Strategy made continued attachment to the fishery profitable, even in the absence of fish. Little wonder, then, that getting people out of the industry has proved considerably harder than getting people into the industry. Six years after the closure of the northern cod fishery, overcapacity remains a serious problem. Virtually everyone agrees on the need to reduce the size of the fishery dramatically, although estimates of the required reductions vary. The Department of Human Resources reports a general consensus that the fishery can support half as many fishermen and plant workers as it has in the past (Harrigan 1998, 9). The Fisheries Resource Conservation Council has recommended greater capacity reductions, ranging from a factor of two to a factor of four (FRCC 1996a, 8; 1997, 16).

Without considerable capacity reductions, the Atlantic fishery has little chance of recovering. Excessive capacity will create enormous pressures on the resource and on those who manage it. Fishermen and processors will urge politicians to reopen the fisheries prematurely and to allow unsustainable catches. If experience is any indicator, the politicians will prove unable to resist.

Messy Information

Can we forgive successive governments for creating overcapacity and allowing overfishing? Would any fisheries managers have made such mistakes? Unquestionably not. Overcapacity and overfishing were not so much innocent mistakes as they were calculated political decisions. Politicians, and the bureaucrats serving them, were warned time and again that the fishery could not sustain the pressures to which they subjected it after the declaration of the two hundred mile management zone. As the fishery expanded, scientists and fishermen alike cautioned that fish stocks were declining. Governments chose to ignore—and worse, to suppress—these warnings.

The first warnings came from Newfoundland's inshore fishermen, the traditional small-boat fishermen who operate during the months when cod migrate inshore to feast on capelin. When, in 1982, the size of both the inshore catch and the individual fish making up the catch began to decline, fishermen accused the offshore fleet of fishing the stocks too heavily. Although inshore catches continued to fall—between 1982 and 1986, landings dropped from 113,000 tonnes to 72,000 tonnes—and inshore fishermen became increasingly vocal about the perils of overfishing, the government dismissed their concerns. Federal Fisheries Information Officer Bernard Brown described the government's attitude: "Essentially they were telling the inshore fishermen who were creating all the uproar about the destruction of the stocks, that you don't know what you're talking about" (quoted in Finlayson 1994, 107).

The government's reluctance to listen to the inshore fishermen reflected, in part, the difficulty that a centralized bureaucracy faces when dealing with decentralized information. The Department of

Fisheries and Oceans obtained from the offshore fishery most of the data that it relied on to assess stocks and set catch limits. The department found it far easier to get information from fifty offshore trawlers owned by a few companies than from tens of thousands of widely dispersed small-boat fishermen using different gear in different ways. Information from the former was systematic, uniform, and quantifiable, while that from the latter, often anecdotal, could not be readily quantified or computerized. In the words of Information Officer Brown, "You just don't want to deal with that kind of messy information" (quoted in Finlayson 1994, 111). Edward Sandeman, former director of the DFO's Science Branch, defended that attitude:

> There is a fundamental reason why, to a large extent, we ignored the inshore cod fishery. The reason being that it was extremely difficult to study. . . . It was just too big an area to cover with the people we had. . . . [T]he comments of the vast majority [of inshore fishermen] are self-serving and extremely restricted in geographical range. For the most part the majority of them have a litany of mumbo-jumbo which they bring forth each time you talk to them. . . . [T]hey were totally unscientific! (quoted in Finlayson 1994, 109–110)

In 1986, the Newfoundland Inshore Fisheries Association became more scientific. It commissioned three biologists to review the government's stock assessments. Their review criticized the government's sources of data, its statistical procedures, and its conclusions about the status of the northern cod stock. It charged that the government, systematically interpreting uncertain information in the most optimistic light, had overestimated the fish biomass (the total weight of the stock) by as much as 55 percent each year; as a result, the government had permitted catch levels that had prevented the stock from recovering from overfishing by foreign boats in the 1970s. True to its habit of rebutting rather than communicating, the DFO dismissed the review as superficial (Finlayson 1994, 35–38, 110; Hutchings, Walters, and Haedrich 1997, 1201).

An Unsteady Hand

Although the inshore fishermen sounded the loudest warnings, they were by no means alone. Scientists within the government also expressed uncertainty about the stock assessments upon which their political masters based catch limits. The scientists' cautions about the unreliability of their data and conclusions, however, were often stifled by a bureaucracy intent on simplifying its findings for political or public consumption. The institutional structure of the DFO could not accommodate ambiguity or uncertainty. Decision makers wanted simple, unproblematic information (Finlayson 1994, 138–139). As a result, scientists were frequently, in the words of Brian Morrissey, former assistant deputy minister of science, "drawing a firm line with a very unsteady hand" (quoted in Finlayson 1994, 133).

Insisting on an appearance of unanimity, the DFO always presented its stock assessments and its recommendations regarding allowable catches as consensus documents (Finlayson 1994, 39). Former employees have complained that the department's determination to have a single official opinion compromised the quality and effectiveness of its work. Stock assessment documents failed to reflect the full range of scientific opinion regarding the health of fish stocks (Hutchings, Walters, and Haedrich 1997, 1198–1204). Senior bureaucrats and politicians accordingly set catch limits without access to information about the full implications of their decisions.

The demand for consensus did not just impede the decision-making process, it also limited intellectual discourse within the department. Former DFO biologist Jeffrey Hutchings described the department's tendency to reject thinking that challenged established positions: "It seemed to behave almost as a tribe, as tribal groups. It was group thinking and group action. . . . And if you got someone from outside of that group analyzing what you've done, I think there was a tendency to downplay or, possibly, discount it" (quoted in Harris 1998, 190). The result could be disastrous. As

Ransom Myers noted, “bureaucratic and authoritarian control over scientific results results in pseudoscience, not science. Such a system will inevitably fail and lead to scientific blunders” (Commons 1997b, 935–940).

In addition to minimizing uncertainty and creating the illusion of consensus, DFO scientists frequently put an inappropriately positive spin on ambiguous information. In assessing cod stock sizes, they tended to interpret ambiguity too optimistically, exploiting the “interpretive flexibility” of the data (Finlayson 1994, 30). Sometimes they did so to meet their own ends. Leslie Harris, chair of the 1989 Northern Cod Review Panel, commented on scientists’ inclination to use data to confirm their projections: “I think our scientists saw their data from a particular perspective that the stock was growing at the rate they had projected, and the data were sort of made to fit the equation” (Harris 1998, 141).

Other times, scientists selectively presented or interpreted data to meet the needs of their political masters. The scientists understood that they derived their funding and authority from politicians who relied on their help to achieve political objectives (Finlayson 1994, 150–151). This understanding tainted the stock assessment process. One critic charged that “the actual dynamics of the CAFSAC [Canadian Atlantic Fisheries Scientific Advisory Committee] process shows it to be more a forum for projecting the political interests of the state into the scientific construction of reality than the other way around” (Finlayson 1994, 143). Jake Rice, former head of DFO’s Groundfish Division, admitted that there were times when political realities prevented him and his colleagues from disclosing the full scientific truth: “Or you can only tell half the answer because the other half is still being debated in Ottawa for its political sensitivities. I, and no other scientist in the Department that I know of, have never been asked to lie. But we certainly have, at various times, been discouraged from revealing the whole truth. Every government has to do that to its civil servants” (quoted in Finlayson 1994, 115).

The tendency to ignore uncertainty and to optimistically interpret ambiguous data affected the political bureaucracy even more severely than the scientific bureaucracy. One DFO employee explained that although decision makers did not falsify documents, "they optimized what they had. The politicians and the senior bureaucrats would run away, pick the very best numbers and come out and present them in the very best light. They would hide any negative notions—numbers, information, anything at all that took the gloss off what they had presented. Any attempt by anyone on the inside to present a different view was absolutely squashed" (quoted in Harris 1998, 301). John Crosbie admitted to sharing this tendency toward optimism: "We have opted for the upper end of the scientific advice always striving to get the last pound of fish" (quoted in Charnetski, Winqvist, Wissing, and Vilkko 1994, 59).

The habit was a long-established one. The 1982 Task Force on Atlantic Fisheries, for example, relied on explicitly tentative scientific documents—documents rife with warnings about their untestable assumptions. But the warnings never made it into the task force's report, which overflowed with wildly optimistic forecasts of stock growth. The northern cod stock, the task force predicted, would grow explosively; within five years, the allowable catch would increase by 75 percent (Kirby 1982, 27, 241). These predictions encouraged further expansion of the industry, justifying unsupportable investments in harvesting and processing. "The government of the day," commented Jake Rice, "did no one a service to drop the qualifiers" from the original scientific documents (quoted in Finlayson 1994, 8).

Scientists who were aware of and concerned about the government's selective use or overly optimistic interpretation of data could not express their concerns. Jeffrey Hutchings explained that public employees must not challenge the government's position: "For a government scientist to publicly disagree or publicly identify scientific risks or scientific deficiencies in the minister's decision is to publicly disagree with and potentially embarrass the minister, and it's simply not allowed" (Commons 1997a, 940–945).

Indeed, suppression inheres in the rules of the civil service. The federal government's communications guidelines advise ministers to "ensure that communications with the public is managed . . . in accordance with the priorities of government." "It is not appropriate," the government warns, for public servants "to discuss advice or recommendations tendered to Ministers, or to speculate about policy deliberations or future policy decisions" (Office of the Prime Minister 1984). The federal media-relations policy authorizes designated spokespersons to speak to the media only on matters of fact or approved government policy (Treasury 1995, F-2). Furthermore, the collective agreement covering DFO scientists specifies that "the employer may suggest revisions to a publication and may withhold approval to publish" (quoted in Canadian Press 1997a). Although the government defends this restriction on the grounds that it applies to policy issues rather than data, it cannot be unaware that rules limiting a scientist's discussions to data make impossible any meaningful communication, since even the simplest facts often have policy implications. The DFO's departmental discipline guide goes even further in its efforts to stifle employees: in the same category as fraud and assault, "public criticism of the employer" may be grounds for dismissal (Canadian Press 1997a).

Such rules intimidated scientists concerned about the cod stocks and suppressed their valid, if controversial, findings. When the House of Commons Standing Committee on Fisheries and Oceans held an inquiry into the role of science in fisheries management, successive witnesses testified about flagrant intimidation. The witnesses were not merely disgruntled former employees. Indeed, Steven Hindle, president of the Professional Institute of the Public Service of Canada, the union representing DFO scientists, appeared on behalf of scientists throughout the department who feared the repercussions of speaking out themselves. He described a "climate of intimidation and mistrust" within the DFO, saying that the department suppressed data, ignored or diluted scientific advice, prevented scientists from publishing or speaking publicly about their findings, and threatened the career advancement—and even the jobs—of dissenters (Commons 1998a, 1010–1025).

As the cod disaster brewed, the DFO did not merely control the information flowing from the department to the public; it also limited the flow of information within the bureaucracy, preventing critical knowledge from reaching upper-level decision makers. Several instances involved the Canadian Atlantic Fisheries Scientific Advisory Committee (CAFSAC), which provided information on stocks to the Atlantic Groundfish Advisory Committee (AGAC), the body that advised senior management about catches. In 1990, CAFSAC's discussion of a conservation-based catch limit for 1991 did not even make it onto AGAC's agenda. Thus, those who ultimately chose a limit of 190,000 tonnes may not even have known that the option of 100,000 tonnes would have allowed for a sustainable catch (Hutchings, Walters, and Haedrich 1997, 1200).

A similar omission occurred two years later. On July 2, 1992, the first day of the northern cod moratorium, the chair of CAFSAC's groundfish subcommittee was scheduled to make a presentation to AGAC. He intended to give AGAC an overview of all of Canada's Atlantic cod stocks—an overview that would indicate that because stocks other than the northern cod were also being overfished, their levels, too, were declining. Apparently senior officials did not want AGAC to hear that the other cod stocks could be in serious trouble. They cancelled the presentation. Jeffrey Hutchings later speculated that the cancellation may have been motivated by the presentation's inconsistency with the deputy minister's announcement, two days earlier, that the troubles in the northern cod fishery were unique (Commons 1997a, 945–950).

Of course, it soon became obvious that stock declines were the rule rather than the exception. By the following fall, the DFO had closed the cod fisheries off the southern coast of Newfoundland and in the Gulf of St. Lawrence. Ransom Myers described the damage done by the suppression of information responsible for the delay in closing the fisheries: "This is a crime beyond imagination. During this year delay, 70 percent of the remaining cod were removed and this caused a much greater collapse in the rest of eastern Canada than was needed. We could have stopped fishing then. It was a direct decision, a bureaucratic decision, to suppress the information" (Commons 1997b, 945–950).

Whistling Past the Graveyard

Despite formidable barriers, ominous news about the health of the cod stocks did emerge. As early as 1986, scientists within the DFO cautioned that their colleagues had grossly overestimated stock sizes, and, as a result, had set Total Allowable Catches (TACs) at unsustainable levels. That year, two DFO scientists estimated the size of 1984's northern cod spawning stock to be less than half that officially predicted, raising the possibility that fishermen had been catching between 40 and 60 percent of the available stock, rather than the 20 percent generally thought to be sustainable (Harris 1998, 100).

Other DFO scientists soon voiced their own concerns. In November 1986, George Winters, head of the Pelagic Fish, Shellfish, and Marine Mammals division of DFO's Newfoundland Region, presented a paper to CAFSAC dismissing his department's northern cod stock assessment as "*non gratum anus rodentum*": it was not worth a rat's rear end. Winters maintained that the DFO had overestimated the size of the cod stock since 1977 and, as a result, had recommended inappropriately high catches. Documenting a statistically significant link between high offshore and low inshore catch levels, he concluded that "the decline in the inshore catches since 1982 has been due to the increase in the offshore exploitation rate" (quoted in Hutchings, Walters, and Haedrich 1997, 1200). The committee agreed with at least some of Winters's findings: Catch levels between 1977 and 1985 had been twice as high as they should have been.

Catch limits for 1987 reflected none of the warnings coming from scientists. Nor did the following year bring more restraint. Although the Task Group on Newfoundland Inshore Fisheries, which was commissioned to investigate the drop in inshore catches, recommended that 1988's TAC for northern cod be held at the previous year's level, the government insisted on raising it by 10,000 tonnes, to 266,000 tonnes (Harris 1998, 106). In its public response to the task group, the DFO glossed over concerns about both the volume of catches and the sizes of the fish in those catches. It affirmed its confidence in both its science and management:

> The Department of Fisheries and Oceans prides itself on world-class scientific capability. The unprecedented rebuilding of the Northern Cod resource since 1977 is ample testimony to sound management practices based on good scientific advice. Having nurtured the resource to a good stage of health overall, the department is now setting out to enhance that all-important achievement by addressing more intensively and more comprehensively other problems in the fishery. (quoted in Finlayson 1994, 53)

By the end of 1988, biological reality made a mockery of the DFO's optimism. CAFSAC confirmed what it had suggested two years earlier: Throughout much of the decade, fishermen had been catching northern cod at twice the sustainable rate. The committee advised the government to reduce 1989's allowable catch of northern cod from 266,000 tonnes to 125,000 tonnes. But those in charge went into denial, setting the TAC at 235,000 tonnes—an astonishing 88 percent higher than recommended (Harris 1998, 106–107).

In fact, setting the TAC at unsustainable levels had already become departmental policy. Earlier that year, the DFO had introduced what it called "the 50 percent rule," allowing managers to ignore their long-standing (if rarely achieved) target of limiting catches to about 20 percent of the spawning stock. If stock estimates declined and if the traditional target would mean large adjustments for the industry, managers could phase in catch reductions rather than imposing tough measures at once: They could recommend TACs halfway between the current catches and the 20 percent target. In other words, when presented with evidence of abruptly declining stocks—a circumstance demanding immediate action—fisheries managers could drag their feet. But even this rule "institutionalizing" overfishing (FRCC 1996a, 7) did not go far enough for the government, which could not bring itself to impose a quota as low as the rule required.

John Crosbie, who announced the 1989 TAC with Fisheries Minister Tom Siddon (and who would become fisheries minister two years later), explained his government's decision to disregard its own scientists' advice:

> A politician has to be concerned about protecting both the fish stocks and the livelihood of fishermen. We couldn't suddenly cut the TAC by more than half. If we did, for historic and political reasons, we would have had to give priority to inshore fishermen or accept the death of their outport communities. Cutting the total allowable catch to 125,000 tonnes overnight would have wiped out the offshore fishery. Two large Canadian companies were primarily involved in the offshore fishery—National Sea Products in Halifax and Fishery Products International in St. John's; both had fish-processing plants along the south and east coasts of Newfoundland. If we accepted the new TAC recommended by the scientists, both National Sea and Fishery Products International would have gone bankrupt. "We are dealing with thousands of human beings, who live and breathe and eat and need jobs . . . so we are not going to, because of the formula . . . immediately go to a quota of 125,000 tonnes," I told a press conference in St. John's. (Crosbie 1997, 378)

With this announcement, the government established a pattern that it would follow until the cod stocks disappeared. Scientists would warn of serious stock declines and advise dramatic catch reductions; the government, afraid of throwing fishermen and processors out of work, would merely inch the TAC downward. The government's refusal to act quickly destroyed the cod stocks, and, with them, the jobs it wanted so desperately to protect.

Historian Leslie Harris, who in 1989 chaired the Northern Cod Review Panel—a review that savaged the DFO's data and methodologies, suggested that the stock size was half of what the DFO had previously estimated, and warned that recent catch levels could not be maintained (Finlayson 1994, 9, 66)—later commented that a more responsive government could have averted the cod catastrophe. "Even in 1988–89, if we had strictly followed the rules then and said, 'Okay, we're going to chop the fishing season from 260,000 tonnes down to 120,000,' then that might have saved the day—probably would have saved the day" (Harris 1998, 296).

But the government just could not bring itself to act decisively. Although warned by scientists that stock levels threatened the very survival of the northern cod fishery, it set the 1990 TAC at 197,000 tonnes. John Crosbie recalled:

> Although Siddon and I knew we were walking a very thin line between scientific advice and economic reality, we were trying to keep the TAC high enough to permit the continuation of part of the offshore fishery and save jobs of people employed by at least one of the three threatened plants owned by Fishery Products International (FPI). . . . I believed, if the quota was a bit larger [than that recommended by the Harris panel], FPI might be able to keep its fish plant open at Trepassey in my constituency. (Crosbie 1997, 379)

Crosbie, in other words, had his eye on votes rather than on the fish, illustrating what he would later describe as "an understandable, if misguided, tendency among politicians of all stripes to put the interests of fishermen—who were voters—ahead of the cod, who weren't" (Crosbie 1997, 373).

Meanwhile, what was happening with annual allowable catches for northern cod was also happening with the allocations of catches of other cod stocks. In March 1991, one hundred fishermen vandalized a DFO office to protest the early closure of the cod fishery off southwestern Newfoundland. The department had closed the fishery because fishermen had caught too many redfish along with the cod. After the protest, it took only two days for the government to find an additional redfish quota and to reopen the cod fishery. The following month, a similar scenario occurred. After sixty fishermen staged a protest at a DFO office, bureaucrats added three hundred tonnes to the fishermen's original four hundred tonne quota (Harris 1998, 138).

Commercial fisherman Stuart Beaton explained that there was nothing unusual in these politically motivated allocations:

> Time and again in the past twenty years, fishermen, plant workers, and companies have hit the streets in often violent protest because the quota for a given year or region was exhausted and there were boats to pay for, mouths to feed, UI to qualify for, or elections in the near future. Most of the time more fish was found. "Paper fish" as it is known. The resource was sacrificed on the altar of political expediency until, at last, the fish refused to cooperate. (Beaton, 1998)

The government brought the TAC for northern cod down by another 7,000 tonnes in 1991. That the stocks could not support a 190,000 tonne catch soon became obvious. Try as they might, fishermen could not catch more than 127,000 tonnes (Harris 1998, 129).

In October 1991, Leslie Harris shared CBC airtime with Brian Morrissey, DFO's assistant deputy minister for science. After the former expressed fears for the very survival of the species, the latter insisted that the cod stock was growing. In the words of Michael Harris, author of the most damning book yet about the cod collapse, "Ottawa's whistling past the graveyard was getting loud enough to wake the dead" (Harris 1998, 141). Ottawa whistled its way into 1992, reducing the northern cod TAC by just 5,000 tonnes. Again, John Crosbie defended the decision: "I'm not going to carry out advice of theirs that I think is wrong. I'm not going to listen to advice that says, oh, reduce the TAC for the northern cod to 125,000 tonnes when there's no scientific advice that says this should be done, or must be done. I'm not going to do something that I think is wrong for Canada" (quoted in Harris 1998, 144).

Ottawa's bravado made even the big offshore trawling companies nervous. Fisheries Products International President Vic Young admitted, "I can't say if they're right or wrong. I can say I'm very uncomfortable with it. Why? Because I now see that there's no fish in 2J [the fishing zone off the southern half of Labrador]. That makes everyone very, very uncomfortable" (quoted in Harris 1998, 146).

It soon became apparent that even the 125,000-tonne TAC that Crosbie had sneered at just months earlier would be hopelessly high. In February 1992, CAFSAC estimated that the northern cod's spawning biomass—the total weight of fish mature enough to spawn—had decreased to 130,000 tonnes and recommended that the TAC for the first half of 1992 be cut to 25,000 tonnes. Crosbie later explained that he was under tremendous pressure: "The political pressures on me . . . to do something—anything—about the fishery made the job almost unbearable" (Crosbie 1997, 372). Perhaps for this reason, while he followed CAFSAC's advice, announcing a six-month TAC of 25,000 tonnes, he maintained that the TAC for the year would be 120,000 tonnes (Harris 1998, 154). But the fish could not support such plans. By July, CAFSAC estimated that the northern cod stock had fallen to between 48,000 and 108,000 tonnes (Harris 1998, 161). Only then did Crosbie impose a moratorium on fishing for northern cod. Was he too late? Crosbie has considered that question: "I wish I could say that we weren't too late in closing the fishery. I wish I could say the northern cod and other species are recovering and that the seas off Newfoundland will once again teem with fish as they did for the first five hundred years of our history. I wish I could say it, but I can't. Not yet. Probably never" (Crosbie 1997, 401).

Plus ça change . . .

Upon taking over the fisheries portfolio in 1996, Fred Mifflin made promising noises about rearranging the government's priorities. "Unless science comes before political, economic, business, social, or other considerations," he admitted, "fisheries are going to be in trouble" (quoted in Harris 1998, 251). Trouble appeared just around the corner. In September, Mifflin, claiming that "the recovery so far has been absolutely phenomenal," announced a weekend-long "food fishery" for cod (Southam News 1996). For three days, fishermen would be allowed to catch up to ten cod per day for their personal use. Fishermen went wild. Over the course of that and a second weekend, they took 21,944 boats onto the water and caught 1,230 tonnes of cod; the effort equalled that of 93,000 people fishing for one day. The fishing alarmed scientists, who knew that the stocks remained extremely low and that any healthy schools should be preserved to permit stock recovery. The Fisheries Resource Conservation Council reiterated its recommendation against the food fishery, noting "the uncontrolled nature of this fishery and the grave consequences this poses for conservation" (FRCC 1996b, 8). A memo from one DFO cod expert sounded a distressingly familiar note: "I am disappointed and disheartened that important decisions are being made that disregard the scientific advice from this region" (quoted in Harris 1998, 230).

The June 1997 federal election again tested Mifflin's resolve to put science before politics. Politics won. In April, shortly before the election was called, Mifflin announced the reopening of the cod fisheries off Newfoundland's southern coast and in the northern Gulf of St. Lawrence. He said "it felt like Christmas" on announcing the reopening (quoted in Strauss 1997a). As irresistible as it must have been to play Santa Claus and to distribute goodies to the electorate, the government was in no position to give away the cod.

To be sure, Mifflin, in reopening the cod fisheries, had followed the advice of the Fisheries Resource Conservation Council. That the council might have given him advice he wished to hear would come as no surprise. The council consisted of members appointed by the minister, senior DFO bureaucrats, and delegates from provincial governments. Its mission included helping the government achieve not only its conservation objectives but also its social objectives for the fishery (FRCC 1997, A9). As the council noted in the introduction to its report recommending the reopening of the fisheries, "Minister, we are *your* conservation council" (FRCC 1996b, viii).

Even so, the council's recommendation came with a number of caveats:

> [T]he Council is recommending, for three of the cod stocks which were under moratorium, a reopening of commercial fishing at a small scale. These recommendations must not be seen as an indication that these stocks have returned to their historical levels of productivity. On the contrary, the Council remains extremely concerned with the status of these stocks. In their 1996 Stock Status Report on Atlantic Groundfish, DFO scientists have clearly indicated that "*Although the declines have been arrested, the rebuilding of groundfish stocks has only partially begun.*" The Council is concerned that the abundance of these stocks remains low, much below historical levels. Recruitment, while improving, remains poor. Growth, despite definite improvements in the condition of individual fish, remains poor. Environmental conditions, while somewhat improved, remain rather cold, particularly in the Gulf of St. Lawrence. (FRCC 1996b, 21)

The council stressed the scientific uncertainty about both the state of the stock and the effects of fishing upon it. Senior bureaucrats also admitted these uncertainties. William Doubleday, director-general for fisheries and oceans science at the DFO, noted "considerable uncertainties about abundances" and acknowledged that some scientists believed the risks entailed in reopening the fisheries to be unjustified (Strauss 1997a).

Indeed, a number of independent scientists expressed consternation over the decision. They warned that stocks were still dangerously low—perhaps as low as 1 or 2 percent of their former levels. Some stocks, they warned, were still declining. Reopening the fishery, they said, was a "risky and irresponsible" "pre-election ploy" (Hutchings 1997; Cox 1997). Fish ecologist Kim Bell, who had just spent three years studying the cod for the Committee on the Status of Endangered Wildlife in Canada and had concluded that the government should add the cod to the endangered species list, was appalled. "I can only hope that they know something I don't know," he said of the reopening of the fishery. "If they don't, it is a big mistake" ("Confidential Report" 1997, 18).

Mifflin also used other groundfish stocks as political pawns in the months leading up to the federal election. Shortly before the election call, he unilaterally increased, by 1,100 tonnes, Canada's share of the turbot quota in Davis Strait, between Baffin Island and Greenland. He did so without consulting Denmark, with which Canada shared the turbot quota. His action contravened the advice of the nearby Inuit, the Northwest Atlantic Fisheries Organization, and his own Fisheries Resource Conservation Council, all of whom were concerned about the dangers of depleting the turbot stock (Harris 1998, 310–311). A federal court later overturned the minister's decision and restored the original quota. In its judgment, the court criticized Mifflin for ignoring his assistant deputy minister, who had warned that raising the quota "would be completely irresponsible" ("Fisheries Lab Director" 1997).

Even the northern cod stock did not escape the fisheries minister's preelection politicking. Three days before the election, Mifflin told the *Evening Telegram* that the northern cod stock was showing encouraging signs, that he would ask the DFO to take a "special look" at it, and that he might be able to open a restricted fishery within a couple of years (Harris 1998, 260). His optimism was baseless. Less than a year later, the Fisheries Resource Conservation Council reported that the stock had been declining since the early 1990s, that the offshore portion of the stock was especially sparse, that few young fish had grown large enough to be considered "recruited" into the spawning biomass, and that natural mortality had increased. The council warned that unless the latter problem was addressed, "the chances for recovery for this stock are limited (at best)" (FRCC 1998, 33). Edward Sandeman, former director of science for the DFO in the Newfoundland region, sounded a less technical warning: "The last thing we should do is polish off the last bit of our remaining spawning stock. If we do there will be nothing" (Commons 1998a, 1055–1105).

Surrendering Control

For too much of the history of the Atlantic fisheries, the wrong people have been making the wrong decisions for the wrong reasons. Politicians have subsidized expansion of the fishery despite countless warnings of overcapacity. They have permitted catch levels far beyond those recommended by their own scientists. With an eye on the next election, they have chosen actions with short-term political payoffs and disastrous long-term consequences.

Faced with successive crises, politicians and bureaucrats have proven to be adept at studying the problems of Canada's troubled fishing industry. Studies provide excuses for inaction, which serves the government's interests. As fisheries biologist Carl Walters noted, bureaucrats "are rewarded not for effective action, but for making every problem disappear into an endless tangle of task force meetings and reviews" (Walters 1995, 49). An endless tangle indeed.

During the twentieth century, well over one hundred official commissions reviewed the numbers, consulted with stakeholders, and penned volumes of recommendations that have gathered dust on governments' shelves, in what one of those countless commissions described as a "traditional cycle of a crisis, followed by a study and perhaps a subsidy, then partial recovery, then back to a crisis again" (Kirby 1982, 3).

Although governments have succeeded in putting off some fisheries problems, they have not succeeded in solving those problems. And how could they? Too often, they themselves have been the causes of the problems. As member of Parliament and then-Fisheries Committee Chair George Baker said of the groundfish collapse, "This is not a natural disaster that's happened. This is a catastrophe made by man. We believe this collapse to a very large degree was caused by the government of Canada" (quoted in Eggertson 1998). Baker has since left the committee. Speculation abounds that he was fired for his sharp criticism of the government (Anderssen 1998c; MacCharles 1998).

Baker's recognition aside, no politicians or bureaucrats have been held accountable for making the decisions that destroyed the groundfish stocks. None have been fired, or demoted, or even—unlike the scientist who dared tell the truth about the collapse—reprimanded. In its 1998 report on the East Coast fisheries, the House of Commons Standing Committee on Fisheries and Oceans did recommend—fruitlessly, it turned out—"that senior DFO personnel who are viewed by the fishing community as being responsible for the crisis in the fishery be removed from the Department" (Commons 1998b, 40). The committee chose its words carefully, intentionally avoiding any suggestion that these bureaucrats be fired (Anderssen 1998a). Regardless, four committee members could not stomach even the mild recommendation; in a "supplementary opinion" they objected that "'witch hunt' justice is no justice at all" and insisted that removing bureaucrats "would certainly do nothing to restore trust between the fishing community and the Department of Fisheries and Oceans" (Commons 1998b, 47).

Fisheries Minister David Anderson echoed the dissenters' reservations about replacing senior bureaucrats, saying "I don't want to spend my time on a witch hunt" (quoted in Eggertson 1998). He had earlier said that although he was keeping an open mind, he had seen nothing so far that would demand that departmental bosses be held accountable for the loss of 40,000 jobs (Canadian Press 1998). MP Wayne Easter, the minister's parliamentary secretary, elaborated on his concerns: "How could you fire somebody? It's pretty hard to pinpoint one individual, or one department or one government as being responsible for the crisis in the fishery" (quoted in Ferguson 1998). As outrageous as such a remark would appear in the private sector, it was to some extent correct. Fault lies not only with a handful of individuals and a succession of ministers but also in the very nature of Canada's fisheries management system. The groundfish collapse illustrates that there is no place for the political in fisheries management.

The solution is not just to punish those responsible, but to depoliticize the fishery. In the words of fisherman Stuart Beaton, "If fisheries are to survive, governments will have to surrender control over them" (Beaton 1997).

Government control is simply not a sustainable method of fisheries management. Political pressures and bureaucratic structures being what they are, government managers have neither the incentives nor the tools to make the best long-term decisions. To worsen matters, when governments control fisheries, fishermen, too, follow a short-term agenda. Self-interest drives fishermen who have no control over fish stocks to catch as much as they can. If a fisherman leaves a fish uncaught to promote conservation, he has no guarantee that it will survive to spawn or to be caught the following year. More likely, it will end up in his competitors' nets—a threat that leads even the most honorable fisherman to race for fish and to catch more than he should.

The transfer of ownership and control of fisheries from central governments to fishermen, fishing companies, or fishing communities changes these incentives. Exclusive, permanent property rights promote stewardship. They ensure that fisheries owners will reap the benefits of conservation, thereby creating incentives to conserve. When fishermen have secure rights to future stocks, overfishing ceases to be in their interest. And as one economist said, "You don't have to be an economist to know that it doesn't pay to kill the goose that lays the golden egg" (Dales 1968, 64). With property rights, fishermen gain powerful incentives to maximize their stock's value, not just today, but in the future. They have a financial interest in monitoring and conserving their stocks, in using them efficiently, and in investing in them and their habitat. The stronger the owners' rights, the more likely they are to profit from investments in conservation. Property rights internalize the benefits of such investments. As the stocks grow, and catches become easier or larger, the value of the rights increases.

Furthermore, putting those who fish in charge of fisheries enables them to use their detailed knowledge of local stocks, fish behaviors, habitats, and environmental conditions to manage their operations sustainably. Fishermen's information—that "messy information" so distasteful to the DFO's central planners—is specific to their time and place, allowing them to choose actions most appropriate to their particular circumstances. Fishermen can also act more quickly than can most government managers. Approval processes for many bureaucratic decisions are painfully long, making governments slow to adjust to change. But time is a luxury that a good fisheries manager cannot always afford, since the resource is rarely in equilibrium. Fishermen and fishing communities are best equipped to respond to its volatility.

Property rights ensure healthy fisheries only to the extent that they fully internalize the costs and benefits of fisheries management decisions. Fisheries owners must understand that if they set unsustainable catch limits and destroy their resource, they, rather than taxpayers, will bear the full consequences of their actions. Knowing that they cannot look to the government to bail them out—knowing, in short, that they depend on their fisheries for their very survival—fisheries owners make wise decisions indeed.

A number of studies of private fisheries around the world—salmon fisheries in Iceland's rivers; commercial netting operations off the Scottish coast; inland fisheries in England; oyster beds in the United States; artificial reefs and inshore fisheries in Japan; quota-based fisheries in Iceland, New Zealand, and a growing number of other countries; and traditional community fisheries around the world—confirm that property rights promote sustainable behavior. Individual, corporate, and communal owners understand that their economic futures are tied to the health of their fisheries. As a result, these private owners regularly limit fishing and invest considerable money and effort in enhancing habitat for the long-term benefit of their stocks (Agnello and Donnelley 1975; Cordell 1989; Crowley 1996; De Alessi 1996; Hide and Ackroyd 1990; Jones and Walker 1997; Lee 1996; Williamson 1993).

Theory and practice alike support a proposal to develop systems of exclusive, transferable, and permanent property rights in fish—systems of self-managed ownership. Self-managed ownership removes decisions about catches and habitat from the political arena. Rights holders, or the associations representing them, set catch limits, monitor fishing activity, enforce regulations, and exclude interlopers. Under such a system, those who wish to acquire rights do not waste resources lobbying government. They simply purchase rights from others in market transactions—transactions that leave buyer and seller better off.

Ownership can take many forms. Individuals, communities, associations, or firms can own specific stocks. They can own fishing areas or fish habitat. Judging from experience around the world, an endless number of configurations are possible. There is no good reason not to experiment with several. As long as they confer secure rights, and as long as they remove governments from the business of managing fisheries, they should have an excellent chance of success.

In January 1998, Ransom Myers commented on the collapse of the cod: "The disaster in the cod fishery is now worse than anyone expected. . . . It may be a generation before we see a recovery of the cod. That a five-hundred-year-old industry could be destroyed in fifteen years by a bureaucracy is a tragedy of epic proportions" (quoted in Harris 1998, 332–333). The destruction of the Atlantic groundfishery is a tragedy that need not have occurred. Freeing fisheries from the political arena and placing responsibility for them with those who have a long-term interest in their success will ensure that the groundfish tragedy will not be repeated.

REFERENCES

Agnello, Richard J., and Lawrence P. Donnelley. 1975. Property Rights and Efficiency in the Oyster Industry. *The Journal of Law and Economics* 18: 521–533.

Alexander, Anne. 1997. *The Antigonish Movement: Moses Coady and Adult Education Today*. Toronto: Thompson Educational Publishing.

Anderssen, Erin. 1998a. Bar Foreign Boats, MPs Urge. *Globe and Mail*, 5 March.

———. 1998b. Fishery Package Spurs Resentment. *Globe and Mail*, 20 June.

———. 1998c. MPs Contradict Chrétien, Insist Baker Was Pushed from Fisheries Committee Post. *Globe and Mail*, 2 October.

Auditor General. 1997. *Report of the Auditor General of Canada to the House of Commons: Atlantic Groundfish Fisheries*. Ottawa: Minister of Public Works and Government Services Canada.

Beaton, Stuart. 1997. Personal communication, 31 July.

——. 1998. Personal communication, 26 March.

Burke, Leslie, and Leo Brander. 1996. *Behind the Cod Curtain: A Perspective on the Political Economy of the Atlantic Groundfish Fishery.* Halifax: Atlantic Institute for Market Studies.

Cameron, Silver Donald. 1998. Why Aren't Heads Rolling? *Globe and Mail,* 20 January.

Canada. Department of the Environment. Fisheries and Marine Service. 1976. *Policy for Canada's Commercial Fisheries.*

——. Department of Fisheries and Oceans. 1981. *Policy for Canada's Atlantic Fisheries in the 1980s: A Discussion Paper.*

——. Department of Fisheries and Oceans. 1992. *Crosbie Announces First Steps in Northern Cod (2J3KL) Recovery Plan.* Press release, 2 July.

——. Department of Fisheries and Oceans. 1993. *Science Branch Council Final Report.*

——. Department of Fisheries and Oceans. 1997. *Integrated Fisheries Management Plan: Atlantic Groundfish.*

——. Fisheries Resource Conservation Council (FRCC). 1996a. *Learning from History: Report of the Historical Perspective Subcommittee.*

——. 1996b. *Building the Bridge: 1997 Conservation Requirements for Atlantic Groundfish.* Report to the Minister of Fisheries and Oceans. Ottawa: Minister of Public Works and Government Services Canada.

——. 1997. *A Groundfish Conservation Framework for Atlantic Canada.* Report to the Minister of Fisheries and Oceans. Ottawa: Minister of Public Works and Government Services Canada.

——. 1998a. *1998 Conservation Requirements for the Gulf of St. Lawrence Groundfish Stocks and Cod Stocks in Divisions 2GH, 2J3KL, 3Ps, 4VsW and Witch Flounder in Division 3Ps.* Report to the Minister of Fisheries and Oceans. Ottawa: Minister of Public Works and Government Services Canada.

———. 1998b. *1999 Conservation Requirements for Scotian Shelf and Bay of Fundy Groundfish Stocks, Redfish Stocks, Units 1-3 and 3-0, and Groundfish Stocks in Division 3Ps.* Report to the Minister of Fisheries and Oceans. Ottawa: Minister of Public Works and Government Services Canada.

———. House of Commons. 1997a. Standing Committee on Fisheries and Oceans. *Transcript of Evidence,* 4 December.

———. House of Commons. 1997b. Standing Committee on Fisheries and Oceans. *Transcript of Evidence,* 9 December.

———. House of Commons. 1998a. Standing Committee on Fisheries and Oceans. *Transcript of Evidence,* 5 February.

———. House of Commons. 1998b. Standing Committee on Fisheries and Oceans. *The East Coast Report.* Ottawa: Public Works and Government Services Canada.

———. Office of the Prime Minister. 1984. *Policy Guidelines for Public Servants: Communications with the Public* and *Communications Roles and Responsibilities.* Press releases, 23 November.

———. Treasury. 1995. *Treasury Board Manual: Government Communications Policy.*

Canadian Press. 1997a. Critics Can Be Fired, Ottawa Says. *Globe and Mail,* 6 August.

———. 1997b. Tobin Denies Hiding Overfishing Report. *Globe and Mail* 23 August.

———. 1998. Fisheries Officials Will Be Replaced If Blame Justified, Minister Says. *Toronto Star,* 6 March.

Cashin, Richard. 1993. *Charting a New Course: Towards the Fishery of the Future.* Report of the Task Force on Incomes and Adjustment in the Atlantic Fishery. Ottawa: Minister of Supply and Services Canada.

Charnetski, Kelly, Gaby Winqvist, Erica Wissing, and Elina Vilkko. 1994. *An Historical Analysis of the Extent to which Policy Decisions Contributed to the Collapse of the Northwest Atlantic Cod Stocks.* Toronto: Canadian Environmental Defence Fund.

Confidential Report Calls Atlantic Cod Endangered. 1997. *Canadian Geographic* (July/August): 18.

Cordell, John, ed. 1989. *A Sea of Small Boats*. Cambridge, Mass.: Cultural Survival.

Cox, Kevin. 1997. Fine Catches of Cod Reported. *Globe and Mail*, 21 May.

Crosbie, John C., and Geoffrey Stevens. 1997. *No Holds Barred: My Life in Politics*. Toronto: McClelland & Stewart.

Crowley, Brian, ed. 1996. *Taking Ownership: Property Rights and Fishery Management on the Atlantic Coast*. Halifax: Atlantic Institute for Market Studies.

Dales, J. H. 1968. *Pollution, Property & Prices: An Essay in Policy-Making and Economics*. Toronto: University of Toronto Press.

De Alessi, Michael. 1996. *Emerging Technologies and the Private Stewardship of Marine Resources*. Washington, D.C.: Competitive Enterprise Institute.

Eggertson, Laura. 1998. MPs Blame Collapse of Fishery on Ottawa. *Toronto Star*, 24 March.

Ferguson, Derek. 1998. Fisheries Probe to Recommend Overhaul. *Toronto Star*, 3 March.

Finlayson, Alan Christopher. 1994. *Fishing for Truth: A Sociological Analysis of Northern Cod Stock Assessments from 1977 to 1990*. Social and Economic Studies No. 52. St. John's: Memorial University of Newfoundland, Institute of Social and Economic Research.

Fisheries Lab Director Grilled by Irate MPs. 1997. *Globe and Mail*, 7 November.

Fitzpatrick, John, and Chris Newton. 1998. *Assessment of the World's Fishing Fleet 1991–1997*. Posted on Greenpeace International Web site: http://www.greenpeace.org/oceans.

Greenspon, Edward. 1998. Ottawa Approves New Aid for Fishery. *Globe and Mail*, 12 June.

Harrigan, Eugene. 1998. *Post-TAGS Review Report.* Ottawa-Hull: Human Resources Development Canada.

Harris, Michael. 1998. *Lament for an Ocean: The Collapse of the Atlantic Cod Fishery: A True Crime Story.* Toronto: McClelland & Stewart.

Hide, Rodney P., and Peter Ackroyd. 1990. *Depoliticising Fisheries Management: Chatham Islands' Paua (Abalone) as a Case Study.* Unpublished Report for R. D. Beattie Ltd.

Hutchings, Jeffrey. 1997. Reopening Two of the Cod Fisheries Is a Big Mistake. *Globe and Mail,* 22 April.

Hutchings, Jeffrey A., Carl Walters, and Richard L. Haedrich. 1997. Is Scientific Inquiry Incompatible with Government Information Control? *Canadian Journal of Fisheries and Aquatic Science* 54: 1198–1210.

Iles, T. D. 1980. The Natural History of Fisheries Management. *Proceedings of the Nova Scotian Institute of Science* 30: 3–19.

Jones, Laura, and Michael Walker, eds. 1997. *Fish or Cut Bait: The Case for Individual Transferable Quotas in the Salmon Fishery of British Columbia.* Vancouver: The Fraser Institute.

Kirby, Michael J. L. 1982. *Navigating Troubled Waters: A New Policy for the Atlantic Fisheries.* Report of the Task Force on Atlantic Fisheries. Ottawa: Supply and Services Canada.

Kurlansky, Mark. 1997. *Cod: A Biography of the Fish that Changed the World.* Toronto: Alfred A. Knopf Canada.

Lee, Philip. 1996. *Home Pool: The Fight to Save the Atlantic Salmon.* Fredericton, New Brunswick: Goose Lane Editions.

Loaves and Fishes. 1998. *Economist* (March 21): 12–13.

MacCharles, Tonda. 1998. Fish Committee Chair Quits Post Suddenly. *Toronto Star,* 2 October.

Matthiessen, Peter. 1959. *Wildlife in America.* New York: Viking.

May, Doug, and Alton Hollett. 1995. *The Rock in a Hard Place: Atlantic Canada and the UI Trap.* Toronto: C. D. Howe Institute.

McGinn, Anne Platt. 1998. The Worldwatch Report: Freefall in Global Fish Stocks. *Environmental News Network,* 7 May.

McKibben, Bill. 1998. Ocean Solitaire. *Utne Reader* (May–June): 60–65, 102–105.

Mittelstaedt, Martin. 1998. Massive Fleets to Blame for Depleting Fish Stocks, U.S. Report Says. *Globe and Mail*, 20 August.

One-Third of Marine Species Overfished, NMFS Says. 1997. *Environmental News Network*, 6 October.

Schrank, William E., Blanca Skoda, Paul Parsons, and Noel Roy. 1995. The Cost to Government of Maintaining a Commercially Unviable Fishery: The Case of Newfoundland 1981/82 to 1990/91. *Ocean Development and International Law: The Journal of Marine Affairs* 26: 357–390.

Scott, Anthony, and Philip A. Neher. 1981. *Public Regulation of Commercial Fisheries.* Ottawa: The Economic Council of Canada.

Southam News. 1996. Cod Fishing by Public to Resume Off Newfoundland. *Toronto Star*, 19 September.

Steele, D. H., R. Andersen, and J. M. Green. 1992. The Managed Commercial Annihilation of Northern Cod. *Newfoundland Studies* 8, no. 1: 34–68.

Strauss, Stephen. 1997a. Partial Cod Fishery Set for May 1. *Globe and Mail*, 18 April.

——. 1997b. Fisheries, Scientists to Debate Accusations. *Globe and Mail*, 5 September.

Thorne, Stephen. 1997. Overfishing, Not Seals, Killed Cod, Buried Fisheries Report Reveals. *Globe and Mail*, 22 August.

United Nations. Food and Agriculture Organization (FAO). 1995. *The State of World Fisheries and Aquaculture.* Rome: FAO.

Walters, Carl. 1995. *Fish on the Line: The Future of Pacific Fisheries.* Vancouver: The David Suzuki Foundation.

Williamson, Robert. 1993. *Scottish Salmon Fishing Rights, A Transferable Property: The Consequences for Administration and Regulation.* Paper presented at ICREI colloquium, 28 January, at Paris.

David Gerard **6**

The Origins of the Federal Wilderness System

Forest Service wilderness reservation policy in western states may have been sincerely inaugurated to meet preservation sentiment which began developing over one hundred years ago. . . . However, the application of the policy in many cases developed into political maneuvers to thwart the Department of the Interior and the National Park Service. . . . The policy was not the result of a "grass roots" movement. . . . It was never intended to reserve specified areas permanently from development.

—James P. Gilligan (1953, 221–222).

Introduction

The Wilderness Act of 1964 established a system of preserving federal land that has outstanding natural and scenic characteristics by placing certain public lands off-limits for road building, commodity use (logging, grazing, mining), and motorized vehicle use. Although it is not surprising that wilderness designations generate considerable opposition, the degree to which the system has proliferated is impressive. The 1964 statute designated 9.1 million wilderness acres. Since then the system has grown to 46.8 million acres of wilderness in the continental United States, and more than 100 million acres overall (a total area approximately the size of California).[1] In addition, another 30 million acres are currently being considered for inclusion in the federal wilderness system.

It is tempting to attribute the origins of the wilderness system to a response to public pressures to preserve remote and scenic areas. After all, the environmental movement came to prominence during the 1960s, and the Wilderness Act was one of many federal environmental laws enacted between 1964 and 1972.[2] Such a story would also be consistent with the often accepted notion that environmental policies develop in response to public demands and grass-roots activism.

The wilderness system, however, did not emerge in response to constituent demands. Rather, the idea of a public land wilderness system originated from within the U.S. Forest Service shortly after World War I, which is surprising because there was little public or Forest Service interest in wilderness preservation at that time. Instead, the Forest Service was an agency committed to the prudent utilization of public land resources through scientific management practices.[3] Accordingly, preservation for preservation's sake was not a popular notion within the agency. Even so, in 1929 and again in 1939 the Forest Service established an administrative wilderness system that included more than eleven million acres by 1953. These regulations provided the template for the federal wilderness system created out of Forest Service land in 1964.

What accounts for the Forest Service's interest in wilderness preservation? Certainly, the efforts of wilderness advocates within the agency, such as Arthur Carhart, Aldo Leopold, and Bob Mar-

1. Even wilderness advocates did not foresee (or even hope for) such a vast system. For instance, the conservation director of the Sierra Club believed that the system could expand to as much as 48 million acres (McCloskey 1966, 289).

2. Elliott, Ackerman, and Millian (1985) examine the development of federal environmental law.

3. See Nelson 1995, Chapter 2.

shall, deserve much of the credit for advancing the preservation cause. Their efforts, however, do not account for the whole story, as these men were not positioned to create such a system nor did they represent the views of most Forest Service personnel.

This chapter examines the role of competition between administrative agencies in the development of the federal wilderness system.[4] Although the General Land Office within the Department of Interior was the principal federal land agency throughout the nineteenth century, in 1905 Congress moved the national forests from Interior to the Department of Agriculture.[5] Soon after this transfer, Interior and Agriculture began competing for administrative control of the vast federal estate in the West. After Congress established the National Park Service within the Department of Interior in 1916, the national forests became targets for Park Service expansion. The Forest Service (within the Department of Agriculture) responded by designating administrative wilderness areas as an alternative to large-scale transfers of its properties to the Park Service.

There were substantial differences between these early designations and the current wilderness system. Prior to the statutory restrictions written into the Wilderness Act, the Forest Service generally allowed some form of development—logging, grazing, and its own road building—within the boundaries of its wilderness areas. Changes in these areas did not have to be approved by Congress. By keeping the land within its jurisdiction, the Forest Service could rescind any designations that interfered with its other development plans, thus maintaining discretion over management of and development options for these lands. Statutory wilderness designations curtail this

4. See Peffer (1951), Gilligan (1953), Dana and Fairfax (1980), Libecap (1981; 1984), and Allin (1982; 1987) for discussions of the interjurisdictional feud between the Forest Service and the agencies within the Department of Interior.

5. The General Land Office and the Grazing Service were consolidated as the Bureau of Land Management (BLM) in 1946. BLM continues to be a principal land-management agency today.

administrative discretion. Consequently, the agency opposed versions of wilderness legislation first introduced in 1956.

The evidence presented in this chapter suggests that the Forest Service's early commitment to wilderness was a means to forward the agency mission. Although the Forest Service was no great champion of the preservation cause, its political maneuvers helped to develop the modern wilderness concept. The present-day statutory protection of wilderness owes a debt to the Forest Service's lip service to preservation between 1929 and 1964.

The Economics of Bureaucracy and Bureau Competition

Congress has the constitutional authority to manage the public lands, but the design and implementation of federal land policy is often left to the federal land agencies. As a result, these agencies often have some degree of autonomy over the development and implementation of federal land policy. At the same time, however, the agencies often have to balance competing pressures, such as appeasing important client interests and convincing Congress to reauthorize funding.

The economic theory of bureaucracy begins with the assumption that agencies act in their self-interest. Models with variations on the budget-maximization hypothesis of Niskanen (1971) are often the starting points for this analysis. These models argue that agencies are free to pursue their own self-interests because congressional oversight is generally handled by the legislators with the highest demand for the agency's output. Even when this is not the case, it is argued that congressional review is often limited, and the information for such reviews is often provided and controlled by the agencies. Thus, agency monopoly power is seen as a critical component in determining output, budget, and costs. In general, these models find that bureaus with a monopoly position will produce too much output at too high of a cost.[6]

Although the empirical validity of the monopoly position and budget maximization has been questioned,[7] it is reasonable to assume that agencies have some degree of autonomy, without strictly adhering to the budget-maximization hypothesis. The operating assumption of agency self-interest has been used to explain the development and growth of federal land agencies. For instance, Libecap (1981) finds that centralized control of federal lands was a source of bureaucratic growth for the Department of Interior, and Johnson (1985) argues that Forest Service behavior has been consistent with the budget-maximization hypothesis.[8]

Self-interested behavior appears to have been important in the development of early federal wilderness policy, as the Forest Service and the Department of Interior actively competed for control of the federal estate. The resultant policies did not always originate from demands by Congress, the executive branch, or client interests, but rather flowed from within federal land bureaucracies.

The effects of introducing competition into the model of bureau behavior, however, are not clear. Some argue that government agencies should be subject to the same competitive pressures as private entities are. In other words, competition would discipline bureaus to perform more efficiently and also to offer a greater range of

6. McCubbins, Noll, and Weingast (1987) provide an alternative perspective that examines the effect of administrative rules on agency behavior.

7. Carroll (1989) shows that federal agencies generally do not maintain monopoly positions, and the edited volume by Blais and Dion (1991) finds little support for the budget-maximization hypothesis.

8. In Johnson and Libecap (1994), the authors refine their views of bureaucratic behavior. In particular, they argue that the fundamental problem of bureaucracy is found in crafting an institutional setting that will ensure accountability and maintain the productivity over bureaucratic behavior. Their review of the economic literature on bureaucracy is in chapter 7.

goods and services. Higgins, Shughart, and Tollison (1989), for instance, construct a duopoly model for the provision of government services. In the absence of collusion, their model predicts that competition will discipline agency costs.

A central assumption of the duopoly model is that the quality of each agency's output is constant and fixed. It is argued that state, rather than private, production might be desirable in cases where cost reductions come at the expense of the quality of output (Shleifer 1998, 136–141).[9] In fact, concerns about the deteriorating quality of the public domain helped motivate the move toward centralized control of much of the western United States (Nelson 1995, chapters 1 and 2).[10] Introducing public-sector competition had the potential to undermine the motivation for state ownership in the first place.

Government and market competition also differ in that bureaucracies are generally not subject to the same penalties as firms in the private sector. Even in cases of monumental cost overruns or of the agency outliving its purported mission, the dismantling of the agency rarely occurs.[11] Thus, there is considerable question whether agency competition will introduce fiscal discipline.

Consequently, the theoretical implications that stem from introducing competition into the model of bureaucracy are sensitive to the underlying assumptions of the model. In practice, the effects

9. This is a highly qualified statement. According to Shleifer (1998), "The modern case for government ownership can often be seen from precisely this perspective. Advocates of such ownership want to have state prisons so as to avoid untrained low-wage guards, state water utilities to force investment in purification, and state car makers to make them invest in environmentally friendly products. As it turns out, however, this case for state ownership must be made carefully, and even in most of the situations where cost reduction has adverse consequences for noncontractible quality, private ownership is still superior" (139).

10. Whether these concerns were valid and their remedies were appropriate is another matter. Nelson (1995) discusses these topics extensively.

11. An excellent example of bureau longevity and renewal is the Bureau of Indian Affairs. See McChesney (1990).

of competition will depend on the type of output being produced. Predictably, the empirical evidence shows that agency competition can have mixed results.

Trends in Public Land Management, 1865–1916

Federal land policy following the Civil War was designed to transfer the public lands to individuals, states, and the railroads.[12] These transfers were made through land sales, scrip locations, cessions to state and local governments, railroad land grants, and disposal to settlers through laws such as the Homestead Act. During this period, the General Land Office within the Department of Interior facilitated these land-disposal tasks. The agency budget depended on the number of claims processed and total acreage transferred, and officials earned commissions by validating and processing these claims. Therefore, for the General Land Office, "budgets, salaries, and long-term employment depended on the piecemeal disposal of federal land" (Libecap 1981, 9–10).

As abuses of the public land laws began to attract national attention in the late nineteenth century, the emerging conservation movement began to challenge the land-disposal paradigm. The conservation program called for the scientific management of land resources retained in public ownership (this did not include land suitable for cultivation by single-family crop farms).[13] The first major piece of conservation legislation was the General Revision Act in

12. Gates (1968) is the standard source for the history of federal land policy, and Nelson (1995) provides a recent treatment.

13. Although the distinction is often lost today, the conservationists differ from preservationists such as John Muir. The major shift brought about by the conservation movement was the scientific management of lands retained in federal stewardship—not the preservation of these lands for their aesthetic values (Nelson 1995, 44–50). Even so, preservation was not absent from public land policy during this period. An executive order in 1902 created the National Wildlife Refuges, and the Antiquities Act in 1906 gave the executive branch power to designate national

1891. The statute gave the president the authority to create forest reserves on the public domain. These reserves were removed from disposal under the various land laws, and timber harvesting and grazing within the reserves became subject to the consent of the General Land Office officials. In practice, however, Congress did not appropriate funding for these tasks until it enacted the National Forest Organic Act in 1897 (Gates 1968, 573). Thus, the degrees of administrative control provided for by these laws were pervasive changes in the status quo, especially for an agency that earned its keep surveying, validating, and processing land claims.[14]

The Organic Act came about partly as a product of recommendations from the National Forestry Committee. A member of the committee, Gifford Pinchot, was the rising star of the conservation movement. He was the self-described first American professional forester and the foremost advocate of the scientific-management principles. Pinchot and the conservation movement each gained considerable momentum when Theodore Roosevelt became president in 1901. At the urging of Pinchot and with the support of the commissioner of the General Land Office and the secretary of the interior, the forest reserves were transferred from the Department of Interior to the Department of Agriculture in 1905. Legislation in 1907 changed the name of the reserves to the national forests.

The fact that officials in the General Land Office and the Department of Interior supported the transfer seems incongruent with the hypothesis that agencies act in their self-interest. Gates (1968, 571), for instance, argues that the General Land Office should have

---

monuments. Early designations included Devil's Tower in Wyoming, the Grand Canyon in Arizona, and most recently the Grand Staircase Escalante in Utah. The national parks also began to flourish. In 1872, Yellowstone became the world's first national park, and by 1916 there were fifteen national parks containing almost five million acres.

14. Interestingly, this provision was attached as a rider. It is not clear whether Congress was aware of the withdrawal privileges for the president. Ise (1972, 109–118) discusses the "peculiar circumstances" of the legislative history.

known that its funding would decrease following the transfer. There are a number of reasons to question this assertion. First, the source of General Land Office funding was land disposal, not administration, and the agency also recognized that hands-on administration of the reserves was completely outside its area of expertise (Department of Interior 1904, 50).

Second, Congress was often reluctant to fund and staff the General Land Office. Thus, it is not surprising that Interior was eager to wash its hands of responsibility of the reserves. Administration of the reserves looked to be an expensive endeavor, and the General Land Office was short of funding. In the year prior to the transfer, the General Land Office commissioner pleaded for additional staff and additional space, on the basis that "there is more business now pending before this office than it will be possible to perform during the next year with the present force" (Department of Interior 1904, 67).

Moreover, the amount of land and funding at stake were probably not clear at the time of the transfer. Figure 1 illustrates the rapid growth of the reserves following the transfer. In 1904, the reserves contained 62.6 million acres, and expanded to 194.5 million acres during the presidency of Theodore Roosevelt.[15] The expansion of budget appropriations and staffing was equally remarkable. When the transfer occurred in 1905, the Forest Service budget was $439,000. By 1908, however, the budget had ballooned to almost $3.6 million,[16] while the number of Forest Service personnel had nearly tripled from 939 to 2,753. By 1909 the Forest Service budget exceeded that of the General Land Office.

15. Pinchot's zeal for Forest Service expansion was not limited to the national forests. He also had an interest in nationalizing all of the nation's forests, including privately held lands (Dana and Fairfax 1980, 124–125). In addition, the Forest Service and the Department of Interior also battled for the public grazing lands, until Congress awarded the spoils to the Department of Interior through the Taylor Grazing Act in 1934.

16. The increase in wholesale prices for this period was just under 5 percent.

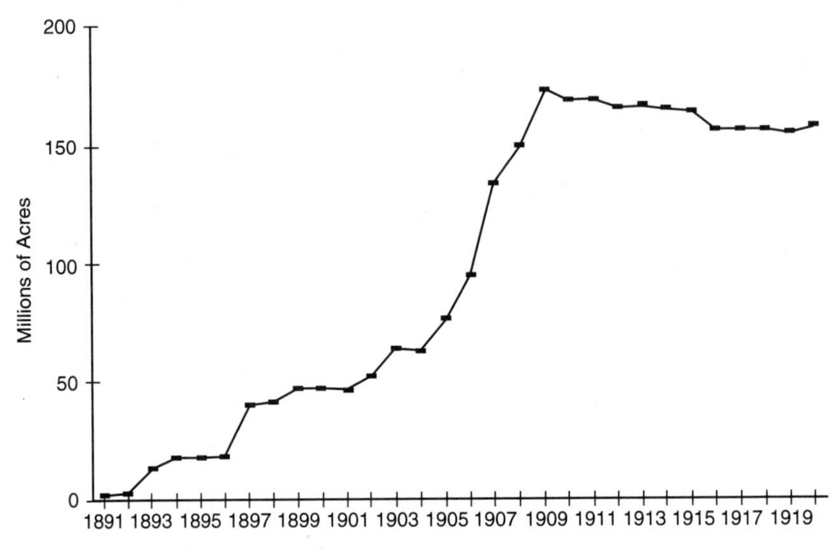

FIGURE 1 National Forest Acreage, 1891–1919

The Forest Service illustrated that centralized control of public land resources could provide a significant source of congressional funding, and Interior officials began to reevaluate their stance toward management of the national forests. The result was the commencement of an ongoing dispute between Interior and the Forest Service for control of public lands. In 1911 the secretary of the interior tried to initiate the transfer of the national forests back to Interior. Between 1916 and 1923, there were a number of bills introduced seeking a unification of land-management agencies (Gorte and Cody 1995). Nevertheless, control of the land did not revert back to Interior, and the Forest Service budget and staff continued to grow.

The degree to which the tide had turned on public land disposal was quite remarkable. To illustrate, the Forest Homestead Act of 1906 gave the secretary of agriculture the discretion to open to disposal reserves that were valuable for agriculture and not needed for public purposes. By 1910, only 632,412 of the 194,505,325 acres of national forests (0.3 percent) had been opened up under the Forest Homestead Act (Dana and Fairfax 1980, 89–90).[17]

Forest Service Wilderness Policy, 1916–1939

Interior failed to regain the national forests, but it did manage to obtain control of the National Park Service in 1916. The parks were in the custodial care of the army, but pressure was mounting for a unified system of park management. Although Pinchot began lobbying for the national parks in 1905, Interior cosponsored several conferences with the American Civic Association—a group concerned with park planning. The support of this constituency helped the Department of Interior to win the parks (Peffer 1951, 175–176).

The wilderness system developed within the context of the emerging debate over national recreation policy. In 1919 a Forest Service employee, Arthur Carhart, went to Trappers Lake, Colorado, to formulate a Forest Service development plan for the area. Instead of providing such a plan, Carhart convinced his superior to leave the area alone. This was quite a departure from Forest Service policy. At about the same time, Aldo Leopold began pressing for the preservation of many large roadless tracts.

These ideas might not have made their way into Forest Service policy had it not been for expanding public demands for recreation coupled with competitive pressures from the Department of Interior.

> Stephen T. Mather, Director of the National Park Service had made his ideas of park expansion at the expense of the national forest system increasingly apparent to the Forest Service. He had generated

17. Despite the limited effect of the legislation, the authors argue that "the homesteader mystique was so powerful that, even during the heyday of Pinchot's administration, it proved an unstoppable threat to the forests" (Dana and Fairfax 1980, 89, 90).

> such support for the park system that there was at least a fair chance of many large areas in the forests being transferred to the Park Service. (Gilligan 1953, 92)

Table 1 illustrates that there were a number of requests and transfers of national forest lands into the Park Service between 1920 and 1928. Mather lobbied against congressional funding for any Forest Service recreation programs, and in 1922 "Congress refused to appropriate recreation funds for the Forest Service, claiming that the Park Service was in charge of recreation on federal lands and that Forest Service involvement in recreation amounted to a duplication of services" (Wilkinson and Anderson 1987, 316).

Between 1917 and 1924, the number of travelers over forest roads increased from three million to more than eleven million (Gilligan 1953, 95). If recreational uses of the public lands continued to

TABLE 1 Major Park Service Expansion Requests, 1920–1928

National Forest Areas	*Acreage Requested by Park Service*	*Acreage Transferred*
Grand Teton and Jackson Hole, Wyoming	850,000	300,000
King and Kern Rivers and Mt. Whitney, California	1,000,000	225,000
Devil Postpile, Red Meadows, and Minarets Country, California	60,000	0
Mt. Rainier, Washington	4,480	4,000
Diamond Lake and Mt. McLoughlin, Oregon	100,000	0
Rocky Mountain, Colorado	65,000	16,000
Mount Evans, Colorado	101,000	0
Grand Canyon (area north), Arizona	154,000	45,000
Grand Canyon (area south), Arizona	12,000	2,000
Total	**2,346,480**	**592,000**

SOURCE: Gilligan (1953, 121).

expand and the Park Service was to be the sole provider of recreation services, the Forest Service stood to lose control of substantial portions of its holdings to the Park Service. In 1927, for instance, 323,365 acres were transferred to Sequoia and Grand Canyon national parks; and in 1929, another 162,649 acres went to Grand Teton, Lassen, Bryce Canyon, and Yellowstone national parks.

By 1926 Chief Forester William Greeley began "seeking some way to swing preservationist support to the Forest Service—and away from the increasing movement for national parks" (Gilligan 1953, 101). Greeley requested an appraisal of roadless areas that revealed seventy-four roadless tracts larger than 230,000 acres—totaling 55 million acres. He instructed his district foresters to designate lands in an administrative wilderness system. In 1929 the Forest Service promulgated its first formal wilderness policy, the L-20 regulations, and by 1933, the agency had classified sixty-three areas containing 8.4 million acres.

Although the original wilderness system was now in place, the Forest Service wilderness policy was not overly restrictive:

> It is not proposed unduly to curtail timber cutting, grazing, water development, mining, or other forms of economic utilization within such areas, but rather to guard against their unnecessary invasion by roads, resorts, summer-home communities, or other forms of use incompatible with the public enjoyment of their major values. (Department of Agriculture 1928, 38–39)

Of the sixty-three areas designated by 1933, logging plans had been approved in twenty-three, and grazing operations in fifty-three (Gilligan 1953, 133–135). Similarly, in 1937 there were seventy-two primitive areas containing 13.5 million acres, but only four of these areas, containing a total of 297,221 acres, had prohibitions on logging, grazing, and road construction. Overall, fifty-nine of the seventy-two areas had logging planned, and sixty-two had approved grazing operations (Gilligan 1953, 193).

So why did the Forest Service bother with these administrative wilderness designations? Certainly the anecdotal evidence suggests that bureau competition was a factor in the early designations:

> At a Congressional hearing at which Greeley was testifying, the subject of wilderness area establishment on national forests was mentioned. One veteran Congressman leaned forward and shook his finger at Greeley, saying, "I know why you set up these wilderness areas, Greeley. Just to keep them out of Steve Mather's hands!" (Gilligan 1953, 108)[18]

But by maintaining control of the land, the Forest Service preserved an option on future management decisions. These decisions were potential sources of present and future congressional funding.

Although client interests did not directly support wilderness designations, they likely preferred Forest Service to Park Service management. For instance, Peffer (1951, 242–243) discusses local opposition of transfers of Forest Service holdings to the Park Service, including protests from lumber, mining, and grazing interests. The evidence suggests that the early designations did little to hinder grazing, logging, or road building.

Empirical Analysis of Wilderness Designations

The remainder of this chapter examines the determinants of individual designations in the western states. There were 125 national forests in Arizona, California, Colorado, Idaho, Montana, Nevada, New Mexico, Oregon, Utah, Washington, and Wyoming. The dependent variable is one if the Forest Service had established an administrative wilderness area within a national forest by July 1933 and zero otherwise.[19]

18. The author cites a 1953 interview with William Greeley.
19. These are taken from Gilligan (1953, Appendix B).

A number of binary explanatory variables capture elements of the competition between Interior and the Forest Service. *National park* is set equal to one if the national forest is on the boundary of a national park. Beginning in 1917, the Park Service expansion efforts included attempts to harness control of the national monuments (Dana and Fairfax 1980, 152). *Monument* equals one if there was a national monument within the boundaries of the national forest.[20] If there were Park Service requests for a transfer of land from a given national forest, *Recommendation* is set equal to one.[21] Overall there were 27 forests adjacent to a national park, 14 national monuments within park boundaries, and 27 areas recommended for transfer from the Forest Service to the Park Service. Of the 125 national forests examined, 46 forests had at least one *Recommendation, National park,* or *National monument.*

The management of wilderness areas in the 1930s was quite different from contemporary wilderness management, mainly because there were very few areas where logging, grazing, and road building were absolutely prohibited. Even if there was a prohibition, however, the Forest Service maintained discretion to make administrative changes without approval from outside the Department of Agriculture. Thus, if wilderness areas were strategically designated to maintain an option on future development, agency interest and constituent interest variables could play an important role.

The data for these variables are available at the state level. The first two variables measure the Forest Service's road budgets. *Road, 1930* contains the Forest Service road-building expenditures for that

20. The monuments and their acreage are listed in U.S. Department of Agriculture (1929, 1044).

21. The recommendations are found in a number of sources. Gilligan (1953, 93–94) cites the 1924 President's Committee on Outdoor Recreation of a Coordinating Committee on National Parks and Forests. Gilligan (1953, 136) references recommendations made in 1925 and in 1932. Finally, the Forest Service's *Report of the Forester* (Department of Agriculture 1930/1931) discusses national forests requested by the Park Service.

year, and *Road, cumulative* contains cumulative road-building expenditures on Forest Service roads for the period from 1917 to 1930. In each case, these variables are dollars spent per acre. The expected coefficients are positive if the building and maintenance of roads is desirable for maintenance and expansion of the Forest Service budget. The expected coefficients are negative if areas with roads reduce the quality of the wilderness and thus reduce the likelihood of a wilderness designation.

Two variables attempt to capture constituent interest characteristics. *Logging* is the value of timber cut per acre of national forest within the state. *Grazing* is the number of cattle per acre of national forest. The expected coefficients for these variables are negative if wilderness designations are likely to reduce commercial logging and grazing. Alternatively, there should be positive coefficient estimates if the Forest Service offered wilderness designations to commercial interests as a superior alternative to Park Service expansion. This fact may have been especially important before 1934, because the Forest Service and Interior were competing for control of the federal rangelands.

Finally, the total acreage of each forest, *Acres*, is included. With all else constant, larger forests should be more likely to contain wilderness areas because the opportunity cost of the set-aside should be lower and because the larger areas are more likely to contain areas deemed worthy of a wilderness designation.

The dependent variable is binary, and several logit models are estimated. The results are reported in table 2.[22] The first set of estimates contains only the interagency competition variables. Each of the variables significantly increased the probability of having a designation. These coefficient estimates remain reasonably stable as the other explanatory variables are added.

22. The baseline for the comparison is seventy-three correct predictions. This can be obtained by guessing that no wilderness designations are made.

TABLE 2 Logit Estimates for Wilderness Designations (standard errors in parentheses)

Dependent variable = wilderness designation within national forest through 1933.

	Model 1	Model 2	Model 3
Recommendation	0.29[1]	0.34[1]	0.41[2]
	(0.13)	(0.14)	(0.15)
National park	0.34[1]	0.43[1]	0.26[3]
	(0.13)	(0.17)	(0.15)
National monument	0.36[1]	0.33[1]	0.38[1]
	(0.16)	(0.14)	(0.19)
Acres	0.06	0.01	0.01
	(0.05)	(0.01)	(0.01)
Road, 1930		0.31[1]	0.56[2]
		(0.15)	(0.19)
Road, cumulative		3.94[1]	6.54[2]
		(1.69)	(2.06)
Grazing			25.99[1]
			(11.98)
Logging			−0.46
			(0.39)
Constant	−0.41[2]	−0.87[2]	−1.48[2]
	(0.14)	(0.23)	(0.34)
N = 125			
Predicted Correctly[4]	93(74%)	91(73%)	96(77%)

[1]Significant at 5 percent level

[2]Significant at 1 percent level

[3]Significant at 10 percent level

[4]Guessing 0 (no designation) correctly predicts 73 of 125 observations (58%).

The addition of the agency interest and constituent interest variables gives seemingly perverse results. *Road, 1930* and *Road, cumulative* each show positive and significant effects on the probability of a designation, suggesting that areas with higher road budgets, both in the current period and historically, were more likely to be assigned to administrative wilderness. If the designations were a maneuver to avert transfers to the Park Service, the agency was protecting lands where its road-building expenditures were largest. This is a reasonable interpretation if the Park Service saw greater opportunities for control in those areas where wilderness (meaning roadless areas) was more scarce.

The number of cattle per acre within a state increased the likelihood of a designation. A possible explanation for this phenomenon is that the Forest Service was using wilderness as a means to foment support from this important client base, especially as Congress was debating whether centralized control of the federal rangelands would be placed within Interior or Agriculture (Libecap 1981, 41–42). In contrast, the value of timber cut per acre within the state did not provide any explanatory power. The latter result may be attributed to the fact that the Forest Service was not competing with another agency for control of timber as it was with grazing.

The evidence is consistent with the hypothesis that agency self-interest played a role in the designation process. In particular, the variables measuring interagency competition suggest that the early designations were closely related to areas likely to be coveted by the Park Service. The constituent interest and agency interest variables also lend support to the hypothesis, though these variables should be viewed with caution because they are aggregated at the state level.

Public Land Management after the Taylor Grazing Act of 1934

With the election of Franklin Roosevelt, the Department of Interior renewed its predatory behavior toward Forest Service lands. The main proponent of consolidation was Secretary of the Interior Harold Ickes. Under Ickes, Interior acquired control of the federal grazing lands under the Taylor Grazing Act in 1934 and effectively

TABLE 3 Transfers from National Forests to National Park Service, 1927–1939

Year	*From National Forest*	*To National Park*	*Acres*
1939	Tongass	Glacier Bay	505,600
1938	Olympic		648,000
	Coronado	Chiricahua	6,408
1933	Sierra	Yosemite	8,785
	Absaroka	Yellowstone	6,360
	National Monuments		384,833
1932	Santa Fe	Bandelier	26,026
	Crater	Crater Lake	973
1931	Arapaho	Rocky Mountain	14,597
	Powell	Bryce Canyon	19,424
	Rainier	Mt. Rainier	34,000
	Harney	Wind Cave	880
1930	Stanislaus	Yosemite	7,726
1929	Teton	Grand Teton	95,185
	Absaroka	Yellowstone	3,072
	Gallatin	Yellowstone	27,008

SOURCE: USDA Forest Service, *Report to the Chief*, various years.

ended the era of large-scale land disposal.[23] Although Interior managed to win several major victories, Ickes fell short of his goal of consolidating public land management into a new Department of Conservation. In the absence of the full-scale absorption of the Forest Service, Ickes began piecemeal acquisition of the national forests.

Table 3 shows that the Park Service successfully acquired more than 1.5 million acres of national forests between 1933 and 1939. These transfers were initiated in a number of ways. An executive

23. Despite a downward trend in land disposal, between 1920 and 1934 homestead acreage ranged from 2.7 million to 13.4 million acres. Total homestead acres were less than 100,000 for each year after 1937.

order authorizing a Park Service reorganization in 1933 gave the Park Service jurisdiction over all the national monuments, including sixteen located on Forest Service land. Not only did the national monuments contain 384,833 acres, they also provided the Park Service with inroads to several national forests. In 1934 the National Resources Board (chaired by Ickes) recommended the transfer of ten of the national forests to the Park Service, in addition to the creation of four new national parks out of Forest Service land. Other pressure was applied in 1936, when the Park Service again tried to establish itself as the sole government recreation planning organization. Ultimately, Congress gave the president power to authorize the Department of Conservation in 1939, but Ickes could not persuade the president to make the transfer (Libecap 1981, 47).

As Interior applied pressure, the Forest Service continued to add acreage to its wilderness areas. Part of this expansion came through the tireless efforts of Bob Marshall, who pressed for massive additions to the wilderness system.[24] Even so, Park Service expansion appears to have been the central reason for Forest Service wilderness expansion:

> [Marshall's] total acreage recommendation to the Forest Service for primitive classification was almost three times more than the Service was willing or able to set aside. Areas in which the Park Service had shown a special interest, however, were almost all formally classified as primitive areas—even those under 100,000 acres in the West which were not of special interest to Marshall. (Gilligan 1953, 199)

Thus, in 1939 the Forest Service was a stroke of a pen away from being absorbed into Interior and was also witnessing a systematic

24. Marshall, one of the founders of the Wilderness Society, worked in the Forest Service before becoming the director of forestry within the Bureau of Indian Affairs within the Department of Interior. In 1937 he moved back to the Forest Service as chief of the Recreation and Lands Division. He died at the age of thirty-eight in 1939.

raid of its land base. In addition, there was some internal agency pressure (especially from Bob Marshall) to implement preservation of some of the national forests. These factors led to stricter wilderness regulations in September 1939. The new U-1 (wilderness) and U-2 (wild) regulations were for areas larger than 100,000 acres and between 5,000 and 100,000 acres, respectively.[25] Timber harvesting, road construction, special-use permits, and mechanized access were prohibited in these areas.[26] What remained to be seen was how the Forest Service would implement this policy.

With the U regulations, the Forest Service planned to review each of the seventy-six existing primitive areas. Progress was not rapid. By the start of World War II, the Forest Service had established three areas as wilderness, six as wild, and consolidated three into the Bob Marshall Wilderness Area in Montana (Hendee, Stankey, and Lucas 1990, 101–102). The Forest Service did no evaluations during the war and, by the late 1940s, had only established two million acres as wilderness.

Although the new regulations were not particularly popular within the agency, Forest Service officials attempted to hide this fact from the public:

> Since regional and staff foresters were unable to prevent the creation in 1939 of the more restrictive U-1 and U-2 Regulations, . . . they nullified the intent of the new regulations by refusing to reclassify most of the primitive areas. This passive resistance . . . was approved by the Washington office with a camouflaging directive which stated that all primitive areas would be managed just as though they were under the new regulations, but not indicating to the public the great probability of future boundary changes. (Gilligan 1953, 221–222)

25. U-3 regulations were also established for roadless areas larger than 100,000 acres, which were applied to three areas in Minnesota.

26. On the other hand, mineral exploration and development, under the Mining Law of 1872 and the Mineral Leasing Act of 1920, and grazing and water development were allowed.

As a result, many of the areas that were thought to have protected status did not. For instance, the designation within the Gila National Forest came partly from the efforts of Aldo Leopold, and the area gained wilderness status in the 1920s. Although Leopold is now revered in environmental circles for his commitment to the wilderness cause, in 1950 the Forest Service approved a plan for commercial timber harvesting of 75,000 acres of the Gila Primitive Area in New Mexico—Leopold's first wilderness recommendation. This was not an isolated incident. For instance, in 1953 the Department of Agriculture approved a project that removed 53,000 acres of old-growth forest from the Three Sisters Primitive Area in Oregon. These proposals affected 20 to 25 percent of the wilderness areas (Wilkinson and Anderson 1987, 342–343).

By the 1950s there was organized opposition to these projects on supposedly protected lands from a growing preservation lobby. This opposition and the Forest Service development plans set the wheels in motion for wilderness legislation. The first bill to develop a wilderness preservation system was introduced in Congress in 1956. The Forest Service opposed these efforts to implement statutory wilderness for a number of reasons. As we have seen, by averting land transfers to the Park Service, the early wilderness designations allowed the Forest Service to maintain an option on the future development plans for the land. Statutory wilderness protection would strip the agency of this discretionary authority. The Wilderness Act upgraded wilderness protection from administrative caveat to statutory mandate.

Once the Wilderness Act was in place in 1964, the Forest Service adopted a very conservative view of what should be classified as wilderness. One explanation for this conservative view is that the agency believed that the congressional intent with the Wilderness Act was for a high-quality wilderness system. This so-called purity principle served to minimize the areas that the agency recommended for inclusion as wilderness. A more plausible explanation for the adherence to purity is that the Forest Service did not want to lose its administrative discretion over large areas of its land (Department of Agriculture 1984, 5–10).

Implications of Bureau Competition

The theoretical implications of agency competition are not clear. It is conceivable that agencies subject to competitive pressures might perform more efficiently or foster policy innovations. Consider this assessment of the origins of the wilderness system:

> It is strange how often we decry in government the same competitive forces that are essential and revered components of the American free enterprise system. . . . In the case of recreation policy and wilderness preservation, however, we see a clear instance of creative competition. The Forest Service was motivated in part by the fear of land transfers to develop and implement a far-reaching program in land preservation. (Dana and Fairfax 1980, 158)

This is a fairly charitable view of the early Forest Service wilderness program. Grazing, timber harvesting, and road development were commonplace within most of the early wilderness designations, and the Forest Service had no intention of reserving lands permanently from development. Thus, there is little evidence that Forest Service wilderness provided superior preservation than would have come about if the land had been transferred to the Park Service.

The benefits of agency competition become even more dubious when viewed in the context of the larger feud between Interior and the Forest Service over the public rangelands. The same authors who herald the government competition that led to the federal wilderness system hold a less favorable view of bureau competition in this instance:

> The Forest Service estimated that the cost of administering the proposed program on 80 to 160 million acres would be at least $1.5 to $2 million. Ickes alleged Interior could do the job for about $150,000 annually. The low estimate would ensure both low grazing fees and a very weak agency to collect them. (Dana and Fairfax 1980, 161)[27]

As noted at the outset, a possible justification for government ownership exists in cases where competition to reduce costs can lead to deterioration of the quality of the output produced. In the case of Interior's management of the federal range, it seems likely that bureau competition contributed significantly to the deterioration of the quality of the public lands.

A recent commentary by Joseph Stiglitz recognizes this problem and the potential downside of introducing competition to the public sector:

> Destructive competition is most prevalent in zero-sum games where the gains of one are at the expense of another. Political games, with position to be won or lost, are particularly prone to this kind of behavior. Competition in political markets is far from perfect, and the scope for destructive competition is therefore all the greater. (Stiglitz 1998, 13)

Conclusions

The origins of the federal wilderness system are not derived from public demands for preservation. Although internal pressures from Forest Service personnel provided the wilderness idea, the threat of Park

27. Libecap (1981, 46–47) also examines how bureau competition strengthened the ranchers' interests relative to the Department of Interior.

Service expansion motivated the Forest Service's early "commitment" to wilderness preservation. The empirical analysis is consistent with the hypothesis that these wilderness designations were systematic adjustments to pressures from a rival agency, a finding consistent with findings of Johnson (1985) and Libecap (1981) regarding the role of self-interest in agency management of federal lands.

The implication from this chapter is that the bureaucratic land grab may be much more far-reaching than previous studies suggest. A number of reasons are typically forwarded to explain why half of the West remains in federal stewardship. For instance, it is argued that these are often arid lands that were not worth homesteading; that federal retention came in response to the general wasteful nature of resource exploitation of public lands; and that the public demanded retention because of the general aversion to monopoly acquisition of public land resources. Although these elements are all part of the story, a more thorough exploration of the issue should include the paramount role of the land-management bureaucracies. Testing this possibility will require a more encompassing theory of bureaucracy that incorporates competition of administrative agencies. The data on early wilderness designations suggest that bureaucratic interests matter.

REFERENCES

Allin, Craig W. 1982. *The Politics of Wilderness Preservation.* Westport, Conn.: Greenwood Press.

———. 1987. Wilderness Preservation as a Bureaucratic Tool. In *Federal Lands Policy,* edited by Phillip O. Foss. Westport, Conn.: Greenwood Press.

Blais, Andre, and Stephane Dion, eds. 1991. *The Budget-Maximizing Bureaucrat: Appraisals and Evidence.* Pittsburgh: University of Pittsburgh Press.

Carroll, Kathleen A. 1989. Industrial Structure and Monopoly Power in the Federal Bureaucracy: An Empirical Analysis. *Economic Inquiry* 23, no. 4: 683–703.

Dana, Samuel Trask, and Sally K. Fairfax. 1980. *Forest and Range Policy: Its Development in the United States.* New York: McGraw-Hill.

Elliott, E. Donald, Bruce A. Ackerman, and John C. Millian. 1985. Toward a Theory of Statutory Evolution: The Federalization of Environmental Law. *Journal of Law, Economics, and Organization* 1, no. 2: 313–340.

Gates, Paul W. 1968. *History of Public Land Law Development.* Washington, D.C.: Zenger.

Gilligan, James P. 1953. The Development of Policy and Administration of Forest Service Primitive and Wilderness Areas in the Western United States. Ph.D. dissertation, University of Michigan.

Gorte, Ross W., and Betsy A. Cody. 1995. *The Forest Service and Bureau of Land Management: History and Analysis of Merger Proposals.* Washington, D.C.: Congressional Research Service.

Hendee, John C., George H. Stankey, and Robert C. Lucas. 1990. *Wilderness Management.* Golden, Co: North American Press.

Higgins, Richard S., William F. Shughart II, and Robert D. Tollison. 1989. Dual Enforcement of Antitrust Laws. In *Public Choice and Regulation,* edited by Robert J. Mackay, James C. Miller, and Bruce Yandle. Stanford, Cal.: Hoover Institution Press.

Ise, John. 1972. *The United States Forest Policy.* New York: Arno Press.

Johnson, Ronald N. 1985. U.S. Forest Service Policy and Its Budget. In *Forestlands: Public and Private,* edited by R. T. Deacon and M. B. Johnson. San Francisco: Pacific Research Institute for Public Policy.

Johnson, Ronald N., and Gary D. Libecap. 1994. *The Federal Civil Service System and the Problem of Bureaucracy: The Economics and Politics of Institutional Change.* Chicago: University of Chicago Press.

Libecap, Gary D. 1981. *Locking up the Range: Federal Land Controls and Grazing*. San Francisco: Pacific Research Institute for Public Policy.

———. 1984. The Political Allocation of Mineral Rights: A Reevaluation of Teapot Dome. *Journal of Economic History* 44: 381–391.

McChesney, Fred S. 1990. Government as Definer of Property Rights: Indian Lands, Ethnic Externalities, and Bureaucratic Budgets. *Journal of Legal Studies* 19: 297–335.

McCloskey, Michael. 1966. The Wilderness Act of 1964: Its Background and Meaning. *Oregon Law Review* 45, no. 4: 288–321.

McCubbins, Mathew D., Roger G. Noll, and Barry R. Weingast. 1987. Administrative Procedures as Instruments of Political Control. *Journal of Law, Economics, and Organization* 3, no. 2: 243–277.

Nelson, Robert H. 1995. *Public Lands and Private Rights: The Failure of Scientific Management*. Lanham, Md: Rowman and Littlefield.

Niskanen, William A. 1971. *Bureaucracy and Representative Government*. Chicago: Aldine-Atherton.

Peffer, Louise E. 1951. *The Closing of the Public Domain: Disposal and Reservation Policies 1900–1950*. Stanford, Cal.: Stanford University Press.

Shleifer, Andrei. 1998. State versus Private Ownership. *Journal of Economic Perspectives* 12, no. 4: 133–150.

Stiglitz, Joseph. 1998. The Private Uses of Public Interests: Incentives and Institutions. *Journal of Economic Perspectives* 12, no. 2: 3–22.

U.S. Department of Agriculture. 1929. *Agricultural Yearbook*.

———. Forest Service. 1928. *Report to the Chief*.

———. Forest Service. 1930/31. *Report of the Forester*.

———. Forest Service. 1984. *The Wilderness Movement and the National Forests*, by Dennis M. Roth. Forest Service History Series 391.

U.S. Department of Interior. 1904. *Annual Report of the Secretary*. Washington, D.C.: U.S. Government Printing Office.

———. various years. *Report of the Commissioner of the General Land Office to the Secretary of the Interior*. Washington, D.C.: U.S. Government Printing Office.

Wilkinson, Charles F., and H. Michael Anderson. 1987. *Land and Resource Planning in the National Forests*. Washington, D.C.: Island Press.

Thomas Stratmann

The Politics of Superfund

Introduction

Is federal spending on environmental goods—in particular spending to reduce environmental health risk—determined only by the severity of the hazard, and thus by the objective to reduce the potential for health problems to the general public, or are other factors important in explaining spending patterns? This chapter sets out to answer this question and to identify spending patterns associated with Superfund, a program instituted to clean up the country's worst hazardous waste sites. This chapter will examine whether political factors, in addition to objective environmental and health factors, are important in determining the disbursement of Superfund monies. Political factors include interest group influence, legislators pressuring the Environmental Protection Agency (EPA) to fund sites in their home states or districts, and EPA bureaucratic discretion in allocating federal funds to meet the EPA's perhaps budget-maximizing or ideological objectives.

Some economists (Barnett 1985; Hird 1990, 1993, 1994) believe that the government acts primarily in the public interest. According to this view, Superfund monies are distributed in accordance with environmental risks faced by the general public, which is the written intent of the Superfund law. If this view is correct, the allocation of funds is consistent with a vision of a benevolent government. Recent work found that representatives in Congress vote for Superfund funding when members of their local constituency live in polluted areas (Hamilton 1997).

Other economists (Peltzman 1976; Olson 1982; Becker 1983) see government actions as being importantly influenced by the self-interests of politicians and interest groups, and these interests are seen as the primary factors determining the allocation of funds. For example, some scholars hypothesize that Superfund monies are allocated in a pork-barrel fashion, meaning that legislators seek funds for their home states or districts in order to benefit their constituency (Stroup and Shaw 1989; Yandle 1989; Stroup 1996). In this case, funds are allocated to serve private interests, not the public interest, and the amount allocated to Superfund sites may not be reflective of a health risk to citizens in the area.

Much of the support for either the benevolent government view or the more cynical self-interested individuals view comes from anecdotal evidence instead of systematic empirical studies. The few statistical studies that exist have limitations in that they examine only relatively short time periods and do not consider health and political economy variables in the statistical analysis, which would shed light on the relative importance of health versus political issues. The purpose of this chapter is to determine the relative importance of both views for Superfund expenditures.

In addition to focusing on how the self-interest of politicians and interest groups shapes Superfund allocation, this chapter examines whether bureaucrats influence the distribution of funds. Liability rules are one important aspect of the Superfund law, and perhaps its most controversial facet (Shanahan 1994). The three main types of liability under Superfund are retroactive liability, joint and several liability, and strict liability. These rules imply that previous and current owners of sites, and parties who have contributed to the contamination of sites, are liable for the cleanup costs and must compensate the federal government for cleanup expenditures. No scholarly work has been done to examine strategies that the bureaucrats who administer the program (the EPA) may follow to obtain the most monies from potentially responsible parties (PRPs). Policy analysts have not examined the spending strategies of the EPA. Does the EPA incur only few expenses on a site where there are no PRPs readily available to sue because the EPA does not want to spend scarce resources if funds cannot be recovered? Or do EPA bureaucrats decide to spend strategically to induce viable PRPs to take over the cleanup activities? This chapter investigates these issues empirically.

A Brief History of Superfund

The Comprehensive Environmental Response, Compensation, and Liability Act (CERCLA), commonly referred to as Superfund, was enacted in 1980. The purpose of CERCLA was to clean up hazardous substances on sites that endanger public health and the environment. The passage of this law has been widely attributed to the environmental concern following the Love Canal incident in 1978. CERCLA also established liability rules for persons associated with these sites. The act established a $1.6 billion trust fund to clean up toxic sites pending cost recovery actions against responsible parties and when no responsible party could be identified. A 1986 amendment to CERCLA, the Superfund Amendments and Reauthorization Act (SARA), authorized an additional trust fund of $8.5 billion over another five years. Once SARA was enacted, cleanup spending on Superfund sites increased significantly (Hird 1994). SARA was to expire in 1991 but was extended until 1994 as part of the Omnibus Budget Reconciliation Act of 1990. In 1994, Superfund was extended again, and an additional $5.1 billion in funding was authorized. To date, the trust fund has increased many times over the originally intended amount, and projections suggest that cleanup activities are likely to take decades and will cost between $106 and $463 billion (Probst, Fullerton, Litan, and Portney 1995).

The Superfund Act, which is administered by the EPA, set forth procedures for allocating funds to sites posing the most hazardous health risk. As of 1998, the EPA has identified approximately 55,000 potential hazardous waste sites. Sites that are considered to be a serious health risk, based on their score on a hazard ranking system (HRS), are placed on the national priority list (NPL) and are entitled to federal funds to be used for cleanup. Only nonfederal NPL sites are eligible for Superfund spending. The HRS is based on a scoring system that measures actual and potential toxic substance pollution through air, surface, and groundwater contamination. The combination of contaminants in these pollution pathways form the HRS score. If a site exceeds a score of 28.5 on the HRS, it is placed on the NPL. The cutoff level HRS score for listing on the NPL was not chosen for its scientific relevance. Rather it was set so that the program would begin with four hundred sites. When the original Superfund law was passed, an HRS score of 28.5 was the level of toxicity at which the politically agreed-upon number of NPL sites was reached. A site can be listed on the NPL with an HRS score of less than 28.5 if it is deemed a health risk by the Agency for Toxic Substances and Disease Registry or if a state designates a site as a top priority (each state is entitled to one designation). Of the potentially hazardous waste sites that have been identified, more than 1,200 sites are currently on the NPL, and the EPA estimates that 3,000 sites will eventually be added to the NPL.

The EPA has broad discretionary power over Superfund allocation decisions and for setting spending priorities (Hird 1994). The statutory requirements of the initial law, CERCLA, were vague. The 1986 reauthorization provided little more guidance regarding which criteria the EPA should use in making decisions regarding NPL site designation, spending, and enforcement. Little direction was given about how the EPA should trade off competing objectives and how it should weigh criteria. There is, however, some guidance for procedures regulating Superfund. The National Contingency Plan (NCP) lists criteria for evaluating the relative merits of alternative cleanup procedures. Guidelines include the protection of human health and community acceptance criteria, which allow for modification of the proposed action. Overall, these guidelines are so broad that there is wide latitude in interpretation. It is this room for interpretation of the law that allows the EPA to use its own judgment in making cleanup decisions.

Congressional committees have influence over writing Superfund bills and appropriating monies to the EPA. In the House of Representatives, the two committees are the Committee on Energy and Commerce and its Subcommittee on Finance and Hazardous Materials and the Appropriations Committee and its Subcommittee on Veterans' Affairs, HUD, and Independent Agencies. In the Senate, the two committees relevant to Superfund are the Committee on Environment and Public Works and its Subcommittee on Superfund, Waste Control, and Risk Assessment and the Appropriations Committee and its Subcommittee on Veterans' Affairs, HUD, and Independent Agencies.

The Economic Framework

The economic theory of regulation provides one pillar of this chapter's conceptual framework. According to the economic model, legislators obtain support from competing constituencies. The model predicts that legislators do not necessarily help one constituency versus another, but rather legislators trade off the gain from helping one group versus another group. In equilibrium, the legislator maximizes support from groups by supporting them both a little rather than alienating one side or another (Peltzman 1976). This model predicts that not only special interest groups, who may supply financial support to legislators' elections, but also the general public, which supplies important votes in legislators' election campaigns, are important for the allocation of Superfund monies. Therefore, both the health hazard from Superfund sites imposed upon citizens and interest group strength in the areas where sites are located are important for explaining allocation patterns.

Models of regulation and interest group competition have no room for bureaucratic involvement in policy decisions and implicitly view bureaucrats as executors of politicians' legislative intent (Peltzman 1976; Becker 1983). Because the EPA does have broad control over spending and procedures, the economic theory of bureaucracy will be marshaled to contribute to the explanation of Superfund spending.

In the bureaucracy literature, there are several competing views regarding the autonomy and objectives of bureaucracies. Some scholars hypothesize that bureaucrats pursue their own interest, an interest that differs from the intent of the law as designed by the legislature (Niskanen 1971). In this case, policy outcomes may result that differ from the legislative intent. Weingast and Moran (1983) put forth a congressional control hypothesis and provide evidence that Congress has influence over decisions made by the Federal Trade Commission. Similarly, McCubbins, Noll, and Weingast (1989) acknowledge that bureaucrats' objectives differ from those of politicians but maintain that administrative rules, oversight committees, and the budget appropriation process provide an effective constraint on bureaucratic behavior. Although there are congressional constraints on bureaucratic behavior, it is not clear how much leeway bureaucrats have in the interpretation of the law and in setting priorities for spending and regulations. Certainly, bureaucratic independence differs from agency to agency, and the EPA is one of the agencies that generally has more leeway than others in making independent decisions (Johnson and Libecap 1994). As noted previously, this leeway is particularly relevant for the Superfund program.

Some evidence is consistent with the hypothesis that the EPA uses discretion in its behavior. Hamilton's (1996) analysis of Resource Conservation and Recovery Act (RCRA) statutes shows that the EPA exhibits strategic behavior involving high initial penalties for polluters. These penalties are reduced once the polluter enters into negotiations with the EPA. The average proposed penalty is significantly greater than the average final penalty after EPA/polluter negotiations occur. Also, the EPA is likely to use informal rather than formal rules to levy higher fines than otherwise possible (Hamilton 1996).

For Superfund, the EPA has wide regulatory latitude for environmental enforcement. Consistent with the view of a budget-maximizing agency, the EPA may want to maximize fund recovery from PRPs. Thus, the issue for the EPA becomes identifying and using the strategy that maximizes fund recovery. If the EPA behaves like agents in a plea-bargaining model, it will accept smaller fines if the PRP agrees to accept responsibility early on in the process, whereas it will levy larger fines if litigation occurs. Thus, the EPA uses the threat of prosecution to elicit smaller financial penalties from PRPs than it may receive through actual prosecuting of PRPs. The agency benefits from offering a "plea bargain" because it reduces lengthy and costly litigation. If the EPA follows this strategy, the test results should show that responsible parties receive lighter penalties if they admit legal responsibility in early negotiations. If parties go through litigation, they are expected to incur fines if they lose in court.

Applied to EPA spending on Superfund sites, the aforementioned strategy implies that the EPA will spend only a little money on its own while negotiating with the PRP so as to hold the potential PRP liability (reimbursement to the EPA) down. In this case, the EPA tries to develop friendly relations with the PRP by holding down spending on cleanup. If litigation occurs, EPA spending will increase.

A different EPA strategy may be to spend more money initially to encourage the PRP to accept cleanup responsibility early to avoid having to reimburse the EPA's expenses. The EPA would then take over the remaining cleanup activities. For example, the EPA may choose to use expensive methods for site cleanup to induce the PRP to take over cleanup activities voluntarily. The logic behind this is that the PRP will prefer the certainty of lower expenses (the PRP will use less costly technologies) over the uncertainty of reimbursing the EPA for large amounts of money.

Alternatively, spending may not be influenced by the presence of a PRP at all. This chapter examines whether the EPA incurs fewer expenses on a site where there are no PRPs readily available to sue. Because it may be rational for the EPA to act in any of these ways, only empirical work can discover the actual method used by the EPA.

In addition to the EPA, legislators have an incentive to exert influence over Superfund regulation. Because funds spent through the Superfund program have beneficial employment effects, legislators prefer having funds coming into their home states and districts as it increases their chances of reelection. Dalton, Riggs, and Yandle (1996) suggest that local interests desire Superfund allocations because no direct costs are imposed on citizens and communities, even if Superfund is not effective in cleanup. However, if a PRP is among the home constituency, Superfund spending can have a negative effect on home electorate. The PRP may have to reimburse the EPA for the cleanup expense incurred. If the PRP is economically important for the region and if the amount of the repayment affects the company severely, the average constituent may incur an economic loss because of EPA Superfund expenditures. Thus, legislators with some influence over the EPA may have different preferences on Superfund spending on sites in their states and districts. (Legislators with influence are defined as those who are more senior and those who are members of oversight committees and committees that allocate funds to the EPA.)

Because of the possibility that legislators influence the EPA in its spending decisions and because the initial Superfund law required that each state had a Superfund site, this environmental program has been referred to as a pork-barrel program (Stroup and Shaw 1989; Yandle 1989). It appears, however, that the Superfund program may be less obviously the result of distributive politics than some other programs are. Typically, pork barrel–like congressional programs that benefit only some home constituencies either are written specifically into bills or are passed separately (for example, amendments to farm bills that increase subsidies to peanut farmers). The Superfund program, however, is passed as a whole, and the EPA has wide discretion as to how to spend the money. Unlike other federal programs designed to benefit specific constituencies, which have the classic logrolling outcome of the average taxpayer paying expenses that benefit a geographically concentrated minority, the Superfund program's benefits are widely distributed. Some characteristics of the Superfund program are consistent with the view that it is a program designed to enhance efficiency by reducing health hazards.

This is not to say that Superfund is void of distributive politics. For example, Superfund could be explained as a giant logroll, where every legislator benefits by helping a subgroup in his or her district at the expense of all taxpayers. Federal highway spending is another program that may be viewed in this light. However, the even allocation of funds across districts—which to some extent is written into the Superfund law, because each state is mandated to have at least one site—makes it difficult to find evidence for the pork-barrel spending hypothesis. Usually, increased spending in districts with legislators on oversight committees or the appropriations committee is viewed as evidence of pork-barrel politics. For example, with programs such as the farm programs it is possible for legislators on the agriculture committee to write special provisions into a bill to benefit their home constituencies. Thus, one would be able to document that more peanut subsidies occur in the home districts of the legislators on the agriculture committee. This is less likely to be the case for Superfund allocations because the EPA has wide discretion as to where to spend the monies.

Legislators have direct control over legislation but less direct control over the bureaucracy. To obtain extra Superfund spending in the home district, legislators have to influence EPA decisions directly. Thus, one predicts that committee membership will be less important in the Superfund program than for some other distributive programs.

If Superfund is nothing but a disguised form of federal aid, one predicts that the same allocation patterns that have been found for other federal aid apply. In particular, Inman (1988) has shown that "federal aid is almost always inversely related to the level of state income" (p. 230). Thus, if Superfund were designed to be a welfare program for the poor, state income would be negatively related to spending. However, spending to clean up hazardous sites is spending on environmental goods. If the environment is a normal good, one predicts that state income is positively related with Superfund spending.

Empirical Model and Data

The economic framework suggests that spending is a function of legislators' characteristics, interest group characteristics, bureaucratic behavior, and health hazards. This empirical model will be applied to explain Superfund spending on NPL sites. Thus, covariates measuring these characteristics and other site characteristics are combined to form the empirical model

$$\text{Spending} = f(\text{Interest Group Strength, Legislators' Characteristics, Bureaucracy, Health Hazard, Site Characteristics}) + \varepsilon.$$

The unit of observation is Superfund spending on an NPL site. The dependent spending variable is the cumulative real (in 1983–84 dollars) spending from 1983 to 1997 per site. This variable is measured in two ways: first, as total spending (ALL EXPENDITURES); and second, as spending on removal and remedial activities (REMOVAL AND REMEDIAL EXPENDITURES). The first measure includes expenditures on feasibility studies and on-site investigation, as well as removal and remedial activities. These data are collected from the EPA database CERCLIS. The universe of the data is spending on all NPL sites; thus, the data set includes sites that have been cleaned up. The analysis is limited to sites that have been put on the NPL prior to 1994. Little spending has occurred on sites that have been put on the NPL after that date. Only nonfederal NPL sites are included because federal NPL sites are not eligible for Superfund monies. Further, the sample size is limited by the fact that a complete set of variables for some sites was unavailable. The sample has 1,052 site observations.

Interest group strength is measured by membership per one thousand state residents in Greenpeace, the Sierra Club, and the National Wildlife Federation in 1990 (ENVIRGRP). The source of these data is the *1991–1992 Green Index* (Hall and Kerr 1991). As the percentage of individuals within a state affiliated with environmental groups increases, that state's legislators have an incentive to appease their constituents by influencing the EPA to allocate funds. In addition, the EPA itself may be responsive to the pressure of interest groups, because these groups may sue or at least create unpleasant publicity for the EPA if they are not pleased with decisions. Or the interest groups may complain to their representatives, which in turn may lead representatives to pressure the EPA bureaucracy. Thus, environmental group strength is predicted to have a positive influence on spending.

To allow for a possible nonlinearity in the interest group variable, the squared term of the variable is included in the regression analysis (ENVIRGRP SQ). The estimated coefficient will not reflect a causal relation if unobserved variables determine both interest group strength and spending. If state interest group membership and

Superfund spending is high due to severe environmental problems in the state (severity of environmental problems being the unobserved variable), then the coefficient on interest group membership is biased upward.

Real state per capita income in 1990 is also included to measure constituency and, perhaps, interest group preferences (INCOME PER CAPITA). If environmental goods are a normal good, then a positive sign is predicted.

Legislator characteristics are measured by seniority and membership on the congressional committees relevant to the EPA. Variables included are the cumulative seniority of members on the House Appropriations Committee by state (APPSUM), the cumulative seniority of members on the Senate Appropriations Committee by state (SAPPSUM), the cumulative seniority of members on the House Energy and Commerce Committee by state (ENSUM), and the cumulative seniority of members on the Senate Environment and Public Works Committee by state (EPWSUM). The variables on seniority and committee membership are collected from the *Congressional Quarterly Almanac* (1982–1997).

To examine whether the EPA behaves strategically in various stages of interaction with the PRPs, the following variables are included: the number of times the EPA negotiates with a PRP during the remedial investigation or feasibility study (the period when the EPA determines if remedial action is necessary and what are feasible cleanup technologies) of the site (RIFSNEG); the number of times during remedial cleanup that the EPA negotiates with a PRP about remedial design or remedial action at a site (RDRANEG); the number of times the EPA negotiates with a PRP regarding cost recovery (CSTNEGOT); the number of times litigation pursuant to Section 107 of CERCLA (which allows the EPA to assign blame and recover costs for cleanup actions without the cooperation of the responsible party) occurred regarding the site (LITIG107); the number of judicial administrative orders (wherein the responsible party admits guilt and thus has to reimburse the EPA for all or part of the cleanup expenses) that have been administered against responsible parties (ADMCNSNT); and whether the site is owned by a private company, as opposed to having mixed ownership or ownership by a state or the federal government (PRIVOWN).

A variable is included for whether an industry can be identified as responsible for the damage (ORPHAN). Superfund was designed to spend on sites for which no responsible party can be identified. If the EPA follows the intent of this law, an orphan site will receive more money from Superfund because there is little hope of finding a responsible party for cleanup. All data for this variable are obtained from CERCLIS.

A site's health hazard measure is the HRS score, which is the primary tool that the EPA uses for measuring the hazard posed by a potential NPL site. Scores were obtained from a Resources for the Future database. Sites for which the HRS score could not be obtained were excluded from the data.

The HRS score combines the measurements of three pollution migration pathways: groundwater (GW), surface water (SW), and air (A). Using a certain set of criteria, the EPA scores each pathway from zero to one hundred, with a larger number indicating a greater environmental problem. The score is influenced not only by the amount of potential pollutants, but also by the size of the population affected, and potentially affected, by the pollution. The scores are combined in the following manner (Hird 1990):

$$\text{HRS} = \sqrt{\frac{\text{GW}^2 + \text{SW}^2 + \text{A}^2}{3}}$$

Sites that achieve a score of 28.5 are placed on the NPL.

There are several problems with the HRS. First, the design of the scoring mechanism biases the score upward. Because the most hazardous substance found at the site is used to score the health hazard, sites such as mines attain a high HRS due to the large amount of waste, even though very little of that waste may pose a health hazard (Stroup 1995). Second, because of the squaring of the individual pathway scores, HRS scores are higher if one of the underlying pathway scores is high, leading to an emphasis on sites with single pollutants. Sites are therefore likely to be on the NPL if pollutants can escape through multiple pathways. Although the final score may not accurately measure the real health risk of a site, it is the best summary measure of toxicity and risk to the surrounding population that currently exists.

Site characteristics are collected from CERCLIS. A control for the size of the site is the number of operable units on the site (UNITS). Cleanup costs are affected by the type of toxicity. Consequently, controls are included that indicate whether the site was originally a chemical plant (CHEMPLNT); whether it has mines or tailings (MINES); whether there are waterways, creeks, or rivers on the site (WATERWYS); and whether the site is radioactive (RADIOAC).

Sites do not have to pass the HRS minimum score criterion if the site is selected by the Agency for Toxic Substances and Disease Registry or if a state declares the site a priority. Thus, two indicator variables for these cases are included (ATSDR and PRIORITY, respectively).

Another control variable in the regression analysis is the number of PRPs on a site (NPRP). These data are obtained from Resources for the Future, and the variable is measured by the number of notifying letters sent to PRPs by the EPA. Unfortunately, these data are not considered very accurate, because the EPA has numerous PRPs that it has not publicly identified. It is unclear what a large number of PRPs at a site means to EPA's strategies. Fewer PRPs could mean that identifying a responsible party is easier, or it may be that a greater number of PRPs makes it more likely for the EPA to get a private party to pay. However, controlling for a potential effect appears desirable. The second motive to include PRPs in the regression analysis is to control for the fact that the EPA will spend less on a site if PRPs have agreed to take responsibility for cleanup.

Lastly, the analysis controls for the date the site was put on the NPL (START), because more spending can have occurred on sites that were put on the list earlier. These data were obtained from RTK-Net (Right-To-Know Network).

Table 1 contains variable means and standard deviations, as well as the variable description.

Results

Regression results are presented in table 2. The second column reports the results with removal and remedial site expenditures as the dependent variable. The third column comes from regressions with total Superfund site expenditures as the dependent variable.

In all regressions, the results show that more toxic sites, as measured by the HRS score, receive priority with respect to funding. Also, consistent with EPA's statutory obligations, orphan sites receive priority with respect to funding.

Some of the variation in spending across sites is explained by the type of site. More spending occurs on radioactive sites and sites with waterways running through them. However, mines and former chemical plants do not receive any more Superfund monies than the left-out categories, such as housing areas, lagoons, or landfills. Radioactive sites may receive more funds because they are most expensive to clean up. Or it could be that the EPA puts priority on radioactive sites because the agency believes that those sites pose a significant health hazard relative to lagoons or landfills.

Some, but not all, of the political economy variables matter for explaining Superfund allocation. States with more senior legislators on the House Committee on Energy and Commerce and the Senate Appropriations Committee receive more funds than states with no members on those committees. The coefficients on the other two

TABLE 1 Data Description Means (Standard Deviations)

Variable	*Description*	*Mean (standard deviation)*
REMOVAL AND REMEDIAL EXPENDITURES	Removal (real 1983–84) expenditures 1983–1997	4.570 (13.581)
ALL EXPENDITURES	All (real 1983–84) expenditures 1983–1997	4.727 (13.789)
ADMCNSNT	Number of administrative orders on consent	0.961 (2.188)
APPSUM	Cumulative seniority of House Appropriations Committee members, by state	13.823 (10.154)
ATSDR	Agency for Toxic Substances and Disease Registry equals one, zero otherwise	0.005 (0.069)
CHEMPLNT	Chemical plant equals one, zero otherwise	0.095 (0.293)
CSTNEGOT	Number of cost recovery negotiations	0.066 (0.309)
ENSUM	Cumulative seniority of House Energy and Commerce Committee members, by state	10.236 (7.886)
ENVIRGRP	State environmental group members per 1,000 state population	9.305 (2.877)
ENVIRGRP SQ	ENVIRGRP squared	94.860 (55.899)
EPWSUM	Cumulative seniority of Senate Environment and Public Works Committee members, by state	23.796 (30.405)
HRS	Hazard ranking system score	40.809 (9.950)

TABLE 1 *(continued)*

Variable	*Description*	*Mean (standard deviation)*
INCOME PER CAPITA	Per capita income, 1990 (real 1983–84)	16,128.4 (2,426.7)
LITIG107	Number of Section 107 litigations	0.240 (0.472)
MINES	Site with mines/tailings equals one, zero otherwise	0.032 (0.177)
NPRP	Number of potentially responsible parties, by site	26.119 (34.271)
ORPHAN	Orphan site equals one, zero otherwise	0.069 (0.254)
PRIORITY	State priority site equals one, zero otherwise	0.022 (0.146)
PRIVOWN	Private ownership equals one, zero otherwise	0.365 (0.482)
RADIOAC	Radioactive site equals one, zero otherwise	0.0124 (0.111)
RDRANEG	Number of remedial design/action negotiations	0.937 (1.054)
RIFSNEG	Number of remedial investigation/ feasibility study negotiations	0.710 (0.642)
SAPPSUM	Cumulative seniority of Senate Appropriations Committee members, by state	37.315 (42.820)
START	Year of NPL listing	1985.98 (2.856)
UNITS	Number of operable units on an NPL site	3.009 (1.648)
WATERWYS	Waterways, creeks, rivers on an NPL site equals one, zero otherwise	0.010 (0.102)

TABLE 2 Spending on NPL Sites
Parameter Estimates and Standard Errors

Variable	*Dep. Var.*: REMOVAL AND REMEDIAL EXPENDITURES	*Dep. Var.*: ALL EXPENDITURES
INTERCEPT	367.56 (294.03)	373.53 (295.91)
HRS	0.184 (0.042)	0.186 (0.042)
RIFSNEG	–2.368 (0.640)	–2.378 (0.644)
RDRANEG	1.018 (0.436)	0.989 (0.439)
CSTNEGOT	6.274 (1.277)	6.299 (1.285)
LITIG107	3.234 (0.875)	3.287 (0.880)
ADMCNSNT	–0.448 (0.187)	–0.443 (0.188)
PRIVOWN	1.305 (0.827)	1.293 (0.832)
ORPHAN	6.932 (1.536)	6.946 (1.546)
CHEMPLNT	1.923 (1.333)	2.016 (1.341)
RADIOAC	13.107 (3.711)	13.423 (3.735)
MINES	0.640 (2.263)	0.732 (2.277)
WATERWYS	10.263 (3.725)	10.186 (3.749)
APPSUM	–1.153 (0.758)	–1.180 (0.763)
SAPPSUM	0.384 (0.215)	0.382 (0.216)
ENSUM	2.128 (0.855)	2.151 (0.860)
EPWSUM	–0.066 (0.245)	–0.060 (0.247)

TABLE 2 *(continued)*

Variable	*Dep. Var.:* REMOVAL AND REMEDIAL EXPENDITURES	*Dep. Var.:* ALL EXPENDITURES
INCOME PER CAPITA	0.00030 (0.00028)	0.00028 (0.00028)
ENVIRGRP	–1.561 (0.691)	–1.554 (0.696)
ENVIRGRP SQ	0.071 (0.032)	0.072 (0.033)
NPRP	–0.00011 (0.012)	–0.00028 (0.012)
UNITS	1.366 (0.271)	1.484 (0.273)
START	–0.189 (0.148)	–0.192 (0.149)
ATSDR	11.182 (6.142)	11.075 (6.182)
PRIORITY	–1.198 (2.608)	–1.257 (2.624)
R^2	0.212	0.217

included committees are not statistically significant. However, the total effect of all committee variables on spending is greater than zero at the 2 percent level of statistical significance. Thus, legislative influence matters when it comes to Superfund spending. The importance of committee membership is dominated by the House Committee on Energy and Commerce, which is consistent with the hypothesis that representatives have a greater interest in obtaining extra spending than senators do. More spending on a Superfund site benefits a larger percentage of representatives' geographic constituency, thus the gains to get extra funding are higher for House members.

State per capita income is important for explaining spending—the coefficient on per capita income is positive and statistically significant. The estimated coefficient in the second column of table 2 implies an income elasticity estimate of 1.1. If one thinks of the regressions as estimating the demand for a clean environment, then the estimates imply that environmental goods are luxury goods. This result is contrary to some findings on federal aid that indicate that more federal funds are being spent in poor communities.

Two caveats apply to the interpretation that the income coefficient reflects demand for environmental goods. First, the coefficient on income is biased upward if unobserved variables lead to more Superfund spending and higher per capita income. An example of an unobserved variable could be past income growth that was associated with polluting the environment. In that case, past income growth leads to higher current per capita income, and past pollution may necessitate more Superfund spending on cleanups. Second, if high-income individuals are more productive than low-income individuals, health hazards in high-income areas may have higher economic costs than health hazards in low-income areas. According to this view, allocating funds to high-income areas may be wealth-maximizing.

Although the coefficient on environmental group membership is negative, the squared environmental group variable is positive. The combined marginal effect of the interest group variable, evaluated at the mean, is negative, which appears to be an anomaly. However, this anomaly can be explained by recalling that EPA Superfund spending tends to be higher on sites where private parties do not assume responsibility for cleanup. In addition to pressuring the government, environmental groups exert pressure on PRPs by threatening boycotts or by threatening negative publicity if PRPs do not accept liability for the site pollution. If pressuring private firms is effective, EPA spending will be lower on sites where groups successfully lobbied private parties. Thus, the negative effect of state environmental interest group membership may reflect that interest groups with large numbers exert strong pressure on PRPs to clean up sites in their state.

All variables that measure EPA discretion in Superfund allocations across sites are important, and an interesting pattern emerges. Initial negotiations (RIFSINEG) are associated with less spending, which can be interpreted as the agency offering a "plea bargain" to the PRP. If the PRP agrees to accept responsibility, only few expenses will have to be reimbursed. However, cost negotiations and litigation are associated with higher spending (coefficients on CSTNEGOT, RDRANEG, LITIG107). Thus, if PRPs did not initially agree to accept responsibility, they are faced with higher reimbursement costs. Finally, once a consent decree has been entered (the EPA knows that it will get reimbursed) spending decreases (ADMCNSNT). A consent decree indicates that a PRP reimburses the EPA for all or part of EPA expenditures prior to the decree.

The results provide strong evidence that the EPA behaves differently, with respect to Superfund spending on sites, at various points of interaction with PRPs. However, two caveats to the interpretation of the bureaucratic control variables apply. First, to the extent that cost negotiations and litigations occur when costs actually have been incurred, the bureaucratic control variables have some elements of the dependent variable in them. Second, sometimes a PRP agrees in a consent decree not only to reimburse the EPA but also to spend its own money on future cleanups. In that case, the negative sign on the administrative consent variable partly reflects that the EPA has to spend less on sites if PRPs pay for cleanup because of a consent agreement.

Summary

This chapter analyzes the determinants of Superfund cleanup expenditures. It examines whether objective environmental criteria can account for all of the Superfund expenditures, or whether legislators, their constituencies, interest groups, PRPs, and preferences of

EPA bureaucrats influence the allocation of funds. The results show that funds are allocated in both wealth-maximizing and wealth-reducing manners. Potentially wealth-maximizing is the fact that sites with more health hazards do receive more funds. Similarly, more money is spent on orphan sites. However, the efforts of legislators to send funds to their home districts are also important in explaining the allocation of Superfund monies, and this aspect of Superfund money distribution is potentially wealth-reducing. Finally, it appears that the EPA behaves differently, with respect to Superfund spending on sites, at various points of interaction with PRPs.

REFERENCES

Barnett, Harold C. 1985. The Allocation of Superfund, 1981–1983. *Land Economics* 61, no. 3 (August): 255–262.

Becker, Gary S. 1983. A Theory of Competition among Pressure Groups for Political Influence. *Quarterly Journal of Economics* 98, 371–400.

Congressional Quarterly Almanac. 1982–1987. Washington, D.C.: Congressional Quarterly Press.

Dalton, Brett, David Riggs, and Bruce Yandle. 1996. The Political Production of Superfund: Some Financial Market Results. *Eastern Economic Journal* 22, no. 1 (Winter): 75–87.

Hall, Bob, and Mary L. Kerr. 1991. *1991–1992 Green Index*. Washington, D.C.: Island Press.

Hamilton, James T. 1996. Going by the (Informal) Book: The EPA's Use of Informal Rules in Enforcing Hazardous Waste Laws. In *Advances in the Study of Entrepreneurship, Innovation, and Economic Growth*, vol. 7, edited by Gary D. Libecap. Greenwich, Conn.: JAI Press.

Hamilton, James T. 1997. Taxes, Torts, and Toxic Release Inventory: Congressional Voting on Instruments to Control Pollution. *Economic Inquiry* 35 (October): 745–762.

Hird, John A. 1990. Superfund Expenditures and Cleanup Priorities: Distributive Politics or Public Interest. *Journal of Policy Analysis and Management* 9: 445–483.

Hird, John A. 1993. Congressional Voting on Superfund: Self-Interest or Ideology? *Public Choice* 77: 333–357.

Hird, John A. 1994. *Superfund: The Political Economy of Environmental Risk.* Harrisonburg, Va.: John Hopkins University Press.

Inman, Robert P. 1988. Federal Assistance and Local Services in the United States: The Evolution of a New Federalist Fiscal Order. In *Fiscal Federalism: Quantitative Studies,* edited by Harvey S. Rosen. Chicago: University of Chicago Press.

Johnson, Ronald N., and Gary D. Libecap. 1994. *The Federal Civil Service System and the Problem of Bureaucracy: The Economics and Politics of Institutional Change.* Chicago: University of Chicago Press.

McCubbins, Matthew D., Roger G. Noll, and Barry R. Weingast. 1989. Structure and Process, Politics and Policy: Administrative Arrangements and the Political Control of Agencies. *Virginia Law Review* 75: 431–482.

Niskanen, William A., Jr. 1971. *Bureaucracy and Representative Government.* Chicago: Aldine-Atherton.

Olson, Mancur. 1982. *The Rise and Decline of Nations: Economic Growth, Stagflation and Social Rigidities.* New Haven, Conn.: Yale University Press.

Peltzman, Sam. 1976. Towards a More General Theory of Regulation? *Journal of Law and Economics* 19 (August): 211–240.

Probst, Katherine N., Don Fullerton, Robert E. Litan, and Paul R. Portney. 1995. *Footing the Bill for Superfund Cleanups.* Washington, D.C.: The Brookings Institution and Resources for the Future.

Shanahan, John. 1994. Superfund Status Quo: Why the Preauthorization Bills Won't Fix Superfund's Fatal Flaws. The Heritage Foundation, Issue Bulletin #204, October.

Stroup, Richard L. 1995. The Use of Knowledge in Environmental Policy. In *L'Environment—A Quel Prix?*, edited by Ejan Mackay and Helene Trudeau. Montreal: Les Editions Themis.

Stroup, Richard L. 1996. Superfund: The Shortcut that Failed. PERC Policy Series, #PS-5, May.

Stroup, Richard L., and Jane S. Shaw. 1989. The Free Market and the Environment. *The Public Interest* (Fall): 30–43.

Viscusi, Kip, and James Hamilton. 1994. Superfund and Real Risk. *American Enterprise* 5, no. 2 (March/April): 36–45.

Weingast, Barry R., and M. J. Moran. 1983. Bureaucratic Discretion or Congressional Control? Regulatory Policymaking by the Federal Trade Commission. *Journal of Political Economy* 91 (October): 765–800.

Yandle, Bruce. 1989. *The Political Limits on Environmental Legislation: Tracking the Unicorn*. New York: Quorum Books.

Andrew P. Morriss 8

The Politics of the Clean Air Act

If there is any type of environmental problem that deserves analysis as a commons problem, it is air pollution. Relatively clean air is necessary for all forms of human activity, and it is a classic public good. Therefore, it would seem that the rationale for the Clean Air Act is straightforward: The air is a vast commons, and without federal environmental protection laws, it would be treated as a waste-disposal medium. The Clean Air Act thus would appear to represent a triumph of the benevolent social guardian vision of government.

The benevolent social guardian story is a good one. It has a clearly defined set of actors, ranging from the public-spirited legislators who, touched by our shared experience of breathing, put aside partisan differences to solve the problem of air pollution, to the villainous industrialists, particularly the auto and utility industries, whose tailpipes and smokestacks belch a toxic cocktail into the atmosphere. The story is moving—a tragedy of the commons is averted by timely governmental action—and ends with an uplifting moral: We have done a great deal, but there remains more to be done to protect the air. Pollutants left unregulated by the current legislation need to be controlled; greater catastrophes like global warming threaten our future. More action is needed.

Although the benevolent social guardian story has a surface plausibility, there are too many places where the details do not fit the theme. If the Clean Air Act was necessary to stop air pollution, why do the downward trends in air pollutants predate the Clean Air Act? If the statutory framework is appropriate, why has every incarnation of the Clean Air Act since 1967 been described as overly cumbersome? If the air is getting cleaner, why do environmentalists regularly decry the act's failure? As early as 1981, after two major rewrites of the act, an Environmental Protection Agency (EPA) deputy general counsel titled his analysis of the act "Why the Clean Air Act Works Badly" (Pedersen 1981). If the Clean Air Act has been so successful, why does so much remain undone after twenty-eight years? Until 1990, the EPA concentrated on only six air pollutants; only since the 1990 Amendments has the EPA seriously addressed toxic air pollutants. The means of controlling pollution have focused not on reducing the production of pollutants, but on keeping them from the air by mandating dubious technologies, such as power plant stack scrubbers and catalytic converters. The pollution is thus not eliminated, but simply shifted to another form, requiring disposal in land or water. Indeed, recent reports suggest that catalytic converters are responsible for 7 percent of total greenhouse gas emissions (Wald 1998, A1). Moreover, the vast majority of the gains in air quality since 1970 are due to a tiny minority of regulations. How then to explain the massive and complex Clean Air Act?

In place of the benevolent social guardian theory, I offer a special interest explanation for the Clean Air Act. The broad coalition supporting clean air legislation is due not to a consensus on a need for action on clean air, but rather to the substantial benefits for multiple interest groups created by the act. State and federal regulators, environmental interest groups, and major source interests all have powerful reasons to prefer the complex, costly, and not particularly effective Clean Air Act to more cost-effective solutions. This chapter examines the major efforts made in the United States since the 1950s to control air pollution. It first describes the key feature of the Clean Air Act—the state implementation plan (SIP) process—and then discusses the various national air quality laws describing the major features that benefit specific interests. The chapter concludes with an argument for simplification of the Clean Air Act to prevent these problems.

Where Are We?

Flaws in the Social Guardian Story

An understanding of air pollution policy in the United States first requires recognizing that it fits all three of Theodore Lowi's (1972) categories of policies: It is simultaneously redistributive, distributive, and regulatory. Air pollution policy is redistributive because it involves massive transfers of funds among different categories of individuals; it is distributive because favored entities and individuals receive valuable rights and sometimes direct payments; and it is regulatory because it seeks to impose standards on individuals and firms through coercion. The social guardian story is unsatisfactory because it concentrates only on the regulatory aspects, which, although prominent in the public debate over the strictness of air pollution controls, pale in significance when compared with the redistributive and distributive aspects. Indeed, the massive complexity of the Clean Air Act is not due to the difficulties of resolving technical problems of pollution control. The complexity seems to exist to hide special favors for regions and industries with powerful legislative advocates, such as West Virginia's high sulfur coal region and Detroit's auto manufacturers.

This complexity can be most clearly seen in the structure of air pollution regulation—a peculiarly complex and obscure process. Rather than relying on a direct permit system (as under the Clean

Water Act)[1] or market-based mechanisms (as with the limited experiment with tradable emissions permits under the 1990 Clean Air Act Amendments), the federal government chose to regulate air pollution largely through a combination of national ambient air quality standards for a tiny number of particular substances and locally created regulations for determining how to meet the national standards. The result is a series of SIPs, which are massive, detailed documents that specify emissions control limits and methods, often down to the individual source level.

State implementation plans are documents whose length and content defy analysis. As early as 1981, one state's SIP was described as "a jumble of unindexed masses of material . . . approximately 2,000 pages long. . . . There is no index and only a brief table of contents" (Pedersen 1981, 1082). Today, SIPs are even more complex, in part due to the extensive requirements added to the Clean Air Act in 1990. New Jersey's SIP, for example, currently fills eight filing cabinets. Further complicating matters, changes in pollution control technology, industrial practices, regulations, and other factors require virtually constant changes in SIP provisions, resulting in hundreds of amendments annually.

The opaqueness of the SIP process means that few members of the general public are aware of the details of air pollution regulation. Most public attention is focused on the national debate over the ambient standards and the EPA's slow pace in producing them. But individuals directly affected by SIPs, those called upon to change their behavior and incur costs, have an enormous incentive to be aware of the details of the relevant SIPs. The result is a textbook public choice problem.

In addition to obscuring information through their complexity, SIPs are embedded in an administrative process that prevents ratio-

1. Title V of the 1990 Clean Air Act Amendments also created a permit system. Rather than simplifying the Clean Air Act, this system made it more complex, as discussed later.

nal policy development. Because SIPs are creatures of both state and federal governments, they generally require notice-and-comment rule making at both levels of government. Maintaining SIPs, therefore, places enormous administrative burdens on both state agencies and the EPA (even if the EPA merely rubber stamps most changes), preventing meaningful policy development or oversight. In addition, the need for constant SIP alterations to reflect changes in plant design and in economic conditions results in a state plan that is never truly final, and in some cases, whose legal status is unclear. Thus, there is confusion not only about what an SIP says but also about the legal status of many of its provisions.

Public choice analysis suggests an explanation for this combination of technical complexity and administrative drudgery. The SIP creates a mechanism through which individual firms can obtain advantages over competitors and potential competitors by negotiating with state governments for favorable provisions in SIPs. State governments are generally more sensitive to the interests of industry than is the federal government. The SIP provisions also overwhelm the EPA with a flood of often minor, technical amendments, immobilizing federal regulators. SIPs give both federal and state regulators employment security, as well as valuable favors to grant or withhold. At the same time, by creating a national debate over the National Ambient Air Quality Standards (NAAQS), the Clean Air Act gave environmental lobbying groups public relations successes. These successes are not based on cleaner air but on the passage of environmental acts far too complex for the public to understand. Even more importantly, the complexity of the many clean air acts offered environmental lobbying groups a perpetual mission: lobbying federal regulators over the ambient standards.

The Effectiveness of Air Pollution Control

How clean is the air today? Emissions from individual sources are certainly less than they were in 1970 because of improvements in pollution control technology. Despite substantial economic growth since 1970, the air is measurably cleaner in many respects (EPA 1997, ES-3–ES-5). In a somewhat self-congratulatory 1997 cost-benefit analysis, the EPA concluded that the net benefits of the Clean Air Act thus far are between $5.1 and $48.9 trillion (EPA 1997, ES-8). In the face of such staggering net benefits, how can the Clean Air Act be seen as anything other than a resounding success?

The EPA's estimate itself suggests that we need a deeper explanation of the Clean Air Act.[2] The EPA attributes to a handful of regulations the most substantial parts of emissions reduction for the criteria pollutants. Thus the "vast majority" of the reduction in lead emissions is due to the phaseout of leaded gasoline; nitrous oxide emission reductions are "mostly" due to catalytic converter use on motor vehicles; sulfur dioxide emissions are lower "primarily" because of scrubbers and fuel switching; VOC and carbon monoxide emissions are lower "primarily" due to motor vehicle controls; and particulates emissions are down "primarily" because of "vigorous efforts in the 1970s to reduce visible emissions from utility and industry smokestacks" (EPA 1997, ES-2–ES-3). The EPA's estimates of the benefits of simple regulations suggest that although air pollution is complex, regulating air pollution need not be. If these few regulations produced such significant improvements, what is the rest of the complex and innumerable statutes, administrative regulations, and implementation plans accomplishing? Even more strikingly, the downward trend for almost every pollutant predates federal controls for that pollutant (Goklany 2000).

2. The EPA compared a hypothetical no-controls-beyond-1970-levels scenario with current conditions to derive its benefits estimate. Because it is unimaginable that no steps would have been taken after 1970 to control pollution if the CAAA70 had not passed, this vastly overinflates the effectiveness of the act. A thorough critique of the EPA study is beyond the scope of this chapter, however.

The Nature of Air Pollution Creates Opportunities for Hidden Choices

Despite the effectiveness of simple rules like the ones described earlier, many air pollution regulations are complex. The structure of these regulations requires many levels of complex, technical choices that can often conceal advantages for particular regulated entities. Regulatory choices are complex and technical because, despite decades of massive investment in research, air pollution remains a complex and poorly understood phenomenon. One recent air pollution text describes the atmosphere as "a reaction vessel into which are poured reactable constituents and in which are produced a tremendous array of new chemical compounds, generated by gases and vapors reacting with each other and with the particles in the air" (Boubel, Fox, Turner, and Stern 1994, 46). The complexity of these reactions "can be staggering" (Boubel et al. 1994, 168).

There are two main results of this complexity. First, as a result of the chemical and physical complexity of air pollution, regulating air quality through ambient standards requires extensive data whose quality is, therefore, critical. Translating ambient standards into emissions controls requires a four-step process of measuring current air quality, compiling an emissions inventory, constructing a model to relate emissions to ambient levels, and setting control levels (Pedersen 1981, 1065). Each step is both complex and "subject to continued change" as data and science improve (Pedersen 1981, 1065).

All aspects of measuring air quality, for example, present choices that can significantly alter control requirements—choices that are not readily transparent to a casual observer. For example, because air pollutants are (for the most part) gases, "[e]ffective regulation require[s] a precise and agreed measurement of dilution" (Hays 1987, 399). Similarly, the time period for measurement is yet another choice: "[t]he longer the average time [for readings], the more higher emissions at one time could be averaged against lower ones at other times and thus be made acceptable" (Hays 1987, 400). Standardizing emissions standards is further complicated by the combination of combustion with other industrial operations (Senate 1974b, 1107). Even something as basic as defining the pollutant presents problems, as "emissions are complexes of chemicals whose ingredients are relatively unknown" (Hays 1987, 399).

Second, air quality determinations and regulatory decisions are frequently based on complex models of atmospheric interaction, the complexity of which increases as our knowledge of the science of air pollution increases (Pedersen 1981, 1065). Model choice, therefore, has enormous implications for the outcomes. Since the technical choices rarely have obvious answers, it does not require bad behavior or ill-intentions on the part of either regulators or regulated for those choices to be influenced by an understanding of a choice's impact on, for example, employment levels at a local plant.

The State Implementation Plan Process

Curiously, for a statute nominally built on concern about a race to the bottom among states (Revesz 1992, 1226–1227), the Clean Air Act relies heavily on states to make the tough choices for allocating the burdens of air pollution control among their industries. While most scholarly and public attention has focused on the national ambient standards set under the NAAQS process,[3] it is the implementation of those standards through the SIPs that has the more serious

3. Even if the SIP process were not obscure, it would still not be possible for environmental pressure groups to pay sufficient attention to them to make a difference. As with other groups, environmental organizations face budget constraints. At the simplest level, environmental organizations have a choice between focusing on the national standards (such as the NAAQS) or focusing on the SIPs. If they choose the former (as they largely have), they face the problems described herein. If they choose the latter, allowing industry relatively more influence on the national standards, the SIPs will become less important as it is the stringency of the national standards that makes the SIPs' allocations of costs meaningful.

impacts on firms. The reliance on SIPs thus delegates to states a crucial step in the pollution control process.

There are three main reasons that the SIP process remains obscure. First, SIPs are complex and difficult to understand. Table 1 lists the SIP sizes reported by each state in telephone interviews along with the number of full-time equivalent employees devoted to maintaining the SIP. As the table shows, even a moderately sized state like Louisiana described its SIP as filling eighteen file drawers. For large states, the SIPs are of such massive size that it is doubtful that any individual fully comprehends their impact. Most SIPs are well beyond the capability of even well-funded public interest organizations to analyze thoroughly. Several state agencies reported that there was no single document containing all the provisions of their SIPs.

Second, the SIPs are in a constant state of flux.[4] State implementation plans must be tightened whenever new data show that either applicable prevention of significant deterioration (PSD) or nondegradation requirements are no longer being met. Conversely, SIPs may be relaxed if new data show they can achieve their goal with less stringent controls. Redesignation of an area under either the PSD and/or the nonattainment rules can also trigger changes. Changes in an NAAQS can trigger changes in an SIP (Pedersen 1981, 1076–1077). State implementation plans also require changes as a result of changes by sources in processes, output levels, fuels, and so forth. Keeping up with the frequent amendments of the SIP requires a significant investment of manpower, one beyond the

4. Over the Clean Air Act's life, Congress has attempted to force SIPs to be drafted and submitted in a relatively rapid fashion. These deadlines have been, at best, moderately successful. For example, thirty-two states failed to meet the 1986 deadline to revise their SIPs to comply with long-term visibility protection (Friedman 1990, 245). EPA approval of SIPs and modifications is a lengthy process—a 1989 survey, for example, found that the EPA was exceeding its own fourteen-month goal for processing as well as numerous court orders to speed up processing (Friedman 1990, 222).

TABLE 1 SIP Size and FTE Estimates

State	*State's Estimate of SIP Size*	*FTE Employees Maintaining SIP*
Alabama	1½ in.	Unknown
Alaska	3 1½-in. binders	4
Arizona	A wall of file drawers	4
Arkansas	50–60 pp	1
California	Many rooms of documents	300+ regional people
Colorado	9 in. plus appendices; total 27 in.	6–7
Connecticut	Thousands of pages	10
Delaware	700+ pp	5
Florida	8 ft of shelf space, about 1000+ pp	4
Georgia	Draft SIP amendment for Atlanta 600 pp; rules are 2 2-in. binders; total file is 2 cabinets	1.5
Hawaii	2 in. of paper	1 assigned but is behind
Idaho	3 to 4 4-ft × 6-ft bookcases, filled with binders	20
Illinois	Not able to answer question	50
Indiana	Multiple filing cabinets, rules are one volume	19.25
Iowa	3 3-inch binders	4
Kansas	State regs, meat of plan, are not large; submission of plan very large; not sure we could find it	2, very busy
Kentucky	"Huge"; 3 filing cabinet drawers	5
Louisiana	18 file drawers	4
Maine	"Voluminous"; 5 5-drawer filing cabinets	6
Maryland	"Substantial"; 12/97 revision was 600 pp; 1993 submission of amendments for 1990 act was 6–7 books, 200–300 pp each	Development: 6; regs: 3

TABLE 1 *(continued)*

State	*State's Estimate of SIP Size*	*FTE Employees Maintaining SIP*
Massachusetts	4 3-in. to 4-in. vols, plus diskettes; "too much"	4–10
Michigan	Very large	6 plus many others scattered over agency
Minnesota	6 ft of paper	1.5
Mississippi	A couple of feet thick	0.5
Missouri	Fairly large; filing cabinet per year	1–2
Montana	2 5-ft × 6-ft bookcases, ring binders	5
Nebraska	4-drawer file cabinet	0.5
Nevada	2 3-in. ring binders (maybe a little more), plus 2 boxes for nonattainment areas	2+
New Hampshire	Fragmented, not in one place; 6-ft high stack of paper. Lots of 3-in.–4-in. thick pieces.	1
New Jersey	18 file drawers	Not enough, 15
New Mexico	Several shelves, about 10 ft of shelf	2.5–3
New York	Narratives: 200 pp; appendices: 1000s of pp; NYC alone about 10 in., fills 4 bookcases	14+
North Carolina	File drawer or two; regs are 1½ in. thick	22 at HQ plus regional
North Dakota	3 in. to 4 in. thick	0.1
Ohio	20 5-drawer file cabinets	7
Oklahoma	No copy in one location, in a lot of different file drawers, with index on computer disk	5
Oregon	"Huge"; more than 3 drawers in file cabinet	6
Pennsylvania	Fills 6-ft × 8-ft × 10-ft room; regs are ½ in. thick book	5 at HQ plus regional
Rhode Island	File drawers	3

TABLE 1 *(continued)*

State	*State's Estimate of SIP Size*	*FTE Employees Maintaining SIP*
South Carolina	Regs are 1-in. thick; can't put hand on SIP as a document	2+ others as needed
South Dakota	100 pp (no nonattainment areas)	0.25
Tennessee	30 4-in. to 5-in. thick vols	3
Texas	6 ft of shelf space in binders	150
Utah	SIP text is 9½ in. single side, plus 1 in. rules; administrative and other documentation make up 7 filing cabinets full	Development: 6; Inventory: 5; PSD: 1; Rules: 1
Vermont	Couple of inches	1.5
Virginia	2–3 file drawers	6–8
Washington	Pretty big; 6-ft shelves	4.5
West Virginia	A file cabinet	10
Wisconsin	3 filing cabinets overall, 1 for 1990–94 submittals	41,000 person-hours per year
Wyoming	A filing cabinet	0.5–0.67 but increasing

SOURCE: Telephone interviews with state environmental agencies.

capability of most state-based public interest organizations. Even after more than two decades of efforts to get the SIP process to work, it is still an unwieldy mess. A 1993 General Accounting Office (GAO) report concluded that "delays continue in the States' submission and the EPA's review and approval of SIPs" and that SIP amendments could languish for months without action to identify the reason for the delay (GAO 1993, 3).

Third, the NAAQS, compared with the SIPs, are more suited to a national organization's agenda. National environmental interest groups must constantly maintain their membership, both as a source of pressure for political campaigns and as a funding source. Doing so requires a continuous process of overcoming the collective action problem. Battles over safe lead levels in the atmosphere, for example, are relatively easy to explain to a lay audience. Such battles offer a clear story with heroes (the environmental group protecting children from lead exposure) and villains (the industry seeking to expose children to higher lead levels). Even more important, national battles motivate the entire membership; because the NAAQS are national standards, they affect us all. An SIP provision, in contrast, is unlikely to motivate members outside the affected region of a particular state.

At the same time, SIPs provide powerful incentives to individual sources to pay close attention to their provisions.[5] State implementation plan provisions directly affect individual sources, costing them resources. Even more importantly, once the NAAQS for a pollutant are set, the SIP becomes a zero-sum game for the sources it covers. Getting favorable treatment in an SIP not only provides an advantage to a firm, it also imposes an additional disadvantage on other firms, because they will have to come up with additional emission reductions to make up for the first firm's favorable treatment. Moreover, requirements can sometimes be met by existing or new facilities being required to obtain emission reductions from other sources, in essence creating a valuable property right for existing sources.

The Clean Air Act's legal requirements for SIPs further complicate matters. Because SIPs are simultaneously state and federal law, states must enact laws and regulations that provide their air pollution control authorities sufficient legal authority to get EPA approval to administer the Clean Air Act within their borders. States must then adopt their SIP through their administrative procedures, a process that almost always requires notice-and-comment rule making under the state administrative procedures act (Pedersen 1981, 1078). When the proposed SIP is submitted to the EPA, however, it must undergo

5. Of course, it doesn't take an SIP for states to engage in protectionist behavior. Many states discriminate in favor of their own coal industries by requiring use of in-state coal directly or through tax incentives (McCarty 1992).

federal notice-and-comment procedures under the federal Administrative Procedure Act. As William Pedersen aptly notes, the two sets of rule making amount to a "double key" procedure (Pedersen 1981, 1078–1079).

How Did We Get Here? A Brief History of Air Pollution Control Legislation

How did we end up with such a complex and opaque process for regulating air pollution? Pollution control need not be either. Water pollution control measures that were enacted contemporaneously to the modern clean air laws have made use of far simpler approaches. Effective incentive-based regulatory schemes have been known for decades. Even mandating particular "end-of-the-pipe" technologies, the approach used in Great Britain for air and in the United States for water, avoids many of the problems of the ambient standard approach. The complexity of the American air pollution statutes is thus not because we lack better alternatives. To explain where we are headed with respect to air pollution requires considering where we started.

The history of clean air legislation at the federal level created three significant features that persist today. First, it introduced a distinction between mobile and stationary sources. Second, it created political coalitions that preserved a significant role for state regulators while limiting the states' opportunities for experimentation. Third, it produced a coalition of interest groups that demanded a federal role.

Before 1970

Before the 1940s there were no public air pollution control programs other than "smoke controls" in a few large cities (Dyck 1971, 18). Dirt and noise were public concerns, but there was little attention paid to the health effects of air pollution until photochemical smogs (mistaken for Japanese gas attacks) hit Los Angeles in 1941 and 1942 (Dyck 1971, 19). Nonetheless, state and local governments created regulatory measures that substantially reduced air pollution (Goklany 1999).

The first federal legislation directly concerned with air pollution was the 1955 Air Pollution Control Act, which created a five-year, $5 million per year research and technical assistance program for the states.[6] (Some legislation had been introduced in Congress earlier in response to local, acute episodes, but none had passed [Dyck 1971, 20–31].)[7] The 1955 law was extended for four more years in 1959,[8] and again for two years in 1962,[9] while a more comprehensive federal approach was studied and negotiated in Congress (Dyck 1971, 47; Reitze 1995, 29).[10] The importance of air pollution control programs to various interests was already becoming clear. As early as 1959, Senator Jennings Randolph of West Virginia sought (and received) assurances that federal air pollution legislation was not intended to discriminate against the use of eastern coal (Dyck 1971, 40).

The 1963 Clean Air Act

The 1962 negotiations over clean air legislation took place in a political environment different from 1955. First, the Kennedy

6. U.S. Pub. L. No. 84-159, 69 Stat. 322 (1955).

7. The major congressional actors on air pollution in the 1950s were the two senators from California, the two senators from Pennsylvania, and a senator from Indiana (Dyck 1971, 207). California, of course, was the first to experience smog and an incident in Donora, Pennsylvania, in 1948, produced concern in that state.

8. U.S. Pub. L. No. 86-365, 73 Stat. 647 (1959).

9. U.S. Pub. L. No. 87-761, 76 Stat. 760 (1962).

10. Between 1959 and 1963, Congress considered numerous proposals to increase the federal role in air pollution control, with most focusing on the problem of automobile emissions (Dyck 1971, 40–50). Repeated attempts by a Republican congressman from Ohio, Paul Schenck, to pass legislation requiring the Public Health Service to set federally enforceable emissions standards for cars went nowhere in Congress (Jones 1975, 33–36).

Administration had a much greater interest in a federal role in air pollution control than the Eisenhower Administration had had (Reitze 1995, 29). Second, the 1960 creation of the Division of Air Pollution within the Public Health Service meant there was now a bureaucratic interest group supporting extension of the federal role (Reitze 1995, 29). Third, the congressional environment changed significantly, with both the House and Senate having committees interested in the subject.[11]

The result was the Clean Air Act of 1963,[12] which provided a modest federal role in enforcement for the first time[13] and a significant increase in funding for air pollution research and control, authorizing $95 million over a three-year period (Dyck 1971, 51; Reitze 1995, 30). The 1963 act was largely the product of the newly formed Senate Committee on Public Works' Subcommittee on Air and Water Pollution.

Several factors contributed to the 1963 act's focus on assistance for state and local governments. First, the chair of the House subcommittee with responsibility for air pollution legislation remained committed to state and local solutions (Jones 1975, 38), and Senator Edmund Muskie of Maine, the leader on the issue in the Senate, was a former governor committed to preserving the states' role (Dyck 1971, 58). Second, the agency responsible for air pollution, the Public Health Service, viewed its role as a research agency and was uninterested in developing an enforcement role (Jones 1975, 71). Moreover, the 1960s were a period of stress in the federal-state

11. The House Committee on Interstate and Foreign Commerce had been conducting hearings on the subject for several years and was thus invested in "solving" the problem of air pollution. The Senate Public Works Committee created a new water pollution subcommittee, chaired by Senator Edmund Muskie of Maine, the chief sponsor of water pollution legislation introduced in 1963 (Jones 1975, 56–57), which then received air pollution jurisdiction as well.

12. U.S. Pub. L. No. 88-206, 77 Stat. 392 (1963).

13. Federal enforcement action for intrastate pollution was authorized only at the request of a state's governor.

relationship in many areas—including civil rights—and any attempt to invade states' traditional areas of authority would have been viewed with great suspicion. Federal officials were thus quick to stress in congressional testimony that they did not seek to invade the states' jurisdiction (Jones 1975, 71).

There was little opposition to the federal role in funding research or in developing criteria programs, although the industry representatives who testified in the hearings opposed federal enforcement authority (Dyck 1971, 58). In general, in the lobbying over the 1963 act,

> The industry groups did not coalesce strongly, and there was a spirit of cooperation in the Senate Subcommittee, particularly between Senators Muskie and [J. Caleb] Boggs [R.-Del.] (the ranking Republican member of the subcommittee) and their respective staffs. Muskie and Boggs had known each other from the days when both had been governors of their respective States, and their staff men . . . formed a very effective working group with [Sen. James] Pearson's and [Sen. Jennings] Randolph's aides. (Dyck 1971, 58)

The 1967 Air Quality Act

Continued public pressure for action, boosted by a New York City inversion in November 1966 and by the Third National Conference on Air Pollution in December 1966, ultimately led to the Air Quality Act (AQA) of 1967.[14] The AQA was modeled after the 1965 Water Quality Act and was shaped largely by Senator Muskie and West Virginia Senator Jennings Randolph.

The 1967 debate over air pollution began with President Lyndon Johnson introducing legislation to establish national emissions standards for major industrial pollutants (Dyck 1971, 77). Senator Muskie opposed national emissions standards. Instead he vigorously pushed for the national role to be limited to ambient criteria, on the

14. U.S. Pub. L. No. 90-148, 81 Stat. 485 (1967).

grounds that the sources of pollution varied greatly across the country (Dyck 1971, 92).

Muskie found allies in industrial sources and the coal industry, which resisted the idea of national emissions standards (Dyck 1971, 111–112). Dyck (1971) calls Joseph Moody, president of the National Coal Policy Conference, "probably the single most important individual in exerting influence upon the formation of the fuels industry coalition," (151–152) noting in particular his role in defeating federal enforcement authority and emissions standards in 1967. Moreover, experience with the 1963 act convinced stationary sources that a united front was important in dealing with the federal government on clean air, as the 1963 act had led directly to sulfur content controls on coal and oil use in New York and New Jersey (Dyck 1971, 111, 151).[15]

Johnson knew of Muskie's opposition to national emissions standards before sending his proposed legislation to Congress; indeed, a Muskie aide told a Johnson aide, "Don't come up here with a bill including national emission standards" (Jones 1975, 79). Johnson proceeded, nevertheless, because the administration thought it could beat Muskie (Jones 1975, 79). This thought proved incorrect, as Muskie attacked the national emissions standards, frequently playing, as Senator Randolph noted, almost the role of a prosecutor in examining administration witnesses (Jones 1975, 80–81).

The administration bill underwent two important changes in the Senate. First, the national ambient standards were changed to a cumbersome framework of national ambient criteria to be enforced through state ambient standards.[16] Second, the Health, Education,

15. A draft of the criteria document for sulfur oxides had been circulating in early 1967 and had produced great concern among the coal industry (Dyck 1971, 111). A 1968 guide to the 1967 act written by coal industry lawyers, for example, singled out the "sulfur oxides controversy" as an example of inaccurate information (Martin and Symington, 1968, 240–241).

16. The Secretary was to produce "air quality criteria," which would reflect current scientific evidence about the effect of various air pollutants. These criteria

and Welfare (HEW) secretary's authority to establish regional air quality regions was limited, with additional authority shifted to the states.[17] Also, in response to coal industry pressures in particular, Senator Randolph, now chair of the Public Works Committee as well as a member of the Subcommittee on Air and Water Pollution, added $15 million for research on sulfur oxide pollution control and instructions to HEW to give high priority to research on reducing pollution from combustion of fuels (Dyck 1971, 113–114).[18]

The AQA did not produce immediate, dramatic results. By December 1970, only twenty-one state implementation plans had been submitted and none had been approved by HEW (Reitze 1995, 32). However, the AQA did produce a significant beginning on scientific research into the health effects of air pollution. The National Air Pollution Control Administration (NAPCA), a part of HEW later folded into the new EPA, produced a twenty-seven volume report in the fall of 1969 covering more than thirty pollutants (Hays 1978, 36). Significantly, the NAPCA report included a schedule for "criteria documents" covering many pollutants during 1969–70, although only six were issued before the Clean Air Act Amendments of 1970 (CAAA70) passed (Hays 1978, 36).

Although the AQA approach was quickly criticized as ineffective, both for its reliance on ambient standards and for its dependence on

---

would then be translated into ambient standards and an implementation plan by states for each air quality control region.

17. The secretary of Health, Education, and Welfare was directed to designate "air quality control regions" based on scientific criteria and consultation with state and local officials. These regions were then the primary jurisdictions for control measures.

18. Unlike stationary source emissions, however, automobile emissions were almost completely federalized, with all states but California preempted from imposing controls. Auto emissions also provoked some debate, with Representative John Dingell making an unsuccessful attempt to prevent California from having stricter standards (Dyck 1971, 122–123). Dingell played (and continues to play) an important role throughout the debates over air pollution, vigorously resisting controls on auto emissions.

state governments to draft the standards (O'Fallon 1968), the AQA produced several important features that shaped air pollution law. First, it established Senator Muskie as the key congressional figure for air pollution. Second, it mobilized two key interest groups, the auto makers and coal industry, to pay attention to the process. Third, it committed Muskie to the ambient approach to federal involvement. Fourth, despite the limited impact of the AQA measures, the AQA did create incentives for state bureaucracies to focus on air pollution control.

The Clean Air Act Amendments of 1970

The combination of the lack of dramatic progress under the AQA and the expiration of the AQA's authorization in 1970 meant that some congressional action was necessary. The 1970 rewriting of air pollution legislation went well beyond tinkering, however, and the 1970 amendments gave air pollution control legislation its modern shape. Although the Clean Air Act was significantly amended in 1977 and in 1990, the basic structure of the Clean Air Act was created by CAAA70.[19]

Understanding the public choice aspects of the CAAA70 requires understanding the political climate preceding their passage. First, by 1970 the federal role in air pollution control had expanded greatly since 1955. Twenty-nine federal employees worked on air pollution issues in 1955; more than one thousand were working on the issues in 1970 (Jones 1975, 113). Federal expenditures rose (in 1955 dollars) from $0.2 million to more than $49 million ($100 million in 1970 dollars) in the same period (Jones 1975, 113).

Second, the environment was a major political issue, "the favorite sacred issue of all politicians, all TV networks, all writers, all good-willed people of any party" (White 1973, 45). Nixon had successfully capitalized on environmental issues in the 1968 campaign

19. U.S. Pub. L. No. 91-604, 84 Stat. 1676 (1970).

(Hays 1987, 57), and public sentiment for action on the environment continued to grow after the election. As one Nixon aide later wrote, "Yet there is still only one word, *hysteria,* to describe the Washington mood on the environment in the fall of 1969. The words *pollution* and *environment* were on every politician's lips. The press gave the issue extraordinary coverage, Congress responded by producing environment-related bills by the bushel, and the President was in danger of being left behind" (Whitaker 1976, 27). The continued and growing public interest ensured attention by both the Democratic majority in Congress and by President Nixon. As Senator Warren Magnuson put it, "Everybody is getting into the environmental business nowadays and all the committees are involved and all the Administrations are involved and even the Department of Justice is getting involved in environment in some way" (Senate 1974b, 1165).

The presidential ambitions of Senator Muskie, then a leading Democratic contender for the 1972 election, also played a major role. Because Muskie was one of two Democrats Nixon feared in 1970 (White 1973, 50) and because Muskie intended to use his environmental record as a major campaign theme, Nixon was determined to undercut Muskie by proving his own environmental credentials (Miller 1972, 11; Davies and Davies 1975, 53).[20] Advocates of a federal role within the Nixon Administration feared that state regulatory efforts would impede national companies' abilities to compete (Bryner 1995, 99). Muskie was also competing within the Democratic Party with Senator Henry Jackson for leadership on environmental issues (Hoberg 1992, 43).

20. Muskie had also been engaged in positioning himself on environmental issues to cut off potential Democratic rivals. For example, Muskie had sought to prevent Senator Henry Jackson (D.-Wash.) from getting credit for the creation of the Council on Environmental Quality by the National Environmental Policy Act of 1969, seeking creation of an Office of Environmental Quality in the Executive Office of the President instead (Whitaker 1976, 49).

Nixon proposed a bill that, although far from meeting environmentalists' demands, would have significantly expanded the federal role in air pollution control beyond its role under the AQA. The administration bill required national air quality standards and national emission standards for new sources and hazardous air pollutants, strengthened automobile emissions requirements, and authorized federal regulation of motor fuels and fuel additives (Davies and Davies 1975, 54). Nixon's plan gave most of the authority over setting automobile emissions standards to the EPA, whereas environmentalists sought to have Congress legislate those standards directly (Bryner 1995, 99). Nixon justified the national standards to prevent a race to the bottom among states. His plan also required rapid submission of state implementation plans (within nine months) and new federal authority to levy significant fines (Whitaker 1976, 34–35). Finally, Nixon pushed some projects that showed his understanding of the means of effective regulation, insisting that the administration pursue a plan to encourage recycling by taxing cars (Whitaker 1976, 40).[21]

With a few, relatively minor changes, some of which weakened the auto emissions provisions (Senate 1974b, 884), the House committee quickly reported a bill that took the administration approach (Davies and Davies 1975, 54). Brought to the floor almost immediately, with less than twenty-four hours' notice and without a committee hearing record available (Senate 1974b, 797), the full House rejected several attempts to further tighten the regulation of auto emissions[22] and passed the bill by a lopsided 374 to 1 on June 10.

21. Similarly, in 1971 Nixon proposed a tax on sulfur emissions (Miller 1972, 26). Although Nixon correctly identified the means of effective control, there is little evidence that Nixon or his administration in general was sufficiently committed to environmental protection as to make obtaining effective regulation worth the expenditure of political capital.

22. The four amendments proposed were (1) to establish the stricter California emissions standards as national standards; (2) to provide for testing of emissions control devices after the car was in use; (3) to give HEW authority to regulate

The short notice precluded several members from offering amendments to strengthen the bill (Senate 1974b, 799). The House leadership offered only a weak justification for the haste when pressed (Senate 1974b, 799).

The CAAA70 restructured air pollution regulation in a number of important ways. Overall, the federal role changed from providing information and assistance to decision making and gave the newly created EPA authority to set NAAQS for "criteria pollutants," where the AQA had left standard-setting to the states.[23] Focusing on the increased federal authority, as many scholars do (Hoberg 1992, 75), neglects the critical importance of the decisions left to the states. Under the AQA, for example, the standards had to be translated into commands to individuals and firms, and this process was left to the states for existing stationary sources.[24] In particular the CAAA70 left to the states the critical issue of the allocation of emissions among the much more politically important existing sources, and it allowed higher emissions from existing sources at the states' discretion.[25]

---

fuels; and (4) to phase out the internal combustion engine by 1978 (Senate 1974b, 835–836).

23. Although EPA's predecessor agency, the NAPCA, had issued a schedule in fall 1969 showing plans to issue many criteria documents, EPA took only the six NAPCA had already issued as the basis for action. The NAAQS would apply, therefore, only to sulfur oxides, particulates, carbon monoxide, photochemical oxidants, hydrocarbons, and nitrogen oxides. (EPA delisted hydrocarbons in 1978 because they were primary contributors to ozone and were regulated under that standard. EPA listed lead in 1983.) Only under the pressure of litigation did EPA add lead to this list in 1976. *Natural Resources Defense Council v. Train*, 545 F2d 320 (2d Cir. 1976). EPA was to set two levels of NAAQS: primary standards had the goal of protecting public health while secondary standards had the goal of protecting public welfare. Primary standards were to be attained by 1977.

24. California, which had significant local air pollution problems related to automobile emissions and an advanced regulatory program, was allowed to retain its emissions standards but no other states were permitted to regulate auto emissions separately.

25. Other new features of the CAAA70 included changes in defining air quality control regions, citizen suits, compulsory licensing of pollution control technology under certain circumstances, and federal authority to regulate toxic air

Even where the environmentalists won by securing tough standards, the CAAA70 began a trend, continued in later clean air legislation, of taking back much of the gains in the details of the legislation. For example, although the tough auto emissions controls were widely seen as a blow to the auto industry, the national emissions standards actually helped the automakers in their contest with stationary sources over allocation of emissions, as several Congressmen noted during the debate (Senate 1974b, 826). Even more important for the auto industry, the final bill adopted the House provisions on testing for compliance, which required only testing prototypes instead of testing each vehicle sold, as had been required in the Senate bill. The final law also dropped Senate provisions that had required public disclosure of emission test result data and pollution control equipment costs. Moreover, the success of the auto industry in obtaining multiple delays in the auto emission standards shows how even a defeat need not be final.

The substance of the CAAA70 set the pattern for subsequent air pollution legislation. Environmentalists won surprisingly easy victories in high profile battles. The translation of those victories into cleaner air, however, was left to an obscure and murky administrative process that was largely in the hands of state regulators.

Two aspects of the creation of the CAAA70 stand out. First, the CAAA70 were created quickly and with little debate, especially for a

---

pollutants. Defining air quality control regions had proven problematic in the AQA, and the CAAA70 sought to jumpstart the regulatory process simply by declaring that every state constituted an air quality control region, while retaining the regions formed under the AQA. States were given the option of breaking the statewide unit into smaller regions without regard to air-shed boundaries. As a result of this mixture of politics and science, "the United States is now a mosaic of multicounty units, all called air quality control regions, some of which were formed by drawing background concentration isopleths and others of which were formed for administrative convenience" (Boubel et al. 1994, 425). Citizen suits were allowed against both sources and the EPA, although suits against the latter were limited. The licensing provisions would not go into effect for at least two years.

complex piece of legislation. Second, the political climate in general, and the jockeying for position between Muskie and Nixon, meant that any interest groups that desired an explicitly weak final bill were shut out of the process early.

The inevitability of legislation and the obvious potential for a series of one-upmanship maneuvers by Nixon and Muskie left those who would bear the costs of the CAAA70 in a difficult position. Because there was a broad consensus on the failings of the AQA, national standards and state responsibility for enforcement were easily incorporated into the CAAA70. There, thus, appeared to be little potential for interests opposed to regulation to undercut the CAAA70 during the legislative process.

Viewing the CAAA70, or environmental legislation in general, as a contest between polluters and environmentalists is naïve, however. The air as a resource was suffering from a commons problem in 1970, and the battle was over how to solve it, not over whether to solve it. Indeed, as Indur Goklany (2000) has shown in considerable detail, states and local governments were solving the problem of air pollution as it was understood at the time. Every major known pollution indicator was already trending downward well before 1970. Moreover, the most organized, and most clearly affected, stationary source interests did not need to wage a high profile battle because they were well represented in the process by members of Congress, such as Senator Randolph and Representative Harley Staggers, both from high sulfur coal–producing West Virginia. These individuals were not shy about making their constituents' interests known during the hearings. For example, in subcommittee hearings Senator Randolph frequently noted that "[a]s you know, I represent a coal state where huge tonnages of bituminous coal are produced and marketed. But most of it is not low in sulfur content" (Senate 1974b, 1010). Administration witnesses were equally forthcoming in their commitment to take care of those interests (Senate 1974b, 1031–1032).

Considered in this light, three features of the CAAA70 stand out: the auto emissions provisions, the switch to national ambient air quality standards, and the differentiation between new and existing sources. The CAAA70 directly hit the automobile industry harder than it did stationary sources. Standards were imposed on the auto industry that could not be met with existing technology. Stationary sources, however, escaped with only unspecified action by states to implement air quality standards, to be written by the administration. Viewed as a contest between mobile and stationary sources, the latter, with Jennings Randolph as their champion, triumphed.

In some respects, car emissions were (and are) a national problem because cars are sold and driven across the nation. The effect of auto emissions, however, were (and are) quite different depending on where the cars were operated. A car's exhaust in Los Angeles, for example, had (and has) a significantly different effect from the same car's exhaust on the windswept plains of Amarillo, Texas. Outside the areas of the Midwest where auto plants were located in the 1970s, measures aimed at auto manufacturers (rather than at auto owners) provided a tempting target for state regulators looking for means of cutting air pollution that did not directly affect local interests. The CAAA70's preemption of state and local regulatory action outside California was thus a benefit to the auto manufacturers, and preemption's value should not be underestimated. Moreover, regulatory methods, such as a fuel tax or emissions charge, which might have restricted auto use (and hence demand), were avoided. Use restrictions, which were likely to be highly unpopular, were left to the more malleable states, which have validated the approach by doing little with their authority since 1970.

Although the auto industry might have preferred no controls at all (although controls did erect a significant barrier to entry of potential competitors), given the political climate the industry could not have been too displeased with the final results in the CAAA70, despite its loud public complaints. Indeed, considering that the political climate included apparently serious discussion of outlawing the internal combustion engine entirely by 1975 and that Congressmen called the engine the "most serious and dangerous source of air pollution in the Nation today" (Senate 1974b, 835), the industry escaped comparatively lightly.

The CAAA70's creation of the NAAQS was hailed as a significant victory for the environment, because the AQA's state-based standards approach was almost universally judged to be a failure. Industrial interests had indeed fought off (with the help of Senator Muskie) national standards in 1967; surely Muskie's conversion and the imposition of those same standards in 1970 counted as a victory for the environment.

The NAAQS were not the crushing defeat for source interests that they appeared to be for several reasons. One hint that this was so is that national standards became part of the debate as a Nixon proposal, not an environmentalist or Muskie proposal. Even as late as the March 1970 Senate subcommittee hearings on the Clean Air Act, Muskie continued to defend the state standards approach (Senate 1974b, 991). The Nixon administration, although theoretically not enthusiastic about government regulation, knew a good thing when it saw one. An administration that was soon to explicitly exploit the fund-raising potential of national occupational safety and health standards could not, after all, have missed the similarity between air quality standards and Occupational Safety and Health Administration (OSHA) standards. Moreover, the administration pushed for national standards partly because it objected to "[run]ning around this country and hold[ing] public hearings on national air quality standards" (Senate 1974b, 1004). Not only were national standards at least partly intended to exclude public participation, but also national standards for sale offered many firms a one-stop rent-seeking opportunity rather than requiring fifty separate purchases of influence.

Moreover, the AQA's state standards had not worked out quite as stationary source interests had predicted. Even if most state governments could be counted on to choose economic development over environmental protection, it only took a few states to inflict substantial costs through adoption of inconsistent standards.

> [A] considerable number of states, under pressure from local communities, established standards more stringent than [industries] thought desirable. In the face of this new development, industries turned to the federal government, seeking to shape a program at that level that would keep the excesses of state standard setting under control. They were not averse to the federal standards required in the 1970 Clean Air Act. (Hays 1987, 444)

The auto industry had learned the value of national standards' preemption of inconsistent state regulations under the 1963 Act. The national standards in the CAAA70 represent the slower learning curve of the stationary source interests. In addition, getting the states and local governments out of the standard-setting business, in which there was a clear metric for the public to evaluate the outcome, and into negotiating about the technical details of individual sources, where there was no such metric, was a desirable outcome for polluters.

The NAAQS also reflected the industry's priorities for the method of pollution control through reliance on ambient standards rather than on technology standards (Hays 1987, 324). As a leading air pollution control text puts it, "[a]doption of air quality standards by a jurisdiction produces no air pollution control" (Boubel et al. 1994, 68).[26] Stationary sources, too, therefore, had reasons to prefer the shape of the CAAA70's regulatory structure to possible alternatives.

26. The NAAQS have been far from an unqualified success, even on their own terms. Consider the following comments made by a political scientist sympathetic to the environmental regulatory process on some of the criteria pollutants. Carbon monoxide: "There is little agreement over the magnitude of the relative contribution of [human activity and natural processes]." Ozone: "Ozone has been one of the most difficult pollutants to regulate . . . air quality levels have not appreciably

The final crucial feature of the CAAA70 was the introduction of the distinction between existing and new sources. Existing source interests feared air pollution regulation not only for its costs but also because it would bestow enormous cost advantages on newer rivals that had the opportunity to engineer their plants' pollution control from the design phase rather than adding it to existing facilities. By mandating that new sources meet stricter emissions standards, the CAAA70 eliminated much of those potential competitors' cost advantage.

In addition to the benefits for sources, existing bureaucratic interests were well positioned by the CAAA70 to reap large benefits. The mandate to produce SIPs quickly would justify rapid expansions of both legal authority and resources for state pollution control agencies. The Department of Health, Education, and Welfare estimated that a 300 percent increase in the number of state pollution control agency personnel would be needed to implement the CAAA70 and warned that the chief difficulty in doing so would be low salaries (Senate 1974a, 254).[27] Even innocuous provisions, such as the designation of all undesignated portions of each state as separate air quality regions, served local interests. (Local governments had competed under the AQA to be included in air quality regions [Senate 1974b, 1225], presumably for both the public relations and the federal grant potential.) The disparate federal air pollution personnel, in the process of being consolidated into the newly formed EPA, were rewarded with the satisfying job of creating the NAAQS framework and overseeing the SIP process. Because federal air

---

improved." Sulfur dioxide: "Sulfur dioxide is generally not the most harmful of the sulfur compounds in the atmosphere, even though it is the form most often monitored." Particulate matter: "Despite tremendous economic growth, progress in reducing such emissions was made even before the first major Clean Air Act was passed, between 1950 and 1970, as industries and power plants became more efficient" (Bryner 1995, 58–73).

27. This inadequacy, widely recognized in Congress (Senate 1974b, 881–882), also left industry the hope of greater influence in drafting SIPs.

pollution officials had indicated during their testimony that federal budget constraints were limiting their ability to act, the CAAA70 also provided a welcome opportunity to enhance their resources.

These features of the CAAA70 should not be seen to diminish the political accomplishments of the newly emerged activist groups or individuals such as Muskie. A finding that the details of the CAAA70 were advantageous to powerful interests does not mean that those features were the result of a grand conspiracy. It merely indicates that, given the existence of those interests, it was likely that the results of a series of closed door proceedings, such as the Muskie committee markup and the conference committee proceedings, would not be harmful to those interests. Far from being bushwacked by the Earth Day crowds, bureaucrats and sources rode the political currents for action on the air to obtain the best outcome they could.

The Clean Air Act Amendments of 1977

Almost immediately after the passage of the CAAA70, both environmentalists and polluters began to seek changes. Although there were a number of single-issue amendments sought and passed between 1970 and 1997, the first major overhaul of the CAA took place with the 1977 Amendments (CAAA77).[28]

Polluting source interests immediately began efforts to soften the effect of the CAAA70 through rule making as well as through statutory amendments (Hays 1978, 59–60). Together with pressure groups in the Office of Management and Budget (OMB), the Department of Commerce, and the Federal Power Commission, industrial interests were successful in weakening the rules implementing the CAAA70, particularly with respect to the guidelines for SIPs (Hays 1978, 60). In the early 1970s, the auto industry also successfully sought amendments four times to postpone auto emission standards

28. U.S. Pub. L. No. 95-95, 91 Stat. 685 (1977) with technical amendments U.S. Pub. L. No. 95-190, 91 Stat. 1399 (1977).

(Bryner 1995, 101). Environmental groups fiercely resisted these attempts to weaken the CAAA70. The Natural Resources Defense Council created an effective strategy built around litigation to toughen the impact of the bill (Hays 1978, 62).[29]

The energy crisis sparked by the Arab oil boycott of 1973 opened the door for changes in the CAAA70, and "energy issues provided a major opportunity to check environmentalists" (Hays 1987, 60). Both automakers and coal interests used the energy issue to refocus the national debate. Detroit was particularly aggressive in resisting the technology forcing envisioned by the CAAA70. Automakers obtained two one-year extensions from the EPA (in 1973 and 1975) and an additional postponement of one to two years from Congress in 1974 (Reitze 1995, 559).[30] Thus, by 1976, both mobile and stationary sources believed they were in a position to renegotiate the Clean Air Act (CAA) on favorable terms.

These delays outraged environmentalists, who were further motivated to seek to change the law, mainly because of the clear evidence that by 1976 the stationary source provisions of the CAAA70

29. Federal administrative law underwent a significant transformation in the late 1960s and early 1970s, greatly enhancing the ability of interest groups to use the courts to contest agency actions (Hoberg 1992, 48, 53).

30. Coal users and producers also aggressively sought relief. In March 1974, for example, the Nixon administration sent a package of proposed amendments to Congress that would have relaxed a number of provisions of the CAAA70 to promote the use of high sulfur fuels (Whitaker 1976, 106–110). Although little action was taken on the Nixon proposals, President Ford resubmitted a similar package the following year (Whitaker 1976, 106). One Nixon-Ford proposed amendment in particular is worth noting: a proposal to give EPA the authority to review SIPs to determine what changes could be made to *increase* the use of high sulfur fuels. As Nixon-Ford environmental aide Whitaker describes it, "[t]his analysis was needed because many state air quality implementation plans were more stringent than necessary to meet national primary health-related standards. If these plans were enforced, they could prevent the use of an estimated 200 million tons of relatively high-sulfur coal annually—about one-third of the nation's total annual coal production" (Whitaker 1976, 109). Even without the change to the statute, EPA worked to encourage states to revise their SIPs to increase the use of high sulfur coal by 130 million tons by the end of 1975 (Whitaker 1976, 109).

did not work. "Not a single steel mill was in full compliance with the CAA. Nearly fifty percent of the refineries, pulp mills, and large commercial boilers were also not meeting CAA requirements" (Reitze 1995, 318).

Given the slow pace of major sources' compliance and the failure of the American auto manufacturers to develop pollution reduction technology fast enough, environmentalists and Muskie had good reason to be dissatisfied with the CAAA70 by 1975. Indeed, most of the environmentalists' successes in the early 1970s were in the courthouse, where they prevailed in a number of suits to force the EPA to act more aggressively. In hindsight, the activists' reliance on a courthouse strategy has led to an overestimation of the CAAA70's effectiveness. Lawsuits against the government, such as those brought by environmental activist groups to force the EPA to take "tougher" actions under the CAAA70, were still a relative novelty in the early 1970s. Congress and source interests had no reason to believe that the vague language of the CAAA70 would produce court rulings reshaping the law. Nonetheless, a Sierra Club lawsuit led to a district court opinion, affirmed by an equally divided Supreme Court, ordering the EPA to create a program for preventing the deterioration of air quality in regions where it was above the NAAQS levels.[31] This judicial intervention created demand for reopening the issue by environmental lobbying groups (who sought a tougher program than the court created), pollution source interests (who sought to weaken the program), and areas with high air quality (who faced unexpected constraints on economic growth).

In early 1976, attempts at comprehensive revision of the CAA began in committees of both houses. The Senate passed an amended version of its committee's bill on August 5 on a 78–13 vote, and the House passed an amended version of its committee's bill on a 324–68

31. *Sierra Club v. Ruckelshaus,* 344 F. Supp. 253 (D.D.C. 1972) *aff'd per curiam* by an equally divided court *sub nom., Fri v. Sierra Club,* 412 U.S. 541 (1973).

vote on September 15. The Senate bill was ninety-one pages (Senate 1979d, 4610–4700), and the House bill was almost two hundred pages (Senate 1979e, 5888–6077). A conference committee met extensively between September 22 and September 24, reporting a compromise that drew heavily from both the House and the Senate bills. With only a week to go in the session, however, western senators opposed to the PSD program, which had been prompted by the Sierra Club suit, filibustered the conference committee bill on the grounds that there was inadequate time to consider such complex legislation.

The 1976 conference committee report was brought to the Senate floor at 10:00 P.M. on September 30, 1976, the penultimate day of the session. Opponents of the bill seized on the rushed nature of the consideration to stop the bill. As Senator Jake Garn noted, he had had the conference report "that looks like chickens have scratched all over it" for less than twenty-four hours when he was being asked to vote on it (Senate 1979c, 4449). There was no printed version of the conference bill (Senate 1979c, 4451). As Alaska Senator Ted Stevens put it, given the enormous impact of the bill on state governments, "until my State government can see this conference report I think it is improper for the Senate of the United States to vote on it" (Senate 1979c, 4498). The 1976 bill died as a result of this filibuster.

When the new Congress met in 1977, the same pressures to amend the CAA in 1976 were still present, namely the judicially created PSD program and the approaching model year 1977 auto emissions standard. The political climate in 1977 was different from that in 1976, however. Not only had Jimmy Carter replaced Gerald Ford, but also energy crisis issues had become more important. The Carter administration proposal for the CAAA77 thus included extensive support for burning domestically produced high sulfur coal. The general outlines of the issues were similar to those adopted by the two houses in 1976, with some changes in the details of the provisions. The House Interstate and Foreign Commerce Committee reported a bill on May 12, 1977, and the full House approved it on May 26 by a 326–49 vote. The Senate Environment and Public Works Committee reported its bill on May 10, and it was approved by the full Senate 73–7 on June 10. A conference committee was appointed to resolve the differences, although the committee did not meet until mid-July. The conference committee bill was reported on and approved by both houses on a voice vote on August 4 and signed by President Carter on August 7. Most striking about the debate is that it provided the same lack of opportunity to consider the complex conference bill as in 1976, yet this time no one objected to the rushed consideration of "chicken scratchings."

The CAAA77 made two major changes to the structure of the CAAA70, in addition to a host of lesser alterations. First, CAAA77 substituted a legislative PSD program for the judicially created one and provided nonattainment restrictions (Hays 1978, 48). Second, CAAA77 postponed the auto emissions standards for two years, while mandating stricter standards in the future (Bryner 1995, 102).[32] The CAAA77 were also far more explicit about requiring consideration of economic factors in decision making than the CAAA70 had been. As a result, "[b]y the 1980s the Executive Office of the President had become the focal point of political leverage for industry in its drive to emphasize the production costs of environmental regulation" (Hays 1987, 371–372).

The CAAA77 expanded on the judicially created PSD program in several ways. First, the amendments mandated that certain areas be given maximum protection instead of allowing states complete discretion in designating these areas. Second, the least protected areas were not allowed to deteriorate all the way to the secondary standard level, as the EPA had allowed. Third, under CAAA70,

32. The CAAA77 also attempted to reduce sources' incentive to delay compliance by introducing financial penalties tied to the savings from noncompliance (Hays 1978, 53).

court-ordered programs had applied only to two of the six criteria pollutants, whereas the CAAA77 extended the PSD program to all six (Hays 1978, 49). Finally, new or modified major sources in PSD areas had to use the "best available control technology," obtain a special permit, and undergo a preconstruction review. Although generally counted as environmental victories, these changes increased the number of discretionary decisions. Not everything in the CAA produced special deals for individual sources, but each new layer of legislation expanded the scope for such arrangements.

The nonattainment provisions of the CAAA77 shifted the focus of the clean air program to total loadings of pollutants. Prior to the CAAA77, the focus had been on sources' reductions from 1970 baselines. The nonattainment provisions of the CAAA77 required consideration of the impact of new sources as well as existing sources. "If growth were to be permitted, the level of clean-up from each source would have to be greater than heretofore envisaged" (Hays 1978, 51). In an attempt to mitigate the adverse consequences for economic growth, the CAAA77 required SIPs to include a growth factor so that some portion of the burden created by new sources would be shared by existing sources. Finally, additional technology requirements were imposed, including the use of "reasonably available control technology" for existing sources and the use of controls that produced the "lowest achievable emission rate."

The CAAA77 included several controversial provisions designed to promote the use of high sulfur coal. These provisions were a particularly stark illustration of how interest groups could manipulate the federal structure of air pollution regulation. Shifting to low sulfur fuel offers a means for reducing pollution that is often both cost-effective and simple to implement. States without high sulfur coal production (almost everywhere except Ohio, Pennsylvania, Kentucky, and West Virginia) could be expected to opt for fuel-switching to solve pollution problems. High sulfur coal interests, therefore, focused their attention on the federal level to force alternative solutions that protected their interests. Senator Randolph's position as chair of the Senate Environment and Public Works Committee allowed high sulfur coal interests a powerful role in shaping federal action. As Ackerman and Hassler (1981) explain, the result was a perverse legislative bargain between the "dirty coal" interests and environmentalists—a bargain that likely has increased sulfur oxide emissions.

As important as what the CAAA77 included is what they did not include. There was no change in the basic structure of the act, with respect to either the ambient approach or the reliance on SIPs. Indeed, the new features introduced by the CAAA77 added additional layers of complexity to the SIPs, requiring a host of revisions and new requirements.

The long debate over amending the CAAA70 spurred environmental interests to organize to protect their earlier gains and led to a coordinated focus in the legislative arena (Hays 1978, 62). Particularly valuable to the coalition was the support of the labor unions, most of which were not formally part of the umbrella "Clean Air Coalition." The environmental–labor alliance divided on the issue of auto emissions, however. As a result, the automakers were able to prevail in obtaining a significant weakening of emissions controls. That the ultimate shape of the CAAA77 depended largely on the positions of organized labor should convince even the most skeptical that nonenvironmental considerations dominated the amendments' creation. Seen as the result of union–environmentalist and eastern coal–environmentalist alliances, there seems little doubt that the CAAA77 had a great deal to do with redistribution.

Most accounts of the CAAA77 score it as if it were the second in a series of games between "environmentalists" and "industry," only sometimes acknowledging even the sector-distinctions between automobile companies and power plants or regional interests. On this scorecard, the CAAA77 produced a mixed result for all sides—automakers succeeded in delaying and weakening standards, eastern coal interests won big, and environmentalists did well in preserving and extending the PSD program. These victories and defeats are only part of the story, however. No one, not even the hardcore of western senators who filibustered the 1976 amendments, challenged the basic structure of the Clean Air Act, despite the convincing evidence that it was not working—automakers were not producing cars that met the standards, and steel plants were not even close to compliance. No one questioned whether the vast bureaucracies being built around the nation, not just in Washington, D.C., were actually producing clean air.

Even if we follow the scorecard approach to evaluating the CAAA77, the success of the environmentalists in obtaining the expanded legislative PSD program is not surprising. A vigorous PSD program was important for preventing not just a race to the bottom (which the national NAAQS would at least slow if not completely prevent), but also a race to the relatively nonindustrialized South and West (where air quality was significantly above the NAAQS primary and secondary standards). Organized labor's strong support of the PSD principle (Hays 1978, 62), for example, is explained by its desire to limit the regional advantages that the nonunion South and West already enjoyed over the Midwest and Northeast. There is little doubt that environmental interests skillfully mobilized their relatively limited resources and that the alliance with organized labor was a major factor in their success. At the same time, however, the focus on the national programs and attempts to constrain states from engaging in a race to the bottom through the PSD and nonattainment programs neglected the importance of the relative burdens imposed by the air pollution programs.

For existing sources, the costs imposed by the air pollution regulations were an annoyance, but one that they could largely pass along to consumers. Utilities, in particular, were well positioned to pass through environmental costs through the cost recovery provisions of state public utility commission regulations. Indeed, capital expenditures on pollution control would produce higher profits, because utilities were guaranteed a return on investment.

Moreover, as long as the air pollution control regime remained complex and obscure, the costs to individual sources could be minimized out of public scrutiny through negotiations in the SIP process. Even the PSD program largely burdened sources attempting change while protecting those who did not want to abandon the skilled, high-wage, union labor force and existing capital investment in plants in the Midwest and Northeast. Those industrial sources that had reached an accommodation with organized labor, for example, had little interest in easing the burden on new, nonunion competitors, who would largely be locating in PSD areas. We should marvel not at the accomplishment of an alliance between organized labor and environmentalists but that the alliance surprised anyone.

What did not happen during the debate over the CAAA77 is equally important. There was no concerted move toward strengthening the technology forcing provisions of the clean air regime. Also, except for the "experimental" provisions on noncompliance penalties, there was little improvement in enforcement (Hays 1978, 66). The SIP structure, already obviously a drag on cleaning the air, not only was left in place but also was made more complex by the new PSD and nondegradation sections.

Nowhere are the public choice issues in the CAAA77 more evident than in the lackadaisical proceedings of the 1977 conference committee. Despite the 1976 filibuster and the passage of bills by both houses by June 10, the conferees did not even meet until July 18 (Ackerman and Hassler 1981, 48). Because the House planned to recess on August 5, this left little time to produce a final bill. Once again, as in 1970 and 1976, the final bill emerged from a middle-of-the-night meeting and was approved the next day by both houses. The conference report totaled a staggering 190 single-spaced pages; the bill obviously received, at most, cursory examination by most members. Moreover, these were exactly the circumstances that prompted Senator Garn's filibuster in 1976, although this time he contented himself with simply a few questions on the details of the PSD compromise (Senate 1979a, 370–374). Midnight lawmaking on this scale is indicative not of carefully considered policy but of the fact that the fix is in. Of course, individual interests, whether they were eastern coal miners and mine owners or automakers, cared deeply about small changes in particular provisions and fought to gain advantages in votes on those provisions. Nonetheless, the lack of effort to obtain a real debate over the many details is strong evidence that those who cared had their interests looked after in the committee rooms.

The Clean Air Act Amendments of 1990

The next major set of amendments to the Clean Air Act did not pass until 1990.[33] These amendments (CAAA90) introduced a number of significant innovations, from marketable SO_2 permits to a new emphasis on mobile source emissions. Congress thought that the CAAA77 would quickly improve the quality of SIPs. By 1980, however, the National Commission on Air Quality found that

> States, particularly those with severe and complex problems, did not analyze air quality problems in detail during revision of their plans. Detailed analyses were not conducted because delays in undertaking plan revisions and statutory requirements for public participation did not allow sufficient time for such analysis. State agencies also did not have adequate resources to use sophisticated analytical techniques. As a result, accuracy and comprehensiveness of emission inventories, upon which the revised plans are based, were not improved significantly. Assumptions for potential emission reductions were often based on crude analyses and air quality modeling techniques were often inadequate to precisely project air quality concentrations. (Friedman 1990, 218)

33. U.S. Pub. L. No. 101-549, 104 Stat. 2399.

Environmental Protection Agency officials were also publicly acknowledging that the SIP process was deeply flawed (Pedersen 1981). Moreover, many of the successes of the Clean Air Act were less than they first appeared. States took credit for emission reductions that even state officials conceded were unrealistically calculated or unlikely to be implemented. Plans routinely underestimated mobile source emissions, government source emissions, and economic growth rates.

Despite these flaws, the "EPA approved virtually all state reductions, notwithstanding these weaknesses" (Friedman 1990, 219). Indeed, the SIP creation and revision process required by the CAAA70 and CAAA77 so overwhelmed the EPA that the breakdown of the entire process was avoided only by the administrative invention of the conditional SIP, which "allowed the EPA to approve SIPs, thereby avoiding sanctions, on the condition that weaknesses in the SIP would eventually be remedied" (Friedman 1990, 219). Although the legal authority for this invention was questionable, it was approved by the courts because a "contrary result would have given EPA an unmanageable regulatory and enforcement burden, rendering futile years of effort to bring nonattainment areas into compliance" (Reed 1982, 10059). Despite these indications that something was seriously wrong with the Clean Air Act, and although the authorization for the Clean Air Act expired in 1981, Congress was unable to revise it. Instead, throughout the 1980s, Congress continued the CAA through a series of appropriations riders while waging a contentious debate over further revisions.

Several circumstances made different interests anticipate achieving gains in the next round of amendments. Finding a more sympathetic hearing in the Reagan Administration, a broad coalition of economists, lawyers, political scientists, and industry officials sought significant changes in the Clean Air Act (Bryner 1995, 105). CAA-imposed constraints that had not been binding in the 1970s became so during the long boom of the 1980s. The gradual accretion of regulations also increased the burden. The automobile industry continued to attempt to weaken and delay the auto emission standards as falling real energy prices boosted demand for larger vehicles. At the same time, the massive noncompliance with the CAAA77, the EPA's continued failure to accomplish many of the goals set by the earlier amendments, and new attention to larger-scale, total-loading problems such as acid rain and global warming motivated environmental interests to seek to strengthen the act. Finally, just as special interest provisions in the tax code prompt periodic reforms to enable members of Congress to collect new rents, so Congress requires periodic reassessment of environmental rules.

The maneuvering through the 1980s pitted regional, industry, environmental, bureaucratic, and other interest groups against each other in shifting coalitions that produced repeated failed efforts to amend the CAA. For example, Representative Henry Waxman, who sought to strengthen the CAA, particularly the auto emissions provisions, chaired the House Subcommittee on Health and Environment of the House Committee on Energy and the Environment. The full committee was chaired by Representative John Dingell, who sought to protect the auto industry from further regulation and to weaken existing mobile source standards. (The battle between Dingell and Waxman dominated the stalemate over amending the act throughout the 1980s.) A group of Republican committee members sought more stringent auto emissions standards as a means of lessening the burdens on stationary sources (Bryner 1995, 110). All involved manipulated the congressional consideration of various proposed amendments to gain an advantage. Waxman, for example, sought to delay consideration of amendments in the early 1980s until closer to the 1982 election, when pressure to vote for clean air would be greater (Bryner 1995, 110). By 1986, however, it was Dingell and the Republicans who were delaying consideration because the political momentum had shifted to amendments that strengthened the act away from the earlier attempts to weaken it.

Similarly, in the Senate, Majority Leader Robert Byrd sought to protect the high sulfur coal industry, repeatedly blocking consideration of acid rain provisions (Bryner 1995, 112). After the political momentum shifted in favor of the environmentalists, however, Senator George Mitchell, chair of the Environment and Public Works Committee, was able to negotiate a compromise with coal interests in 1988, particularly the United Mine Workers union. Overestimating their strength, environmentalists rejected the Mitchell compromise as inadequate and killed it (Bryner 1995, 112).

Two events unblocked the process. First, when George Bush became president, he sought to use the environment to distinguish himself from Ronald Reagan (Bryner 1995, 113). Second, prospects for change were enhanced when Mitchell succeeded Byrd as Senate Majority Leader in 1989 (although Byrd retained significant power as chair of the Appropriations Committee) (Bryner 1995, 113).

Unlike with earlier clean air legislation, which had been shaped largely in the Senate, the House was the main mover behind the CAAA90. Dingell and Waxman continued to have major differences over the shape of the legislation, particularly with respect to auto emissions. However, they resolved some of their differences by agreeing to a compromise that committed all involved to support the bill produced through the conference committee with the Senate (Bryner 1995, 118). Dingell had successfully limited Waxman's influence in the subcommittee by packing it with his supporters, but he feared that Waxman would be able to reverse subcommittee votes on the House floor. Waxman, on the other hand, feared that Dingell could reverse any gains on the House floor in the conference committee (Bryner 1995, 117–118).

Despite the temporary agreement between Waxman and Dingell, midwestern Congress members slowed the bill's progress through the Subcommittee on Energy and Power, which had jurisdiction over the acid rain provisions. Complaining that the Dingell-

Waxman alliance was ignoring their efforts to shift some of the burden of compliance from the Midwestern coal utilities, the Midwesterners "let it be known that they would lend their support in key committee votes on other issues to whatever faction would best help them minimize the costs of acid rain controls" (Bryner 1995, 119). In addition, a group of Western representatives opposed further sulfur oxide regulation on the grounds that the regulations would limit growth in the West (Bryner 1995, 119). The compromise held, however, partly because the Midwesterners did not deliver on some earlier votes for Waxman (Bryner 1995, 126), thus preventing a coalition between environmentalists and coal interests like the one that had shaped the CAAA77.

The final debate over the CAAA90 involved extensive negotiations among environmentalists, industry, and the Bush Administration. In the Senate, Majority Leader Mitchell pulled the Senate bill from the floor for "a series of extraordinary closed-door meetings with Bush Administration officials for a second markup of the bill," (Bryner 1995, 121) a process opposed by environmentalists because it enabled members to escape public votes on changes to the bill. The final compromise that emerged a month later delayed the phase-in time for meeting automobile emission standards and for Midwestern utilities to comply with emission reductions, moved toward the administration proposal on air toxics, added a requirement for alternative fuel use in major cities, and dropped fuel efficiency standards aimed at reducing greenhouse gas emissions (Bryner 1995, 123). Environmentalists were displeased both by the process and the result; industry groups were generally pleased (Bryner 1995, 123). The compromise held despite strong pressure from environmental groups on the Senate floor (Bryner 1995, 124).

The CAAA90 are, like their predecessors, complex. The eleven titles cover so many different air quality issues that a brief summary is difficult. Some provisions of the CAAA90 attempt to address the problems experienced under the CAAA77. For space reasons, I will limit my summary to five provisions: nonattainment, auto emissions, acid rain controls, toxics, and the new air pollution permit program.[34]

The nonattainment provisions of the CAAA90 are themselves among "one of the most detailed and complex laws ever enacted by Congress" (Bryner 1995, 146). They introduce an elaborate new classification system for nonattainment areas, six for ozone alone. Steady reductions in pollution levels in nonattainment areas are now mandated, replacing the earlier law's vague requirement of "reasonable further progress." There are more smaller stationary sources included within the definition of "major source," allowing state regulators more authority. The extraordinary level of detail in the CAAA90 "is Congress' response to the failure of the Clean Air Act [Amendments] of 1977 to produce attainment" of the NAAQS (Bryner 1995, 152).

The acid rain provisions are also complex and innovative. The main issues in the debate over acid rain throughout the 1980s had centered on how much emissions should be reduced, how they should be reduced, and who would pay for the reduction (Bryner 1995, 170). The Bush Administration abandoned the Midwestern utilities, leaving them with the lion's share of the costs, and used its toughness on acid rain to buy flexibility on toxics and other provisions (Bryner 1995, 173). (Bush's maneuver also put Midwestern Democrats in the difficult position of leading the opposition to acid rain controls, disrupting existing political coalitions in a way that "opened up" the legislative process [Bryner 1995, 173].) The use of the emissions trading process, one of the few clear win-win environmental programs, mitigated some of the costs of the program and won support from many proponents of market mechanisms. The

34. There are also a host of other provisions designed to implement the Montreal Protocol on ozone depletion by regulating the use of CFCs, updating penalties, providing a new grant program for workers displaced by compliance costs, and dealing with other, smaller air pollution problems, such as offshore oil exploration.

market for emissions permit trading enables those holding emissions permits to sell or trade them, thus creating a valuable asset in existing sources. (New sources could receive permits from a pool created by the EPA.) At the same time, overall NO_x and SO_2 emissions were to be cut significantly.

Mobile sources were required to meet more stringent standards; inspection and maintenance programs for cars increased; and new controls on related sources, such as gas pumps, were imposed. These provisions partially eased the burden of increased regulation on stationary sources. Inspection and maintenance programs for autos, however, produced widespread dissatisfaction among drivers. States were given a choice with respect to auto emissions: They could require either the national standards (set by the EPA) or the stricter California state standards. This prevented states from creating a patchwork of conflicting emissions requirements while allowing states to shift some of the burden of compliance away from stationary sources to mobile sources.

The CAAA90 provisions on hazardous air pollutants were also a significant departure from the earlier structure. Recognizing that the NAAQS model had produced action on only a limited number of pollutants, Congress abandoned it for hazardous air pollutants and mandated development of national emissions standards according to industrial category. The toxics regulatory system thus shifted regulatory authority from the states to the EPA while attempting to constrain the EPA's discretion through a detailed series of requirements. The toxics program also offered existing sources a chance to gain a six-year extension of the rigorous technology standards that the EPA was required to draft. This extension allowed those that entered into a binding commitment to reduce their emission of toxics by 90 percent before January 1994 and to achieve the reduction before the particular EPA standard that was proposed got a six-year extension. Because the 90 percent reduction was measured against self-reported data, companies had an incentive to inflate their pre-reduction emission levels and, thus, to reduce their actual emissions by less than 90 percent.

Finally the CAAA90 created a new permit program to assist with enforcement.[35] Faced with the reality that the SIPs were unusable, the CAAA90 required consolidation of sources' responsibilities into a single document. In theory, both regulators and the public can then review this document to determine if a source is in compliance.[36] The permit program is less clear than it might be, however. It did not simplify the regulatory regime as it might have if the point-

35. The CAAA90 also requires that SIPs include for nonattainment areas "a comprehensive, accurate, current inventory of actual emissions from all sources of the relevant pollutant or pollutants in such areas, including such periodic revisions as the Administrator may determine necessary to assure that the requirements of this part are met." Inventories do not avoid the problems discussed earlier; they merely shift the problems to a slightly higher degree of generality.

Creation of an inventory requires a list of the sources for the area, a determination of the type of emissions from each source, determination of "emission factors" for each pollutant of concern, a count of the number and size of sources, and then a calculation of total emissions (Boubel et al. 1994, 93). Two problems exist with this methodology. First, emission factors, "the key to the emission inventory," are descriptions of the amount of a pollutant produced by a particular source. These are found in the air pollution control literature, and it is "not uncommon to find emission factors differing by 50 percent, depending on the researcher, variables at the time of emission measurement, etc." (Boubel et al. 1994, 93). Second, the total emissions, which are critical in determining the regulatory impact, depend on estimates of many sources. Thus, while the number of steelmaking furnaces is likely to be exact, the number of home fireplaces is more likely to be estimated (Boubel et al. 1994, 93). The combination of these leaves a considerable fudge factor available to the agency performing the inventory.

36. Polluters initially misread the permit provisions as "highly technical" and showed little interest in them during the negotiations between the Senate and White House (Bryner 1995, 179). By the time the bill reached the Senate floor, however, industry lobbyists actively opposed the permits (Bryner 1995, 179–180). Attempts to weaken the permit provisions were defeated by only one vote in the Senate (Bryner 1995, 180). Language in the conference report suggesting that compliance with permits could serve as a shield against charges of violating the act prompted some concern among environmentalists (Bryner 1995, 180). State and local officials opposed EPA review of the permits but not the permits themselves (Bryner 1995, 180).

less SIPs were abandoned. Instead it added another layer of regulatory requirements. As Bryner (1995) concludes, "One of the many paradoxes of clean air regulation is the attempt to clarify and facilitate compliance and enforcement by adding a new layer of regulatory requirements" (144). The EPA's rules on the implementation of the permits further undercut many of the permit system's proposed advantages (Bryner 1995, 197).

Like the CAAA77 (and unlike the CAAA70), the CAAA90 were the result of a long legislative process, filled with the explicit vote-trading and strategic behavior that makes public choice analysis so compelling. Moreover, by the time Congress began working on the CAAA90, almost twenty years after the CAAA70 were written, no interest group could be accused of being asleep at the switch. Indeed, the fund-raising potential of clean air legislation was now abundantly clear to members of Congress. Bryner (1995) summarizes the enormous amounts of campaign contributions that clean air issues produced in the nonelection year of 1989. More than $612,000 in Political Action Committee (PAC) contributions to members of the House Energy and Commerce Committee alone (5 percent of all money raised in Congress) was from interests in the clean air debate, an average of almost $15,000 per member (113).

Not only does the process of creating the CAAA90 raise public choice issues, but the substance of the amendments does as well. Continuing the trend begun twenty years earlier, the CAAA90 piled additional layers onto the already almost unmanageably complex scheme. Moreover, specific programs, such as the toxics program, created opportunities for existing sources to gain exemption from potentially burdensome new rules that would apply to new sources. The stricter standards on mobile sources, most of which affect consumers (inspection and maintenance programs) rather than car manufacturers (stricter standards on new cars) also helped stationary sources shift significant burdens away from themselves and onto mobile sources in ways that state regulators had refused to do. The revolts by drivers who had been made subject to inspection and maintenance programs, and the resulting political uproar in states like Ohio, suggest that the state regulators' earlier political judgments about the lack of viability of these programs was correct.

Where Are We Headed?

The success of the modern environmental movements in influencing the national legislative process is a compelling and important story. Innovations, from the League of Conservation Voters' election guides to Environmental Action's annual "Dirty Dozen" list of the twelve congressmen with the worst environmental voting records, have made the environmental vote a powerful force on Capitol Hill. Similarly, pollution source interests of many varieties have poured tens of millions of dollars into lobbying and campaign contributions over the past thirty years.

Despite all this effort and despite major overhauls in 1977 and 1990, the basic structure of the CAA has remained unchanged. Are environmentalists unaware that the SIP process is unworkable? Have pollution source interests given up resisting the costs that air pollution regulation imposes and accepted their responsibilities to protect us from air pollution? Or is there simply a stalemate that only another Earth Day can undo? None of these seems likely. A more plausible explanation is that the structure of the CAA serves the interests of all the major players in the air pollution debate.

Environmental membership organizations have succeeded in creating a national policy on clean air that elevates them to a major role. It implies no cynical self-interest in such groups to see the necessity of a federal structure for air pollution control for them to influence policy; their sincere (and correct) belief that they play a vital role as watchdogs is sufficient. National environmental groups continuously play significant roles in federal administrative proceedings and regularly bring lawsuits that constrain EPA's ability to cheat on environmental quality. Environmentalists, therefore, correctly favor a significant role for the national government—one that serves both their substantive policy interests and their organization interests.

As appealing as the "industry bushwacked by popular opinion" story about the CAAA70 is, it is inadequate to explain pollution source interests' long-term acceptance of the basic structure of the CAA. Pollution sources have good reason to find the CAA structure beneficial. As noted earlier, polluters found the CAAA70 an improvement over the AQA in several respects, most notably in that the federal NAAQS were seen as an improvement over some more stringent state standards (Hays 1987, 445). Moreover, administrative politics and state administrative politics in particular, rather than legislative politics, are required for success in the SIP process. Here environmental interest groups lag far behind their industry counterparts. Environmentalists rarely have the resources to participate extensively in state administrative proceedings (Hays 1987, 476), particularly the mundane sorts involved in SIPs. Mobilizing a legislative coalition behind clean air is considerably easier than overcoming the collective action problem in considering the impact of increased emissions from a single source when the overall plan still purports to meet the general health-based ambient standard.

Not only do administrative politics require technical skills to understand the choices that agencies make in implementing complex regulatory regimes, but they also often require local knowledge about the facts of particular cases. An SIP that proposes to provide a plant's boiler with a level of emission control different from other boilers in the same industry (based on the fact that the physical layout of the plant does not allow sufficient space for installing a particular piece of pollution control equipment) requires knowledge of the building structure in question. If only a few such decisions were being made each year, then environmentalists could lobby for rules that require documentation to be placed in a record.

Environmentalists could then review the record and seek to overturn overly lenient decisions in court—just as they do with decisions about the ambient level of SO_2 required under the NAAQS process. When the boiler decision is one of hundreds or thousands each year, however, it becomes more difficult for an environmental group to maintain a consistent level of review.

Even this example oversimplifies the SIP problem. Administrative decisions typically involve "[m]yriad specific aspects of administration, greater in range and number than in the legislation itself" (Hays 1987, 469). Moreover, by locating crucial decisions at the state level, the SIP process grants significant advantages to current source interests. States tend to be far more sympathetic than the federal government to the problems that air pollution control pose for economic development. "More frequently than not, legislators, agencies, and governors were attuned to developmental rather than environmental goals. Only in those few states where levels of environmental interest were especially high, such as California, did the relationship between the two approach a roughly even balance" (Hays 1987, 435). Moreover, state agencies are often "prone to alter advisory committees, substantive policies, and decision-making procedures so as to make the expression of environmental concerns difficult" (Hays 1987, 436).

The CAA, whether by design or not, is an example of an institutional design that actively hinders public monitoring of its implementation. Several features in particular obscure its operation, allowing special interests to obtain preferential treatment. First, the federal government's role in setting the NAAQS created an opportunity for the type of proceeding that favored parties with "the financial resources to command expertise" (Hays 1987, 61). The "highly technical" battles over the NAAQS were "carried out far from public scrutiny or knowledge" (Hays 1987, 75). Second, the SIP process allows dispersion of the difficult and opaque decisions to fifty locations, maximizing the potential for capture. Third, by creating a diffuse decision-making process in which hundreds or thousands of decisions must be made annually, the process favors parties with the institutional means to be persistent players. A decision to modify an SIP provision concerning a particular plant is of intense interest to the owner of the plant and the people who work there. It is of considerably less interest to people living in another part of the same state, let alone those living in other states. Because the primary route for the business community to exert influence in environmental regulation has been through the "persistent presence of its institutional power" rather than through public debate over the merits of particular actions, this provision favored those with existing interests to protect (Hays 1987, 320).

The CAA structure also offers enormous benefits to both state and federal air pollution control bureaucracies. The federal role has steadily grown from the small staff engaged in research and technical support in the 1950s to the massive staff at the EPA today. Federal bureaucracies have thus captured increasing resources. State regulators preserved, and even enhanced, their authority, gaining a role as allocators of a valuable resource, thus increasing their value to state politicians.

Environmentalists frequently tout anecdotes of mandated pollution controls saving a polluter money by forcing it to operate more efficiently. Bryner (1995), for example, cites a Dow Chemical plant that reportedly saved $18 million in the first year after a $15 million pollution control expenditure and a Du Pont plant that saved $1 million a year by "simply using less of one raw material" (175). Thus, pollution control not only creates jobs building the necessary equipment, monitoring emissions, and so forth, it also saves the polluters money: "Environmental regulations ultimately push companies to do what is in their own economic interests" (Bryner 1995, 175).

Of course, this is nonsense as a general theory. Pollution, and air pollution in particular, happens because pollution sources are getting a resource for free—the capacity of the air to disperse waste material. When that disposal capacity begins to cost the source, it is not surprising that a positive price induces changed behavior. Getting the resource for free or getting it for less than competitors and potential competitors remains in the source's interest. The problem with the CAA in all its many forms is that it facilitates practices that are designed to reduce existing sources' costs of using the air as a disposal mechanism relative to the costs of those sources' competitors, existing and potential.

Those who favor regulation face a difficult burden to justify the CAA. Even by EPA's own calculations, the CAA has imposed significant costs on the American economy. To justify those costs, statisticians must, and do, tout the great benefits of the act. Yet they must simultaneously concede that "only modest progress" has been made in implementing the vast machinery the CAA created; that "[t]he implementation of the Clean Air Act largely fails to satisfy the conditions for effective implementation;" and that "we are still far from achieving the goal of clean air that meets national air quality standards, especially for particulate and ozone pollution, and protects human health with an adequate margin of safety, as promised in the Clean Air Act of 1970" (Bryner 1995, 245, 247). Having picked all the low-hanging fruit from the tree, the real question for those concerned about the quality of the air we breathe is why we have tolerated the failures of the CAA for so long.

There are superior ways to clean the air. Although a comprehensive solution requires much more discussion than can be provided here, I offer three principles that might shape such a solution: transparency, universality, and property-rights-based regulation.

Transparency. All requirements for pollution control must be clear, available, and readily comparable across media, type of source, and regulatory authority. State implementation plans that fill file drawers, let alone those that fill rooms, should simply be discarded as a failure. Only when pollution control requirements are open to meaningful public inspection and comprehension can we avoid the creation of special favors. If regulations cannot be written in such a form, they should be abandoned.

Universality. All requirements must be generally applicable to new sources and to old, to steel plants and to automobiles, to avoid opportunities for rent-seeking.

Property-Rights-Based Regulation. Applying the same standards to all sources has the potential to produce enormous inefficiencies. To avoid these inefficiencies, sources must be allowed to develop contractual means of reallocating burdens, which requires property-rights-based regulation.

These three principles could shape a real Clean Air Act, one that attempts to actually clean the air rather than creating rents and hindering competitors. These principles are based on creating a Clean Air Act that is as much the opposite of the current law as possible. Is our political structure capable of producing a real Clean Air Act? Perhaps not, because every participant in the political debate over environmental regulation has a huge stake in the continuation of the current Rube Goldberg scheme. On the other hand, if clean air is as important as it seems, can we afford not to try?

REFERENCES

Ackerman, Bruce A., and William T. Hassler. 1981. *Clean Coal/Dirty Air.* New Haven, Conn: Yale University Press.

Boubel, Richard W., Donald L. Fox, D. Bruce Turner, and Arthur C. Stern. 1994. *Fundamentals of Air Pollution,* 3rd ed. San Diego: Academic Press.

Bryner, Gary C. 1995. *Blue Skies, Green Politics: The Clean Air Act of 1990 and Its Implementation,* 2nd ed. Washington, D.C.: CQ Press.

Davies, J. Clarence, III, and Barbara Davies. 1975. *The Politics of Pollution*, 2nd ed. Indianapolis: Bobbs-Merrill.

Dyck, Robert G. 1971. Evolution of Federal Air Pollution Control Policy 1948–1967. Ph.D. diss., University of Pittsburgh, Graduate School of Public and International Affairs.

Esposito, John C. 1970. *Vanishing Air: The Ralph Nader Study Group Report on Air Pollution*. New York: Grossman Publishers.

Friedman, Frank B. 1990. The State Implementation Plan Process, Nonattainment, PSD, and Other Clean Air Act Issues. Conference Proceedings, February 15–17, 1990. In *Environmental Law*. Philadelphia, Pa.: American Law Institute.

Goklany, Indur. 2000. Empirical Evidence Regarding the Role of Federalization in Improving U.S. Air Quality. In *The Common Law and the Environment*, edited by Roger Meiners and Andrew P. Morriss. Lanham, Md.: Rowman & Littlefield.

Hays, Samuel P. 1978. Clean Air: From the 1970 Act to the 1977 Amendments. *Duquesne Law Review* 17: 33–66.

Hays, Samuel P. 1987. *Beauty, Health, and Permanence*. Cambridge: Cambridge University Press.

Hoberg, George. 1992. *Pluralism by Design: Environmental Policy and the American Regulatory State*. New York: Praeger.

Jones, Charles O. 1975. *Clean Air: The Policies and Politics of Pollution Control*. Pittsburgh: University of Pittsburgh Press.

Lowi, Theodore. 1972. Four Systems of Policy, Politics, and Choice. *Public Administration Review* 33 (July–August): 298–310.

Macy, Jonathan R., and Henry N. Butler. 2000. Federalism and the Environment. In *The Common Law and the Environment*, edited by Roger Meiners and Andrew P. Morriss. Lanham, Md.: Rowman & Littlefield.

Martin, Robert, and Lloyd Symington. 1968. A Guide to the Air Quality Act of 1967. *Law & Contemporary Problems* 33: 239–274.

McCarty, Jess M. 1992. Coal, State Protectionism, and the 1990 Clean Air Act Amendments: Why Keeping Sears in Illinois Withstands Commerce Clause Scrutiny, But Keeping Coal Mining Jobs Does Not. *University of Illinois Law Review:* 1119–1181.

McGarity, Thomas O. 1987. Presidential Control of Regulatory Agency Decisionmaking. *American University Law Review* 36: 443–489.

Miller, James. 1972. Air Pollution. In *Nixon and the Environment: The Politics of Devastation,* edited by James Rathlesberger. New York: Village Voice Books.

O'Fallon, John E. 1968. Deficiencies in the Air Quality Act of 1967. *Law & Contemporary Problems* 33: 275–296.

Pedersen, William F., Jr. 1981. Why the Clean Air Act Works Badly. *University of Pennsylvania Law Review* 129: 1059–1109.

Reed, P. O. 1982. Circuit Courts Endorse Conditional SIP Approval, Connecticut's Construction Plan Restored. *ELR* 12: 10055–10060.

Reitze, Arnold W., Jr. 1995. *Air Pollution Law.* Charlottesville, Va.: Michie Butterworth.

Revesz, Richard L. 1992. Rehabilitating Interstate Competition: Rethinking the "Race to the Bottom" Rationale for Federal Environmental Regulation. *New York University Law Review* 67: 1210–1254.

Schmandt, Jurgen, and Roderick Hilliard, eds. 1965. *Acid Rain and Friendly Neighbors.* Durham: Duke University Press.

U.S. Environmental Protection Agency (EPA). 1997. *The Benefits and Cost of the Clean Air Act, 1970 to 1990.* Washington, D.C.: EPA.

U.S. General Accounting Office (GAO). 1993. *Air Pollution: State Planning Requirements Will Continue to Challenge EPA and the States.* Washington, D.C.: Government Printing Office.

U.S. Senate. Committee on Environment and Public Works. 1974a. *Legislative History of the Clean Air Amendments of 1970,* vol. 1. Washington, D.C.: U.S. Government Printing Office.

U.S. Senate. Committee on Environment and Public Works. 1974b. *Legislative History of the Clean Air Amendments of 1970*, vol. 2. Washington, D.C.: U.S. Government Printing Office.

U.S. Senate. Committee on Environment and Public Works. 1979a. *Legislative History of the Clean Air Act Amendments of 1977*, vol. 3. Washington, D.C.: U.S. Government Printing Office.

U.S. Senate. Committee on Environment and Public Works. 1979b. *Legislative History of the Clean Air Act Amendments of 1977*, vol. 4. Washington, D.C.: U.S. Government Printing Office.

U.S. Senate. Committee on Environment and Public Works. 1979c. *Legislative History of the Clean Air Act Amendments of 1977*, vol. 5. Washington, D.C.: U.S. Government Printing Office.

U.S. Senate. Committee on Environment and Public Works. 1979d. *Legislative History of the Clean Air Act Amendments of 1977*, vol. 6. Washington, D.C.: U.S. Government Printing Office.

U.S. Senate. Committee on Environment and Public Works. 1979e. *Legislative History of the Clean Air Act Amendments of 1977*, vol. 7. Washington, D.C.: U.S. Government Printing Office.

U.S. Senate. Committee on Environment and Public Works. 1979f. *Legislative History of the Clean Air Act Amendments of 1977*, vol. 8. Washington, D.C.: U.S. Government Printing Office.

Wald, Matthew L. 1998. Autos' Converters Increase Warning as They Cut Smoke. *New York Times*, 29 May, A1.

Whitaker, John C. 1976. *Striking a Balance: Environment and Natural Resources Policy in the Nixon-Ford Years*. Washington, D.C.: American Enterprise Institute.

White, Theodore H. 1973. *The Making of the President 1972*. New York: Atheneum.

Index